LITERATURE, MAPPING, AND THE POLITICS OF SPACE IN EARLY MODERN BRITAIN

Mapping has become a key term in current critical discourse, describing a particular cognitive mode of gaining control over the world, of synthesising cultural and geographical information, and of successfully navigating both physical and mental space. In this timely collection, an international team of Renaissance scholars analyses the material practice behind this semiotic concept. By examining map-driven changes in gender identities, body conception, military practices, political structures, national imaginings and imperial aspirations, the essays in this volume expose the multi-layered investments of historical 'paper landscapes' in the politics of space. Ranging widely across visual and textual artefacts implicated in the culture of mapping, from the literature of Shakespeare, Spenser, Marlowe and Jonson, to representations of body, city, nation and empire, *Literature, Mapping, and the Politics of Space* argues for a thorough re-evaluation of the impact of cartography on the shaping of social and political identities in early modern Britain.

ANDREW GORDON is a Research Fellow in the School of English and Humanities at Birkbeck College, University of London. He is the author of a study guide for Thomas More's *Utopia*, as well as several articles on aspects of Renaissance culture.

BERNHARD KLEIN is lecturer in the Department of English at the University of Dortmund in Germany. He is the author of *Maps and the Writing of Space in Early Modern England and Ireland* (2001), and of several essays, reviews and book chapters on Renaissance culture and on contemporary Irish literature.

LITERATURE, MAPPING, AND THE POLITICS OF SPACE IN EARLY MODERN BRITAIN

EDITED BY

ANDREW GORDON

Birkbeck College, University of London

AND

BERNHARD KLEIN

University of Dortmund, Germany

CAMBRIDGE
UNIVERSITY PRESS

PUBLISHED BY THE PRESS SYNDICATE OF THE UNIVERSITY OF CAMBRIDGE
The Pitt Building, Trumpington Street, Cambridge, United Kingdom

CAMBRIDGE UNIVERSITY PRESS
The Edinburgh Building, Cambridge CB2 2RU, UK
40 West 20th Street, New York, NY 10011–4211, USA
10 Stamford Road, Oakleigh, VIC 3166, Australia
Ruiz de Alarcón 13, 28014 Madrid, Spain
Dock House, The Waterfront, Cape Town 8001, South Africa

http://www.cambridge.org

First published 2001

Printed in the United Kingdom at the University Press, Cambridge

Typeface Baskerville 11/12.5pt   *System* Poltype® [VN]

A catalogue record for this book is available from the British Library

ISBN 0 521 80377 2 hardback

Contents

Illustrations

Notes on contributors

CATERINA ALBANO is a freelance researcher in early modern literature and culture. Her current research interests include the history of medicine and Renaissance dietary practices. She has worked on various projects exploring the links between art and science and has been involved in the organisation of several exhibitions, including the multi-media event *Spectacular Bodies*.

OLIVER ARNOLD is assistant professor of English at Princeton University. He is the author of *The Third Citizen: Shakespeare's Theater, the Early Modern House of Commons, and the Tragedy of Political Representation* (forthcoming).

BRADIN CORMACK is assistant professor of English at the University of Chicago. He is working on a book about the relationship between legal jurisdiction and literary authority in the sixteenth and seventeenth centuries.

LESLEY B. CORMACK teaches history of science in the Department of History and Classics at the University of Alberta. She is the author of *Charting an Empire. Geography at the English Universities, 1580–1620* (1997), as well as several articles examining the interrelationship of geography, mathematics, imperialism and the scientific revolution. She is currently working on a book re-examining the role of mathematical practitioners and the rhetoric of utility in the scientific revolution.

JOHN GILLIES is professor in literature at the University of Essex. He is the author of *Shakespeare and the Geography of Difference* (1994) and numerous articles and book chapters. He is co-editor of *Playing the Globe: Genre and Geography in English Renaissance Drama* (1998) and *Performing Shakespeare in Japan* (2001). Interests include: Shakespeare, Renaissance drama, modern theatre, performance, multimedia and cultural poetics – with a particular emphasis on the poetics of space and place.

ANDREW GORDON is an AHRB research fellow at Birkbeck College, University of London, working on the correspondence of Francis Bacon for the Oxford edition of his collected works. He is currently also writing a book on space and community in early modern London and has research interests in graffiti, libel and costume.

RICHARD HELGERSON is professor of English at the University of California, Santa Barbara. His most recent book is *Adulterous Alliances: Home, State, and History in Early Modern European Drama and Painting* (2000). He is also the author of *The Elizabethan Prodigals* (1976), *Self-Crowned Laureates: Spenser, Jonson, Milton and the Literary System* (1983) and *Forms of Nationhood: The Elizabethan Writing of England* (1992), which won the British Council Prize in the Humanities and the Modern Language Association's James Russell Lowell Prize.

BERNHARD KLEIN is lecturer in English at the University of Dortmund, Germany. He is the author of *Maps and the Writing of Space in Early Modern England and Ireland* (2001). He is currently working on literature and the historical imagination in contemporary Ireland; other research interests include a project on modern maritime culture and the sea as a historical space.

ANDREW MCRAE is senior lecturer in Renaissance studies at the University of Exeter. He is the author of *God Speed the Plough: The Representation of Agrarian England, 1500–1660* (1996), and the co-editor of *The Writing of Rural England, 1500–1800* (forthcoming). He is currently working on issues of internal travel and space in the early modern period, while also pursuing another project on early Stuart political satire.

PHILIP SCHWYZER is junior research fellow in English at Hertford College, Oxford. He is the author of essays on Milton, early modern Wales, and antiquarianism and identity. He is currently writing a book on the construction of British antiquity and national identity in the Tudor era.

NINA TAUNTON is lecturer in English at Brunel University. She has published widely on Chapman, Fletcher, Marlowe and Shakespeare. With Darryll Grantley, she is co-editor of and contributor to *The Body in Late Medieval and Early Modern Culture* (2000). She is the author of *1590s Drama and Militarism: Portrayals of War in Marlowe, Chapman and Shakespeare's Henry V* (2001).

JOANNE WOOLWAY GRENFELL is a priest in the Church of England, working on an outer housing estate in Liverpool. Previously, she was lecturer in English at Oriel College, Oxford University, and associate editor of *Early Modern Literary Studies*. She has edited for that journal, with Richard Helgerson, an electronic collection of essays entitled *Renaissance Literature and Geography*. Her DPhil is on Edmund Spenser and the Culture of Place, and her current academic interests include ideas of space, religion, and culture in modern and early modern writing.

Preface

The idea for this collection first took shape at a conference organised by the editors at Queen Mary and Westfield College, University of London, in July 1997 under the title *Paper Landscapes: Maps, Texts, and the Construction of Space, 1500–1700*. Although, sadly, only a fraction of the papers presented at that event could be included in this book, we hope that the collection has managed to capture the co-operative spirit and interdisciplinary excitement of that meeting. In the course of producing the book we have relied on the help, advice and support of many individuals and institutions. For some crucial editorial advice early on, we would like to thank John Gillies. For passing on some invaluable tricks of the trade, thanks are due to Sue Wiseman and Alan Stewart. For their support of the project at various key moments we are indebted to Tom Healy, Lisa Jardine and Peter Barber. Richard Helgerson, whose seminal work on maps and chorography got so many of us started on the topic, has been exemplary in his encouragement of junior scholars in the field. For their financial support of the initial conference, we would like to thank The British Council, Cologne and Queen Mary and Westfield College. For a grant towards the cost of illustrations we are grateful to The British Academy and The Society of the Friends of the University of Dortmund. At Cambridge, thanks are due to Ray Ryan and Nikki Burton for their editorial guidance, and to the two anonymous readers whose comments have helped make this a better book. Bernhard Klein wishes to thank Ina Habermann for tolerance, patience and encouragement, again.

Introduction

Andrew Gordon and Bernhard Klein

'It was always one of the dubious geographical facts locked away in every schoolboy's [sic] head', the catalogue of a recent art exhibition on 'mapping' informs us, 'that the entire population of the world could stand on the Isle of Wight.'[1] A bold claim, surely, and one imagines some puzzled youths unwilling to lend it much credence without more tangible evidence. But it is not to dispute the mathematics of the equation that we draw attention to this didactic wisecrack. Clearly the insight that the whole may easily, if only hypothetically, fit into one of its tinier parts is principally the result of a mental exercise that feeds on the surprise of the unexpected. The immediate pedagogical point may have been to create an affective link between the abstract and global on the one hand, and the intimate and local on the other – two spatial paradigms traditionally kept apart in geographical thought, under the Ptolemaic rubrics of cosmography and chorography. What interests us most about this odd equation, though, is how behind its presumed mathematical impartiality lurks the image of a fantastic cultural congress that is no less suggestive for being the unintended consequence of simply taking the idea too literally.

To be sure, the Babylonic image of a common humanity gathered in a British offshore island is probably not what the early modern map lover Thomas Blundeville had in mind when he praised cartography for making visually accessible 'the whole world at one view'.[2] But to dismiss it too swiftly as the absurd metaphorical excess of a clever schoolteacher's trick that aimed merely to raise awareness of the sheer immensity of space is to make the opposite mistake of assuming, against the historical evidence, that geography deals only in surfaces and numbers, not in cultural issues. Comparison with another ruthlessly arbitrary conflation of the spatial and the social reminds us of the losses

I

incurred in holding that view. In his *Histories*, Herodotus records the following method employed in the reckoning of the vast army assembled by the Persian leader Xerxes:

A body of ten thousand men was brought to a certain place, and the men were made to stand as close together as possible; after which a circle was drawn around them, and the men were then let go: then where the circle had been, a fence was built about the height of a man's middle; and the enclosure was filled continually with fresh troops, till the whole army had in this way been numbered. When the numbering was over, the troops were drawn up according to their several nations.[3]

Carving out 'a certain place' – a featureless, unnamed Isle of Wight – from its surrounding physical space purely to produce a pragmatic vehicle for the quantification of people is an operation strikingly at odds with any notion of territorial and cultural belonging, and the subsequent need to regroup the soldiers in 'national' units seems almost like an embarrassed attempt to make up for this harsh disjunction.

It is, of course, a general feature of cartographic representation that it severs the ties between people and land – for all their historical significance as records of human settlement, modern maps are generally depopulated, often void of human traces, visually 'empty'. But if maps have been instrumental in giving rise to a purely functional conception of space largely divested of its broader social implications,[4] their impact on how we make sense of the physical world, and thus of our social environment, has been immense. To return to the opening image, it is precisely the conceptual hold over our geographical imagination of the *cartographic* construction of the Isle of Wight – rather than the body memory of any direct spatial experience – that enables the mathematical abstraction and which renders it, for our purposes, such a strikingly imaginative exercise. In this operation the enforced silencing of cultural difference in computing the army of Xerxes is compounded in a universal confusion of citizenry which at the same time obliterates all traces of the cultural investment that lent significance to the cartographic inscription in the first place. The image of the Isle of Wight, its conceptual territory saturated by this imaginative influx, raises questions crucial to the central concern of the present volume, the relation of the cartographic paradigm to the politics of spatial representation: if space, through its visualisation in maps, could be redefined, re-imagined, and appropriated for radically new purposes, what effects did the cultural work of cartography – both the mental and material 'acts of mapping'[5] –

have on the shaping of social and political identities in early modern Britain?

'Mapping', the inscriptive practice of the cartographer, has become a key theoretical term in current critical discourse, describing a particular cognitive mode of gaining control over the world, of synthesising cultural and geographical information, and of successfully navigating both physical and mental space. The often inflationary usage of this suggestive semiotic concept in recent critical work tends to ignore perhaps too easily the boundaries between the metaphorical and the material. Yet both realms mutually determine each other, and the intention of *Literature, Mapping, and the Politics of Space* may be best described as the attempt to relate models of cognitive mapping back to a specific historical moment – the early modern period – which saw an unprecedented rise in the use, availability, and conceptual sophistication of the material artefact at the centre of this analytic terrain, the topographical map. As has frequently been noted, its phenomenal career from the fifteenth century onwards points to significant changes in European spatial consciousness.[6] A spatial model that required a geographical *centre*, an *omphalos*, in order to describe, in degrees of civilisation, its difference from a diffuse *periphery*, was slowly replaced by a framed geometric image fully available for European inscription: 'The point of view was elevated, to the point of grasping in a single instant the convexity of the terraqueous globe ... [showing] the plenitude of a universe revealed at last in its totality.'[7] In thus providing a conceptual paradigm for the mental organisation of human experience, the cartographic image is revealed as more than a mere functional tool, or neutral scientific record, emerging instead as a crucial representational site of cultural and historical change.

The statement that all maps are political no longer results in many raised eyebrows.[8] Nor are studies considered unusual that argue at length for the cultural, social and epistemological changes in which early modern cartography was implicated, or in which it was even the central agent.[9] The present collection aims to expand the current research in this field by placing maps and related cartographic products firmly within the many cultural contexts of which they formed a part, and by probing their often troubled (and troubling) relationships to these contexts. The realisation that 'maps excited, moved, informed and remade everyone who had contact with them, and [that] through the social, political, economic and intellectual remakings they prompted, they changed the lives even of those who didn't', as Richard Helgerson puts it in this book, seems perhaps more obvious to us than it did to contemporaries. But even in early modern times maps could be seen as having a socially and politically disruptive influence. Consider, for instance, this view voiced by a fictional farmer in John Norden's *Surveyor's Dialogue* (1607), an early modern treatise on land surveying. '[W]e poore Country-men', the farmer complains,

doe not thinke it good to haue our Lands plotted out, and me thinks in deede it is to very small purpose: for is not the Field it selfe a goodly Map for the Lord to look vpon, better then a painted paper? And what is he the better to see if laid out in colours? He can adde nothing to his land, nor diminish ours: and therefore that labour aboue all may be saued, in mine opinion.[10]

Reminiscent as the 'goodly Map' is of the more recent literary maps at a scale of one-to-one devised by Lewis Carroll and Jorge Luis Borges,[11] the farmer is clearly less intent on ridiculing the mimetic pretension of maps than on giving voice to a genuinely felt anxiety: with the assistance of the map the intimate and closed social microcosm of the estate is in danger of turning into the quantifiable, anonymous and inherently desocialised object of commercial speculation. The estate map, that is, might change the nature of the agrarian space it puts on open display and, more significantly even, it might change the landlord's attitude towards that space, transforming a formerly paternal figure into a ruthless speculator.

Norden was himself a practising surveyor when he wrote that dialogue, and such views are included in his promotional text only to be convincingly refuted. But the farmer's anti-mapping attitude is surely not wholly unfounded. Depending on context and genre, maps could serve many functions, and in each specific instance their objectives were rarely impartial: the individual map could be a facilitator of economic 'improvement', a political or military tool of government, the fetish of an emerging nationalism, or the agent of some other currently little appreciated ideological purpose. Nevertheless, maps in general are not inherently predisposed towards one side or another, and the farmer's fears were generated less by their inevitable complicity with structures of power than by the uses to which they were historically put. The economic context in which Norden's text is implicated – and with it the whole practice of land surveying – is only one of the many areas of cultural experience affected by new mapping techniques. By examining map-driven changes in gender identities, body conceptions, military practices, political structures, national imaginings, civic culture, and imperial aspirations, the essays in this book explore a wide range of contexts influenced by the spatial re-visions that maps both initiated and recorded. In doing so, the essays all share common ground in emphasising the conceptual and semiotic interplay between cartographic discourse and related forms of spatial representation.

For, as a textually and visually highly articulate 'paper landscape', the modern scale-map is not an isolated phenomenon but located within a complex cultural network of spatial signifying practices. Thus, although maps of various genres – national and regional maps, world maps, city views, etc. – feature strongly throughout the pages that follow, they are discussed alongside many other cultural artefacts: paintings, geographical frontispieces, anatomical illustrations, and a wide range of textual genres, covering drama, the military manual, historiography, poetry, civic pageantry, juridical, political and constitutional writings, chorography and biblical texts. The interdisciplinary range and thematic diversity of the essays collected here thus demonstrate, we hope, that the contemporary preoccupation with the epistemological category *space*, most clearly visible in the ideological investments inscribed on the surface of early modern maps, affected the production of cultural artefacts on a variety of mental and material levels. If among the discursive terrains investigated here, literature claims pride of place, this is not simply because most contributors work in literature departments but also a result of the productive tension between the visual and the verbal, between word and image, which most immediately and suggestively evokes the conceptual struggle over the cultural meaning of place and space.

The early modern 'politics of space' attendant on this conceptual struggle, the collection as a whole argues, centres on the deeply felt clash between the various physical and imaginary investments, often contradictory or mutually exclusive, in the shifting landscapes of modernity. One obvious instance of this clash is the contemporary use of the last term in our title, 'Britain'. The stability of geopolitical reference implied by this term can hardly be taken for granted. Cartographically, 'Britain' received its first sustained description in the work of John Speed whose atlas *The Theatre of the Empire of Great Britain* (1611) was expressly devoted to celebrating the political aspirations of the Scottish king new to the English throne, James, 'the Inlarger and Vniter of the British Empire'.[12] There were, of course, earlier maps of 'Britain' but not until Speed's atlas did the word (as a label on a map) take on fully the imperial meaning it had in the *Theatre* where it defined, or claimed to define, the political and spatial cohesion of an archipelago, not just some geographical or political subsection of the 'British Isles'. Saxton's atlas of 1579, for instance, covered only England and Wales. But the nomenclature was still blurred even in Speed who called his map of England and Wales simply 'the Kingdome of England'. Like Speed, many of his contemporaries often made no consistent distinction between 'England' and 'Britain', although the example of the Welsh nationalist Humphrey Llwyd – evocatively discussed in this volume by Philip Schwyzer – is an obvious exception.

Even before James propounded the Union of Crowns, Wales officially 'joined' England in 1536, and Ireland was made a kingdom under the rule of the English monarch in 1541. The island trope, so frequent in historical writing about Britain since medieval times, further blurred geographical boundaries, famously leading John of Gaunt in Shakespeare's *Richard II* to consider England a 'sceptred *isle*',[13] or William Cuningham to declare that 'vnder the name of Englande, I comprehend the whole Ilande conteyning also Schotlande, & Irelande'.[14] Such spatial and political idiosyncracies are too often recorded in writing not to have had an effect on the contemporary geographical – and hence national – imagination. In the period under consideration here, the nation that maps helped to construct was still in the process of defining itself, both socially and culturally – in its internal configuration – and territorially – in its external shape. Stable political referents were often the stuff of cartographic dreamwork, and throughout the sixteenth century, the nation that contemporaries imagined spatially with the aid of maps was largely provisional and experimental, just as it was still, in many ways, no nation at all but a dynastic realm.

The essays that follow are arranged in two sections. The first is more generally problem oriented, combining five essays on the spatial implications of political representation, historiography, geography, civic ceremony and anatomy. The second section focuses on links between literature and landscape, grouping three essays on drama with three on poetry. The aim of this two-part structure is not to establish mutually exclusive categories but to foreground the internal links and overlaps between diverse cultural contexts. Taken as a whole, the essays consider a range of mutually dependent spatial paradigms, progressively pushing further their metaphorical and/or physical boundaries. Thus, while some essays deal with the human *body* as the most intimately experienced spatial unit, others move on to focus on the *stage*, the *city*, the *nation*, and the *imperial* vision, to arrive, finally, at the *epistemological* frameworks surrounding specific spatial constructs. In this way, body, stage, city, nation, empire, and – in a sense – epistemology, circumscribe and define lived cultural spaces in a series of imaginative enclosures, but in so doing they also assume a metaphorical currency in cultural discourse that transcends the immediacy of any direct spatial experience. Contemporary rhetorical usage instrumentalises these spaces for a wide variety of purposes: for the description of socio-political analogies, for instance (the *discordia concors* trope of the body serving as an image of nationhood), the definition of cultural opposites (the dissonance between city vice and proclaimed national virtues), or the exploration of imagined affinities between different topological constructions (such as the conceptual overlap of stage and empire – best illustrated, perhaps, by the generic links in the early modern period between *atlas* and *theatre*). Connections of this kind are central issues of debate throughout the present volume and make appropriate a brief presentation of the individual essays, not in the sequence in which they appear in the book, but in the order established by their discussion of progressively widening spatial paradigms.

In cosmographical thought the world has always been imagined in terms of the human body, and the conceptual identity between cartographers and anatomists is one of the founding tropes of mapping. 'And here first we will', explained John Speed in the preface to his *Theatre*, '(by Example of the best Anatomists) propose to view the *whole Body* and *Monarchy* intire ... and after will dissect and lay open the particular Members, Veynes and Ioynts (I meane the Shires, Riuers, Cities and Townes)'.[15] According to such views, which were frequent in cartographic texts, the internal organisation of spatial entities – cities, nations, empires – resembled that of the body. In the early modern period, as Caterina Albano's analysis of the conceptual links between anatomy and cartography reveals, the mutually enabling strategies of spatialising the body and humanising the cartographic image gave the 'archetypal' land-body analogy a new allegorical twist; a twist that emerges most clearly in the gendering of exotic, 'virginal' lands as female, where the representational techniques that rendered both bodies and spaces culturally visible were governed by a 'politics of specialisation', a desire to penetrate ever further into virtual interiors. The body-space nexus is analysed from a different angle by John Gillies. The map brought on stage in the opening scene of Shakespeare's *King Lear*, Gillies shows, is only fully understood when read against the theatre's own deeply somatic language of space. In contrast to other examples of cartographic props on the early modern stage, Lear's map clearly retains the semiotic power and theatrical rhetoric of cartography as a productive site of suggestive 'nation-scapes'. Yet this national icon not only fosters an uninhibited geographic voyeurism, it also brings into focus the principal spatial contrast of the play – the phenomenological distinction between inside and outside – obliquely aligned to the opposition between the material, even amoral, geography of Lear's map, and the intimate, body-bound chorography of the Dover cliff scene. In *Lear*, the stage might be initially appropriated as the 'scene of cartography', but only to challenge this new master discourse of spatiality with the more theatrically responsive idiom of the naked, unaccommodated, and ridiculed human body.

Nina Taunton further explores the staging of space by focusing on the deeply gendered context of the military camp, ambivalently addressed in Christopher Marlowe's *Tamburlaine* plays through a dramatic *tour de force* rich in cartographic allusions. Analysing Marlowe's female characters with a view to the presence (or absence) of women in Elizabethan theories of warfare, as well as to their representation in sixteenth-century German genre painting, Taunton shows how male subjectivity, in a military context, was predicated on the simultaneous denial and absorption of the disturbingly transgressive cultural spaces defined by women. Bodies and stages are brought into implicit contrast in Andrew Gordon's examination of the construction of early modern London in both map and ritual. While the city served as the stage where a model of social order was imprinted onto urban space in formal procession, the performance of the ceremonial city on ground level increasingly yielded to the cartographic vantage point on high. But despite the infiltration of the representational strategies of ceremony by the geometric space of mapping, Gordon shows, the performative spatiality of civic ritual nevertheless continues to permeate and even determine the cartographic description of the city. Quite a different conception of the city emerges when it is imagined not from outside or above, as on a map, but from within and below. London, as it is produced in the everyday spatialisation of its 'users', not as it is encoded in geometric construction or ceremonial procession, is discussed by Andrew McRae. Drawing on theories of postmodern geography, McRae considers Ben Jonson's neglected poem 'On the Famous Voyage' – a narrative journey through the filthy and grotesque urban body of London – as a text deeply and disruptively engaged in the transformation of an early modern sense of civic space. The 'vitally alternative spatiality' McRae discovers is one that aligns space – the city – again with the human body; not, however, as a trope of hierarchical order but as a continuous cycle of excretion and consumption.

Strategies of absorption are fundamental to maps where people are drawn into landscapes, cities into nations, countries into empires. In the political realm, Oliver Arnold exposes the concept of absorption as central to the ideology of parliamentary representation inherent in the configuration of the House of Commons as both a representative *body* and itself a representation of the realm. The frequent juxtaposition of maps depicting England's physical space with pictorial representations of parliament thus reflect the Commons' rhetorical claims to represent England's inhabitants even as they help to enact the MPs' radical absorption and displacement of the realm and its people. Two further essays demonstrate that the space of the nation could be appropriated from many ideological perspectives. Philip Schwyzer explores a fascinating historical instance of a consciously political usage of the patriotic potential endemic in cartographic representation. His 'Map of Greater Cambria' is an inspiring study of Humphrey Llwyd's map of Wales (1573) which argues, with reference to contemporary historical and poetic works, that Llwyd's early modern Welsh nationalism implicitly draws on a notion of 'essential geography' that still informs present-day political debates – as the more recent political maps of 'Greater Serbia' or 'Greater Bulgaria' amply testify. Competing narrative conceptions of national space in written chorography and epic poetry are examined by Bernhard Klein who argues that the early modern poetics of national space oscillated between the conceptual opposites of plan and itinerary which informed, respectively, the static textual topography of Drayton's *Poly-Olbion* and the dynamic space 'performed' in Spenser's *Faerie Queene*.

Wider spatial frameworks are explored in two essays on empire. As Lesley Cormack shows, imperial aspirations were already implicit in contemporary geographical thought. Her sensitive analysis of the frontispieces gracing a series of geographically inspired historical works shows how an imperial imagination had already begun to take root in Elizabethan England, even if the vision of English superiority – still only a dream on paper – could not yet claim much iconographic or ideological coherence. Bradin Cormack then turns to the theme of imperial expansion as imagined in the interplay between international law and maritime cartography. Contextualising Shakespeare's *Pericles* with an analysis of the legal definition of marine boundaries in English and Welsh coastal waters and a detailed semiotic reading of the compass roses on John Speed's maps of Britain, Bradin Cormack exposes the full range of Shakespeare's dramatic strategies to realise a spatialised reimagining of kingship within the context of the emergent international law. In the concluding essay of the last section, Joanne Woolway

Grenfell turns to the epistemological assumptions of spatial representation by examining the impact of the New World on European spatial
consciousness. Focusing on Edmund Spenser's rich poetic exploration
of place and culture in *The Faerie Queene*, Woolway Grenfell's discussion
of biblical maps and texts, and of the hermeneutic implications of New
World geographies, demonstrates that physical space, for Spenser,
cannot be subjected to its cartographic rationalisation until it has been
fully tested, both morally and politically, for its cultural integrity and
Christian value.

In the final contribution to the volume, intended as both a kind of
epilogue and a timely reminder that too often we find only ourselves in
everything we study, Richard Helgerson considers the moment when
maps as widely celebrated icons of modernity were made to serve quite
another, distinctly anti-modern purpose. For maps both promoted and
ridiculed the newly acquired geographical knowledge that cartographic
images proudly flaunted to the world, a knowledge that had made their
production technically possible in the first place. This tension, poignant-
ly captured in the Fool's Cap Map now gracing the cover of *The Norton
Shakespeare*, generates the ambivalent meanings of maps in Dutch genre
painting where items of cartographic wall decoration signal both a
recently acquired sense of national pride, and the danger and folly of the
worldliness attendant on all profane earthly pursuits, including the vain
contemplation of maps. Yet even the traditional message of *contemptus
mundi* couched in the midst of radically new images of the world
eventually metamorphosed, as Helgerson shows, into quite another
configuration of the modern – the new primacy of the domestic which
mid-seventeenth-century Dutch genre paintings so self-consciously celebrated. Such spatial transformations fostered by the art of mapping,
and their impact on changing notions of cultural identity, are the theme
of this book. While critical approaches vary across the collection, it is
one of our principal intentions throughout to offer a new assessment of
why, in the words of Elyot and Dee, contemporaries suddenly waxed
lyrical about the 'inexplicable delectation'[16] generated by 'Mappes,
Chartes, & Geographicall Globes',[17] and thus to reclaim the lost landscapes of meaning hidden beneath the paper 'wherin all the world is
painted'.[18]

NOTES

1. *The Centre of the World*, intr. and ed. Stephen Foster (Southampton: John Hansard Gallery, 1991), n.p.
2. Thomas Blundeville, *A Briefe Description of Vniversal Mappes and Cardes* (London: Thomas Cadman, 1589), sig. c4r.
3. Herodotus, *The Histories*, trans. George Rawlinson (London: Everyman, 1997), vii, 60, p. 536.
4. On social space see especially the seminal work by Henri Lefebvre, *The Production of Space*, trans. Donald Nicolson-Smith (Oxford: Blackwell, 1991 [French original 1974]). For further influential work on the 'theory of space' see particularly Edward W. Soja, *Postmodern Geographies. The Reassertion of Space in Critical Social Theory* (London: Verso, 1989); and David Harvey, *The Condition of Postmodernity. An Enquiry into the Origins of Cultural Change* (Cambridge, Mass.: Blackwell, 1989). A preoccupation with the use and deployment of spatial metaphors has long been notable in philosophy, semiotics, cultural, social and intellectual history, as well as, more recently, postcolonial theory; see, for instance, Michel Foucault, *Discipline and Punish. The Birth of the Prison*, trans. A. Sheridan (London: Allen Lane, 1977); Edward Said, *Orientalism* (New York: Vintage Books, 1978); Louis Marin, *Utopics: The Semiological Play of Textual Spaces*, trans. Robert A. Vollrath (Atlantic Highlands, New Jersey: Humanities Press, 1984); and Homi Bhabha, *The Location of Culture* (London: Routledge, 1994).
5. Recently summarised by Denis Cosgrove as 'acts of visualizing, conceptualizing, recording, representing and creating spaces graphically'. See his 'Introduction: Mapping Meaning', Cosgrove (ed.), *Mappings* (London: Reaktion, 1997), p. 1.
6. See especially Michel Foucault, 'Of Other Spaces', trans. Jay Miskowiec, *Diacritics* 16 (1986 [French original 1969]), 22–7.
7. Frank Lestringant, *Mapping the Renaissance World. The Geographical Imagination in the Age of Discovery* (Cambridge: Polity Press, 1994 [French original 1991]), p. 5.
8. In many ways, recent work by cartographic historians has been crucial in creating an awareness that maps are more than mere neutral containers of geographic data. See especially a number of seminal articles by J. B. Harley: 'Maps, Knowledge and Power', Denis Cosgrove and Stephen Daniels (eds.), *The Iconography of Landscape* (Cambridge University Press, 1988), pp. 277–312; 'Silences and Secrecies: the Hidden Agenda of Cartography in Early Modern Europe', *Imago Mundi* 40 (1988), 57–76; 'Deconstructing the Map', *Cartographica* 26, no. 2 (1989), 1–20. See also the ongoing, multivolume *History of Cartography*, edited by the late J. B. Harley and David Woodward for Chicago University Press. This work has been supplemented by experts from other disciplines, see especially Denis Wood, *The Power of*

Maps (London: Routledge, 1993); and Jeremy Black, *Maps and Politics* (London: Reaktion, 1997).

9. Even an incomplete list of recent studies in early modern literature, history and culture which deal with cartography, or in which maps play a central role, would have to include Richard Helgerson, *Forms of Nationhood* (Chicago University Press, 1992); John Gillies, *Shakespeare and the Geography of Difference* (Cambridge University Press, 1994); Lestringant, *Mapping the Renaissance World*; William Sherman, *John Dee. The Politics of Reading and Writing in the English Renaissance* (Amherst: University of Massachusetts Press, 1995); Andrew McRae, *God Speed the Plough. The Representation of Agrarian England, 1500–1660* (Cambridge University Press, 1996); Tom Conley, *The Self-Made Map* (Minneapolis: University of Minnesota Press, 1996); Lisa Jardine, *Worldly Goods* (London: Macmillan, 1996); Lesley Cormack, *Charting an Empire. Geography at the English Universities, 1580–1620* (Chicago University Press, 1997); Jerry Brotton, *Trading Territories* (London: Reaktion, 1997); Garrett Sullivan, *The Drama of Landscape. Land, Property, and Social Relations on the Early Modern Stage* (Stanford University Press, 1998); *Early Modern Literary Studies* 4, no. 2 (1998), special issue on 'Literature and Geography', edited by Richard Helgerson and Joanne Woolway Grenfell; Cosgrove (ed.), *Mappings*; and Bernhard Klein, *Maps and the Writing of Space in Early Modern England and Ireland* (London: Palgrave, 2001).

10. John Norden, *The Surveyors Dialogue* (London: Hugh Astley, 1607), p. 15.

11. See Lewis Carroll, *Sylvie and Bruno Concluded* [1893], *The Complete Works of Lewis Carroll*, ed. Alexander Woollcott (London: The Nonesuch Press, 10th edn 1966), pp. 556–7; and Jorge Luis Borges, 'Of the Exactitude of Science', *A Universal History of Infamy*, trans. Norman Thomas di Giovanni (Harmondsworth: Penguin, 1975), p. 131.

12. John Speed, *The Theatre of the Empire of Great Britain* (London: John Sudbury and George Humble, 1611), dedication (n.p.).

13. *Richard II*, 2.1.40. *The Norton Shakespeare*, ed. Stephen Greenblatt, *et al.* (New York and London: Norton, 1997), our italics.

14. William Cuningham, *The Cosmographical Glasse* (London: John Day, 1559), fol. 119.

15. Speed, *Theatre*, preface (n.p.).

16. Sir Thomas Elyot, *The Boke, Named the Governovr* [1534] (London: T. East 1580), fol. 31r.

17. John Dee, *The Mathematicall Praeface to the Elements of Geometrie of Euclid of Megara* [1570], intr. Allen G. Debus (New York: Science History Publications, 1975), sig. A4r.

18. Elyot, *The Boke, Named the Governovr*, fol. 31r.

PART I

Contested spaces

Absorption and representation: mapping England in the early modern House of Commons

Oliver Arnold

I want to begin with a vision of the House of Commons as a living map of England. The vision belongs to an anonymous MP, who, in a remarkable speech in 1571, argued that the Commons' effectiveness as a representative institution was being undermined by the many knights and burgesses who did not reside in – and often knew little about – the shires and boroughs they had been elected to represent. 'Howe may her Majestie or howe may this court knowe', he asked his fellow MPs,

the state of her frontiers, or who shall make report of the portes, or howe every quarter, shiere, or countrey is in state? Wee who nether have seene Barwicke or St Michaelle's Mount can but blindly guess at them, albeit wee looke on the mapps that come from thence, or letters of instructions sent from thence: some one whome observacion, experience and due consideracion of that countrey hath taught can more perfectly open what shall in question therof growe, and more effectually reason thereuppon, then the skillfullest otherwise whatsoever. And that they should bee the very inhabitors of the severall counties of this kingdome who should bee here in tymes certaine imployed, doubtles it was the true meaninge of the auncient kings and our forefathers who first began and established this court might be founde.[1]

On this account, then, the House of Commons represents not only the people of England but the physical nation as well, and maps, our MP suggests, are wholly inadequate representations of the various places that constitute the realm precisely because they are merely imperfect signs of absent towns and terrains. Human agents, by contrast, fully embody their native boroughs and shires: 'Since we deale universally for all sortes and all places', our speaker concluded, 'there [should] bee here all sortes and all countrys'.[2]

This metonymical elaboration of representation – the Commons, can represent all sorts of people and all sorts of places only if all sorts of

Figure 1 Engraving, *House of Commons* (1640)

people from all sorts of places serve as MPs – seems to reach a kind of pictorial fulfillment in Figure 1, an engraving of the Commons from 1640.[3] On all sides, the MPs are surrounded by maps: on the right and left, bird's-eye plans of England's enfranchised boroughs; in the lower left corner, a map of all the shires which sent MPs to parliament; and in the lower right corner, an elaborate map and view of London. The MPs we see engaged in the business of representation make the places we see depicted on the borders present in the Commons' Chamber. But, as we shall see, they do so – at least according to what I will claim is the dominant ideology of political representation from the Elizabethan Commons onwards – not because they collectively resided in all the towns and shires of the realm. Indeed, the literalist construction of representation lost out to a radical account of representation according to which a mere handful of men could, through the power of representation, make the entire realm and its inhabitants present in the House of Commons.

In the pages that follow, I will argue that our anonymous MP's implicit argument for the necessity of representative bodies – because even 'her Majestie' is incapable of knowing her entire realm, a properly constituted Commons must supplement her deficiency – is ironically supplanted by an absolutist account of representation in which a single MP might claim, after Shakespeare's Jack Cade, 'my mouth shall be the parliament of England' (*2 Henry VI*, 4.7.14–15).[4] Indeed, as early as 1567, we find an anonymous MP making just such a boast: 'I speke for all England, yea, and for the noble English nation'.[5]

I

The House of Commons did not have a permanent meeting place until 1549, when Edward VI granted the knights and burgesses the use of St Stephen's Chapel in Westminster. That physical space was the positive condition for the Commons' creation of what I will call representative space: a virtual space in which the whole realm was, according to Commons' rhetoric, present. Our earliest description of the Commons in St Stephen's comes to us from John Hooker's *The Order and usage of the keeping of a Parlement in England* (1571): the Commons Chamber, according to Hooker,

is made like a Theater, having four rowes one aboove an other round about the same. At the higher end in the middle of the lower rowe is a seat made for the Speaker, in which he alwaies sitteth; before it is a table boord, at which sitteth

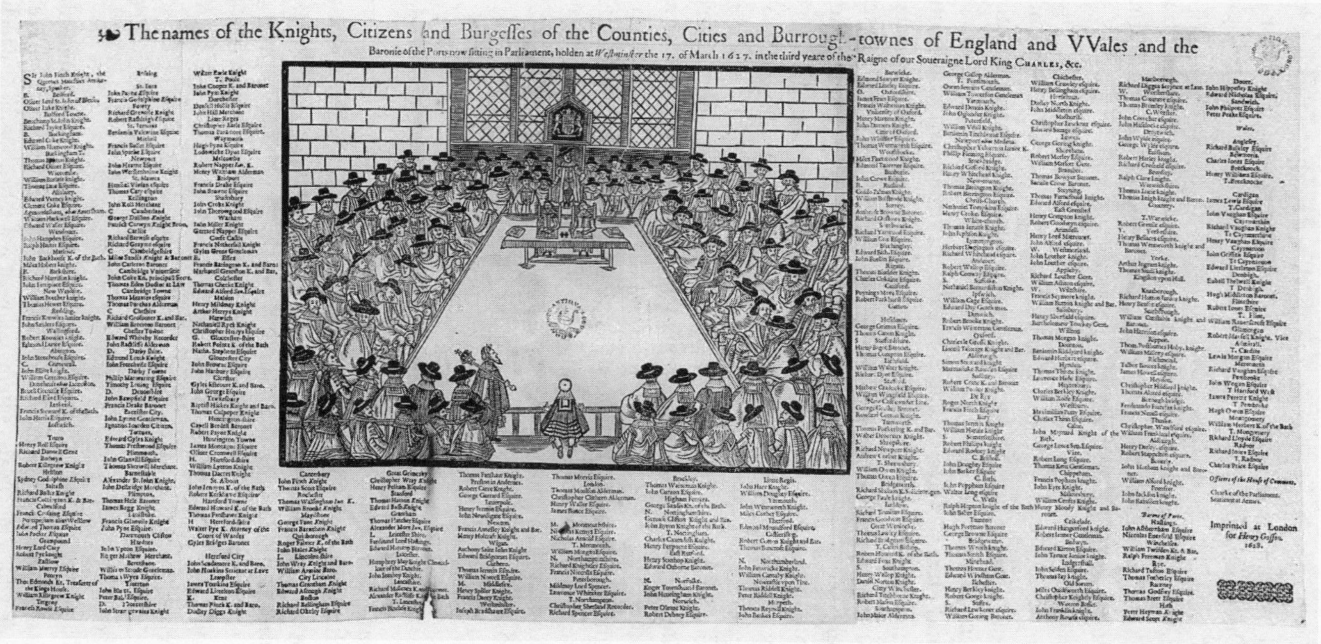

Figure 2 Woodcut, *House of Commons* (1628)

the Clark of the house and there upon [he] layeth his Books, and writeth his recordes.[6]

Hooker had, as an MP, seen the structure for himself, and Figure 2, one of the first pictorial representations of the MPs in St Stephen's, confirms his architectural analogy between the Chamber and a theatre.[7] The engraving, moreover, seems to embrace theatricality as a strategy for representing political representation by staging St Stephen's itself: the whole of the chamber and the MPs in intense activity have been thrown open to the viewer's scrutiny. But the Commons we see is an entirely mythic place, not only because, as we shall see, it was very often nearly empty, but also because it was entirely closed to public inspection. The MPs, to be sure, figured their new home as a radically public structure – a place where all matters of public interest could be openly and freely debated and where the people themselves were 'deemed personally present'.[8] But, in fact, the MPs used St Stephen's to secure unprecedented isolation from the public and to maintain secret proceedings. Thus, the analogies between theatre and the Commons are remarkably infelicitous: for, as the engravings ultimately – perhaps ironically – reveal, St Stephen's may be made like a theatre, but the House of Commons lacks the definitive feature of theatre: it makes no room for spectators. The elevated benches are filled entirely with performers and where the stage and parterre should be there is a void. Indeed, the closest the electorate ever got to seeing the inside of St Stephen's was as an audience to *representations* of the Commons. I want to turn now to the ways in which the early modern Commons managed to establish itself as a representative space and a public authority not by effacing the boundaries between itself and the people, but, paradoxically, by rhetorically absorbing and confining publicness within the narrow walls of St Stephen's Chapel.

Consider, for example, the Commons' peculiar definition of public speech. In 1593, Edward Coke scolded some of his fellow MPs for whispering in the House of Commons: 'Mr. Speaker, perceiving some men to whisper together, said that it was not the manner of the House that any should whisper or talk secretly, for here only publick Speeches are to be used'.[9] Covert speech disturbs Coke because it undermines the Commons' status as a distinctly *public* institution. Private speech might, on the one hand, suggest that members were pursuing personal rather than public ends.[10] On the other hand, whispering might signify an even more damaging timidity: MPs afraid to speak their minds could hardly maintain the Commons' central claim that no matter of public concern would ever be sacrificed to restrictions on speech. According to the institutional ideology articulated in 'A Petition for the Parliament's Liberty' (1610), it was the 'ancient, generall and undoubted right of parliament to debate freely al matters, which do properly concerne the subject, and his right, or State: which freedome of debate being once forclosed, the essence of the libertie of Parliament is with all dissolved'.[11] In order to protect the subject, one MP argued in 1566, the Commons must be free to 'utter in this House all that is beneficiall or dangerous' to the common good.[12] If the MPs failed to maintain that liberty they would become the Adams of the nation: for just as the MPs 'doe feele the smart of [Adam and Eve's] disobedience . . . so shall all our posteritie doe unto the worlde's end'.[13] Thus, within the logic of representational politics, Coke protects the freedoms of the English subject and his posterity by censoring the whispered speech of the MPs.

The public sphere Coke seeks to preserve, however, is strictly circumscribed by the walls of St Stephen's Chapel. For the publicness of Commons was threatened not only by members who whispered in parliament, but also, ironically, by members who reported Commons proceedings to the public. Indeed, the day after Coke admonished the whisperers, Sir Henry Knivett 'moved that for the freedom of the House it might be concluded amongst them a matter answerable at the Bar, for any man to report any thing of any Speech used, or matters done in thise House'.[14] Coke preserves the credibility of the House by prohibiting the concealment of speech in the chamber; Knivett wants to protect 'the freedom of the House' by concealing all speech within the chamber from the outside world – by reducing it to a whisper. Knivett's circumspection was typical: parliament men of all dispositions routinely supported the enforcement of the institution's codified prohibitions on breaching the secrecy of proceedings. Thus, the walls of St Stephen's functioned as a boundary marker of public discourse and defined a radically contained and paradoxical public sphere: within the walls, all speech was public; but nothing spoken within the walls could be reported to the public itself.

Commons' rhetoric, however, claimed that secret proceedings were necessary to protect the MPs from the oppressive scrutiny of the Lords and the Crown: only when they were 'out of the Royal sight of the King, and not amongst the great Lords so far their betters'[15] could they fully protect the subject's liberties.[16] The spectre of a royal audience, however, is largely a red herring; any experienced MP knew that the Lords and the monarch had relatively easy access to Commons' business.[17]

The MPs were far more anxious about being exposed before a public and popular audience and thus frequently punished particular members who spoke of parliament matters outside of St Stephen's.

Let me turn briefly to a case history. In 1572, the Commons forced the MP Arthur Hall to recant 'sundry lewd speeches, used as well in this House as also abroad elsewhere' in which he had both mildly defended Mary and Norfolk and insisted that the Commons should leave their fates up to Elizabeth.[18] Defending Mary and disparaging the Commons' competence in the House was certainly provocative. But the internal prosecution of Hall focused on the words he spoke 'abroad elsewhere'.[19] William Fleetwood's distinction between freedom of speech within and outside of St Stephen's shaped the debate on Hall's case:

[I]n all cases the tyme, place and person ought to bee considered . . . We have nowe greate matters in hande and the arreignement of a queene; and therefore he would have speech to be more liberalie suffered *within* the Howse . . . But here is mencion of speech *without* the Howse: nowe the case is changed . . . words tollerable in this Howse are not sufferable at Blunte's table.[20]

Fleetwood isn't worried about Elizabeth learning of Hall's speech; she did and was apparently grateful for his deference to her will: Blunte's table was a tavern, not a royal council chamber. Thus, when Fleetwood recommends that 'Hall be put to aunswere sutch speach as he used out of the House',[21] he is concerned with publicity.[22] In the end, Hall participated in an elaborate show trial in which he venerated the Commons and confessed his folly.[23] But, to his cost, Hall never learned to stop talking politics at Blunte's table: in 1581, the Commons expelled him because he had 'published the conferences of the Howse in print' in two irreverent pamphlets.[24] The Commons made every effort to destroy all copies of the two pamphlets.[25]

Why exactly was discussing parliamentary affairs at Blunte's table taboo? Or, to put the question more sharply, why were 'private' citizens – the very political subjects who supposedly empowered the Commons – alone denied routine access to information about Commons' business, which members typically shared not only with the nobility, but also with their own professional and social peers (lawyers, judges, important merchants and so on)?[26] The MPs wished, I suggest, to usurp all public debate and to control exclusively the power of acting in the name of public opinion. This desire to monopolise publicness is richly, ironically at play in Robert Cecil's outrage over leaks during the 1601 debates about the Queen's right to grant commercial and manufacturing monopolies to her favourites:

I fear we are not secret within ourselves . . . [and] whatsoever is subject to public
expectation cannot be good, while the parliament matters are ordinary talk in
the street. I have heard myself, being in my coach, these words spoken aloud:
'God prosper those that further the overthrow of these monopolies! God send
the prerogative touch not our liberty!' . . . I think these persons would be glad
that all sovereignty were converted into popularity.[27]

But making sovereignty a function of popularity is, of course, exactly
what the ideology of Commons promises to do; the members, after all,
claimed to derive their authority from popular elections. For Cecil, shut
up in his private coach, Commons ceases to function properly precisely
when it threatens to fulfill its own ideology.[28] Cecil, to be sure, is a
conservative and a paid counsellor to the Queen, but his desire that the
MPs remain 'secret within [themselves]' was shared by all but a few
radicals.

To remain 'secret within [themselves]', the Commons not only had to
prevent particular MPs from leaking information to the public but also
had to prevent the public from witnessing for themselves the proceedings of Commons. Thus, John Hooker stipulates that the Sergeant at
Arms must 'not suffer any to enter into thise house during the time of
sitting here, unlesse he be one of the house'. But 'if any forain person
doo enter into that house, the assembly therof beeing sitting . . . he ought
. . . to be punished'.[29] Despite many such prohibitions, however, dozens
of 'strangers to the House' – to use a favourite phrase of the MPs –
managed to make their way past the Sergeant at Arms during the
Elizabethan and Jacobean parliaments.[30] Strangers to the house were
almost always imprisoned in the Gatehouse – which the MP William
Lambarde described as 'a prison to th[e] House.'[31]

The practices of figuring members of the public as 'strangers' and
'forain person[s]' and barring them from St Stephen's seem extraordinarily inappropriate for an institution that claimed to be empowered by
the people. But, in fact, the Commons instituted its secrecy rules and
exclusionary procedures during precisely the same period when many
members began routinely to argue that Commons was a sovereign
authority because it was a public institution and a representative body.[32]
According to Coke, the Commons could more than hold their own with
the Lords and the Crown because 'his Majesty and the Nobles being
every one a great person, represented but themselves; but . . . [the]
Commons though they were but inferior men, yet every one of them
represented a thousand of men'.[33] An MP in 1593 similarly claimed that
'there is no knight of any shire here but representeth many thousands'.[34]

The MPs boasted, moreover, that the Commons' representative operations actually made all the subjects of the realm 'representatively
present in us of this house of Commons'.[35]

II

Making the people 'representatively present' in the House of Commons
was the distinctive myth of Commons' ideology throughout the Tudor-
Stuart period. As early as 1565, Sir Thomas Smith had claimed that,

> the parliament of England ... representeth and hath the power of the whole
> realme ... For everie Englishman is entended to bee there present, either in
> person or by procuration and attornies ... from the Prince ... to the lowest
> person of England.[36]

By the time James I ascended, it was typical for the Commons to claim
that 'the whole body of the realm, and every particular member thereof,
either in person or by representation (upon their own free elections), are
by the laws of the realm deemed personally present' in St Stephen's
Chapel.[37]

Why, then, bar the people from an institution in which they are
already present? Because the fiction of the people's presence – the
fiction that empowered the Commons – could be maintained only by
excluding the people. For illicit eyewitnesses discovered that the MPs,
far from magically filling St Stephen's with a plenitude of presence,
frequently left the chamber almost empty. In 1584, Speaker Puckering
created a commotion when he revealed to the MPs that John Bland, a
London currier, had publicly reported,

> that this house passing the Bill of the Shoomakers had proceeded contrary to an
> Order taken in the same House, which he [Bland] said was, that the
> Shoomakers Bill should not be further read till the Curriers Bill were first read
> before; and hath likewise reported, that the Curriers could have no Justice in
> thise House; and also that this House passed the Shoomakers Bill when there
> were scantly fifty persons in the House ... And further reported, that the Bill for
> the Tanners lately read in this House was not all read out, but some leaves
> thereof left unread ... Which Speeches being very slanderous and prejudicial
> to the State of this House ... it was thereupon resolved, that Bland ... be
> examined.[38]

Reporting minor deviations from parliamentary practice – considering
bills out of order, reading only portions of a bill – hardly undermined the
fundamental integrity of Commons; but publicising the fact that only
50 out of some 450 members were sitting during a session did. The
absence of members rendered St Stephen's doubly empty: empty of the

representatives themselves, and, consequently, empty of the millions of people those representatives, according to the most important institutional myth of the Commons, made present at the centre of governance. But Bland's report slandered Commons, above all, because it demonstrated not only that the people were neither personally nor representatively present in St Stephen's but also that Commons continued to act despite their absence.

Absenteeism in the Elizabethan and Jacobean Commons was remarkably high: 'attendance', according to J. E. Neale, 'was a constant problem'.[39] The work of Neale, David Dean and Jennifer Loach indicates that throughout the reigns of Elizabeth I and James I the House was frequently only half full and that it was not at all unusual for only one quarter of the members to be present during business.[40] On quite a few occasions, St Stephen's was almost empty: one recorded vote in 1610 lists fifteen ayes and fifteen nays;[41] on 1 July 1607, Robert Bowyer's diary entry strongly remarks that a bill was read with only twenty MPs sitting.[42] On those days over 400 MPs were absent. (We can now justly call the engravings of the Commons – with the members crowding a packed St Stephen's – propaganda.)

In theory, absenteeism was discouraged and could be punished. William Lambarde's tract on parliament warns that 'no Knight or Burgess should depart without license of the House or of the Speaker, to be entered with the Clerk upon pain to lose their wages'.[43] An anonymous author's 1606 manuscript notes on parliamentary procedure make special mention of the many official rules against absenteeism.[44] There were, moreover, sporadic practical measures to curb absenteeism. To encourage attendance, the House could institute roll calls.[45] Thus, during the 1580 session, 'it was Ordered that the House should be called on *Wednesday* next . . . that so it might appear who did diligently intend the business of the House, and who did negligently absent themselves'.[46] And in 1581 at end of Session fines were levied against members who had been absent for the whole session.[47]

These measures, however, produced absolutely no improvement. More important, with few exceptions the MPs never expressed any real concern over the effect absenteeism might have on the day-to-day operations and efficacy of Commons. By contrast, leading members of the House were acutely aware of the threat *the public discovery of absenteeism* posed to the mythology of the Commons. During the especially severe attendance problems of 1606, Sir Thomas Holcroft argued against a proposal to send county and borough officials letters recalling the many absent members. While Holcroft agreed that the missing members must somehow be contacted, he nonetheless 'misliked the Course, for he wished no Writing to be'.[48] Holcroft argued that recording the Commons' emptiness in letters risked damaging publicity: 'it will be a Scandal, to shew, what we have done [during the session] is done with so small a Number'.[49] Holcroft recognised that absenteeism was scandalous not because it revealed a dysfunctional Commons but because it demonstrated, on the contrary, that the Commons could meet, debate and act when the people were neither physically nor representatively present.[50]

But by 1606 some MPs recognised that Commons' own mythology of representation made the issue of absenteeism virtually irrelevant. Robert Bowyer, for example, claimed that it was entirely unnecessary to recall the absent members:

[I] could wish the Company full in regard of the business which is expected, yet will I not soe narrowly impound the . . . Sufficiency of those that remaine, as to think them unable to proceed in such matters as they shall have in hand, and for that which remaineth, it will suffice that all that are absent, Yea all the realme is intended present.[51]

The Commons, whether full or nearly empty, constituted 'all the realme'. Thus, Bowyer suggested, it makes no sense to argue that the Commons requires the presence of all its members, for if some members are *physically outside* of St Stephen's, they, like everyone else in England, are *representatively inside* St Stephen's.[52]

Bowyer, then, doesn't diminish the importance of representativeness; on the contrary, he conceives the Commons' powers of representation in almost mystical terms. Bowyer's elaboration of the Commons' 'sufficiency' has a Derridean quality: those who are absent, Bowyer claims, are present in virtue of their absence.[53] Indeed, absence, as a category, is evacuated in Bowyer's rhetoric. The Commons is no longer a metonymy for a greater but absent whole because it is the whole. Richard Hooker similarly claimed that the parliament, through the representative operations of the Commons, became not a reflection of the body of the realm but instead its incarnation:

The *Parliament of England* . . . is that whereupon the very *ESSENCE* of all government within this kingdom doth depend. It is even the body of the whole Realme; it consisteth of the *King* and of all that within the *Land* are subject unto him; for they all are there present, either in person or by such as they voluntarily have derived from their personal right unto.[54]

James I, frustrated by similar claims for the miraculous power of

representation, once reminded his Commons that they did 'not so represent the whole commons of the realm as the shadow doth the body but only representatively'.[55] But James finally underestimates the rhetoric of Bowyer, Hooker, and many others; according to these MPs and theorists, the people are the shadows of a body that takes their place.

The construction of representation as absorption critically shaped the Commons' relationship to the public. For example, the myth of representative presence allowed the MPs to transform their accountability to the realm and people beyond St Stephen's into an internal accountability. Thus, during the enclosure debates of 1597, the MPs acknowledged the desires of the various groups interested in land management even as they effectively effaced those interest groups by imaginatively relocating them inside St Stephen's. On 26 November, an anonymous speaker, noting that 'the ears of our great sheepmasters do hang at the doors of this House',[56] acknowledged that the MPs could serve their own private interests by gratifying those rich constituents. But he argued that the Commons should nonetheless preserve for small farmers the land those wealthy husbandmen coveted for grazing:

A lawe framed out of the private affecions of men wil never tend to the generall good of all; and if every one may putt in a caution to save his owne particuler it will never prove a lawe of restraint, but rather of loosenes and libertie. The eyes of the poore are upon this parliament, and sad for the want they yet suffer. The cryes of the poore doe importune much, standing like reedes shaking in every corner of the realme. This place is an epitome of the whole realme: the trust of the poore committed to us, whose persons we supplie, doth challenge our furtheraunce of theire releife. This hath bene the inscripcion on mayne bills. If our forwardnes procede from single-hartedness we can noe waye effect this so well as by leadinge their handes to the plough and leaving the success to God. We sitt now in judgment over ourselves.[57]

The speech is quite beautiful and astonishingly modern; it is also, I think, heartfelt. And yet it is precisely as he articulates a representation of selflessness that our MP reveals what is deeply disturbing about political representation. Because he and his fellow MPs supply the persons – an extraordinary phrase – of the people of the realm, they assume an enormous accountability, but an accountability they can feel only to themselves. We see this in the odd self-reflexiveness of the speaker's final admonition – 'We sitt now in judgment over ourselves' – which should, one feels, recall the poor: the eyes of the poor are upon us and they sit in judgement over us. This displacement of the poor by a representative 'we' fulfils the mimetic figure of Commons as 'an epitome of the whole realm'. If the Commons rather than metonymically representing the realm simply is the whole realm in miniature, there is nothing outside it which is not also in it. Thus, even as the speaker articulates the Commons' moral and political accountability to the public, that public is relocated within the Commons itself. What remains, after political representation, is an 'abroad elsewhere' – an insubstantial, otherworldly place inhabited by the ghostly people, the shadows of the body.

The construction of the Commons' representative operations I've been recovering here establishes the House of Commons not merely as a representative body but as a representation. That is, the Commons, on this account, is not merely a collection of representative agents who speak for the absent people they represent; rather, the House of Commons is itself a representation of the realm: 'This *place*', our anonymous MP claims, 'is an epitome of the whole realme'. If the Commons is a representation of the realm, the engravings of the Commons can be understood as representations of representation (though we must bear in mind here the incarnational mode of representation that characterises so much parliamentary discourse), and I want to conclude this essay by suggesting that we can understand what kind of a 'place' the House of Commons is by revisiting the engravings of the MPs in St Stephen's.

But consider first Figure 3, a licensed broadside of the House of Lords. This representation is truly theatrical in the great art historian and theorist Michael Fried's sense of the word: here, the great display themselves, turn themselves toward the viewer; here, all eyes seem to solicit and return our gaze.[58] The engravings of the Commons, by contrast, depict MPs whose absorption in their own activity renders them oblivious to our presence. Their gazes are directed in every direction but ours. These representations of the House of Commons thus refuse to acknowledge the presence of any potential viewer; the viewer, I suggest, is thus absorbed by their absorption.

Let me elaborate this distinction between theatricality and absorption by suggesting that the difference in the way the two houses choose to represent themselves derives from their divergent institutional ideologies. The Lords' power is inherent in their persons not in their representative status – recall the MPs' claim that while knights and burgesses represented thousands, the Lords represented 'but themselves'. Thus, the engraving of the Lords depicts the power and authority of the institution simply by putting the Peers on spectacular display.

By contrast, the Commons' authority, according to its ideology,

Figure 3 Woodcut, *House of Lords* (1628)

rested on its capacity to make all England present within its walls. Thus, we see in the engravings the MPs busy at the business of representing us. The MPs, that is, are absorbed in the activity of absorption. Thus, the representational strategy of the engravings – that is, absorption – repeats the representational strategy of the House of Commons: that is, absorption. The reason, in short, that the MPs do not return the viewer's gaze is that there simply is – according to the Commons' rhetoric – no viewer to gaze.

NOTES

1. T. E. Hartley (ed.), *Proceedings in the Parliaments of Elizabeth I, Vol. 1: 1558–1581* (Wilmington, Delaware: Michael Glazier, 1981), p. 227.
2. *Ibid.*
3. This engraving is in the collection of the Print Room at the British Library and is reproduced here with the permission of the British Museum. I am grateful to the Print Room staff for all their valuable assistance and to Princeton University for the Humanities and Social Sciences Research Grant which made my visit to the collection possible.
4. *The Riverside Shakespeare*, ed. G. Blakemore Evans *et al.* (Boston: Houghton Mifflin, 1974).
5. Hartley, *Proceedings in the Parliaments of Elizabeth I*, p. 137.
6. John Hooker, *The Order and usage of the keeping of a Parlement in England* (1571). Rpt. in John Snow, *Parliament in Elizabethan England* (New Haven: Yale University Press, 1977), p. 163.
7. Figure 2 is in the collection of the Society of Antiquaries, London, as is Figure 3.
8. *Statutes of the Realm*, 12 vols., ed. A. Luders *et al.* (London: Record Commission, 1810–28), vol. II, p. 1018.
9. Simonds d'Ewes, *The Journals of all the Parliaments During the Reign of Queen Elizabeth, both of the House of Lords and House of Commons* (London: John Starkey, 1682), p. 487.
10. Although private bills were often used to accomplish what we would consider public works (road repair, dam modifications, and so on), some private bills pursued strictly personal ends. To take one example among hundreds: on 27 May 1572, Frances Alford, the important London MP, introduced a bill to settle a disputed real estate deal in his favour (Hartley, *Proceedings in the Parliaments of Elizabeth I*, pp. 291–3). For the role of private bills in Commons, see D. M. Dean, 'Public or Private? London, Leather and Legislation in Elizabethan England', *Historical Journal* 31 (1988), 543, 545. J. D. Alsop has suggested that the entirely routine granting of subsidies during the Elizabethan parliaments – there is no evidence, he claims, that any Elizabethan MP 'ever attempted to refuse a request for taxation' – enabled the MPs to devote much of their time to using the lower house as 'a

forum where private interests could achieve realization of their own priori-
ties' ('Parliament and Taxation', D. M. Dean and N. L. Jones (eds.), *The
Parliaments of Elizabethan England* (Oxford: Basil Blackwell, 1990), p. 100).

11. I quote here from a very early printed copy of the 'Petition', included by an
    anonymous editor in *A Record of some worthy Proceedings; in the Honourable, wise
    and faithfull Howse of Commons in the late Parliament* (Amsterdam [?]: G. Thorp
    [?], 1611), p. 16. The MPs composed the document after James I publicly
    declared that he could establish impositions by prerogative and then sought
    to restrain debate on the matter. See Elizabeth Read Foster, *Proceedings in
    Parliament, 1610*, 2 vols. (New Haven: Yale University Press, 1966), vol. II,
    p. 371.

12. Hartley, *Proceedings in the Parliaments of Elizabeth I*, p. 136.

13. *Ibid.*

14. D'Ewes, *The Journals of all the Parliaments During the Reign of Queen Elizabeth*,
    p. 487.

15. *Ibid.*, p. 515.

16. This is perhaps a good place to acknowledge that I frequently refer here to
    the ideology or the rhetoric of the House of Commons; there were, of
    course, many ideologies and rhetorics in play in the Commons. The
    Commons was not a homogeneous institution. Rather, the members of
    Commons pursued diverse agendas, had diverse interests and loyalties,
    and, to be sure, had very different ideas about their own institution's role in
    contemporary political culture. At one extreme, we have the Wentworths
    and Robert Snagge; at the other, members of Commons who were also
    paid officers of the Crown. I have tried here to focus on ideas, practices and
    ideologies that were endorsed by the vast majority of Elizabethan and
    Jacobean MPs.

17. Both Whigs and Revisionists give far too much credence to MPs' protests
    over the Crown's access to their proceedings: for Whigs such protests count
    as fiery opposition; for Revisionists, they demonstrate Commons' fear of
    and subservience to the Crown.

18. This was Hall's maiden speech and it gives ample evidence of the rashness
    that so frequently made him the subject of the Commons' wrath. For a
    summary of Hall's career, see *The House of Commons: 1558–1603, Vol. II
    (Members, D-L*, ed. P. W. Hasler (London: HM Stationery Office, 1981).

19. The Commons, to be sure, also censored members solely for speech within
    St Stephen's. Such restrictions on speech were sometimes motivated by the
    Commons' fear of offending the monarch, but a fine article by J. P.
    Sommerville suggests that the Commons' censoring of its own members did
    not decline as the body asserted greater independence from the Crown.
    Thus, while the MPs sent Sir Christopher Piggot to the Tower after he
    spoke in 1607 against James' cherished Union plans, the MPs of 1624 voted
    to strike from the record Sergeant Higham's defense of James' impositions
    (see 'Parliament, Privilege, and the Liberties of the Subject', J. H. Hexter
    (ed.), *Parliament and Liberty from the Reign of Elizabeth to the English Civil War*

(Stanford University Press, 1992), p. 75).

20. Hartley, *Proceedings in the Parliaments of Elizabeth I*, p. 360.
21. *Ibid.*, p. 327.
22. Compare the position of the MP William Fennor, whose 'infinite ... estimation of liberties' (Hartley, *Proceedings*, p. 361) and desire for 'libertie of speech without restraint' (p. 355) moved him to urge that Hall not be punished at all but instead 'held as a mad man' (p. 361).
23. See Hartley, *Proceedings*, pp. 330 and 366 for two different accounts of Hall's performance.
24. *Ibid.*, p. 509.
25. After being dismembered, Hall was imprisoned in the Tower until he produced a suitable recantation. After nearly a year, Hall finally won his release by proclaiming his 'reverence' for all those aspects of Commons mythology that he had debunked (see H. G. Wright, *The Life and Works of Arthur Hall of Grantham* (Manchester University Press, 1919), p. 191). Thus, for example, he acknowledged the antiquity of Commons he had so carefully disproved in his pamphlets (see Arthur Hall, *A letter sent by F.A. touchyng a quarell betweene A. Hall, and M. Mallerie. With an admonition to him* [Hall] *being a burgesse of the parliament, for his better behauiour therein* (London: H. Bynneman, 1576), sig. D4).
26. Notestein and Relf's careful discussion of publicity in and before 1629 makes it quite clear that before 1610, and really before 1621, the circulation of manuscripts of Commons speeches and proceedings was very limited. Moreover, these reports were always made to men of a quite select class: 'Members of Parliament, important country families, great nobles, politically affected clergymen, ambassadors from foreign states, Privy Councilers and less important people.' Footnotes supply examples for all the types mentioned in this list except, revealingly, 'less important people'.
27. D'Ewes, *The Journals of all the Parliaments*, p. 653.
28. Cecil was similarly distressed by the appearance outside of Parliament of 'a multitude of people who said they were commonwealth men and desired [the House] to take compassion of their griefs' – a multitude who, in other words, asked the Commons to do precisely what the Commons habitually claimed to do (see Penry Williams, 'The Crown and the Counties', Christopher Haigh (ed.), *The Reign of Elizabeth I* (Athens: University of Georgia Press, 1987), p. 135). Williams suggests that Cecil's famous outburst 'reflects ... some remarkable views on the proper relationship between Parliament and the people' (p. 136). But, as I am trying to suggest here, most MPs seem to support Cecil's views, at least on this count. When the quite progressive Robert Snagge, for example, moved in 1571 that the people be consulted about the Commons' debates over the fate of the Duke of Norfolk, even his usual cohorts failed to second him (Hartley, *Proceedings in the Parliaments of Elizabeth I*, p. 392). Of course, when it served their purposes, the MPs did treat the electorate as a primitive constituency. During the debate over impositions in 1610, for example, many members, sensing that the financial

burden would be unpopular, suggested that the knights and burgesses return to 'their several countries' to 'take intelligence' (Foster, *Proceedings in Parliament*, Vol. II, p. 292). To this end, Sir William Twysden prepared an argument based on precedent to prove that the MPs could 'go into the country and receive a resolution from them [the voters]' (Foster, *Proceedings*, p. 366). Cf. *Commons Journals*, p. 427.

29. Hooker, *The Order and usage*, pp. 173, 170.

30. See, for example, the cases of Edmund Moore and John Turner (D'Ewes, *The Journals of all the Parliaments*, p. 394); 'two younge gentlemen' (Hartley, *Proceedings in the Parliaments of Elizabeth I*, p. 200); and William Hanney (D'Ewes, *The Journals of all the Parliaments*, p. 288–9).

31. William Lambarde, *Notes on the procedures and privileges of the House of Commons* [1584], ed. Paul L. Ward (London: HM Stationery Office, 1977), p. 76. For the use of the Gatehouse as a holding pen for 'strangers to the House', see the cases of Charles Johnson (D'Ewes, *The Journals of all the Parliaments*, p. 248), Charles Morgan (p. 334), Richard Robinson (p. 334), and Roger Dodswell (p. 565).

32. Prior to 1571, for example, the Commons had never claimed a right to secret debate (Conrad Russell, *The Crisis of Parliaments: English History, 1509–1660* (Oxford University Press, 1971), p. 222). And while Hooker's 1571 tract harps on barring strangers from St Stephen's, the *Modus tenendi Parliamentum* itself makes no mention of excluding the public.

33. D'Ewes, *The Journals of all the Parliaments*, p. 515. Coke's interpretation of the three estates very much reflects the Commons' account of English governance. That is, Coke assumes not only that parliament is comprised of the three estates but also that the monarch cannot claim to represent anyone but himself. The monarchy, when it admitted of the sovereignty of the king-in-parliament, had its own strategy for figuring the king as the representative of the whole realm. Coke's account of parliament closely echoes, among others, Lambarde, John Hooker and Aylmer. Hooker, for example, argues that while the King is 'a ful whole degree of him self' (*The Order and usage*, p. 152), by calling Commons he can 'seek & aske the advice, councel and assistance of his whole Realme' (p. 145). In representational ideology, being a whole degree unto oneself is a deficiency. The Lords were also keenly aware of this rhetoric: they strenuously objected when Snagge allegedly claimed that 'the noble men represented their own voices only' and were thus 'unable to deale in matters of common weale' (Hartley, *Proceedings in the Parliaments of Elizabeth I*, p. 403). The Lords' alarm over Snagge's speech would seem to indicate the increasing political capital attached to representativeness.

34. Jennifer Loach, *Parliament Under the Tudors* (Oxford University Press, 1991), p. 148. Because each MP represented many people, he was a public rather than private person. Thus, Carleton argued that a particular MP who had been detained from the House, must be brought to St Stephen's: 'forasmuch as hee nowe was not a private man but to supply the roome, person

and place of a multitude especially chosen and therfor sent ... for the liberty of the House' (Hartley, *Proceedings in the Parliaments of Elizabeth I*, p. 238).

35. *The Commons' Apology* [1604], quoted in J.R. Tanner (ed.), *Constitutional Documents of the Reign of James I: 1603–1625* (Cambridge University Press, 1961), p. 219.

36. *De Republica Anglorum* [1583], ed. Mary Dewar (Cambridge University Press, 1982), pp. 78–9.

37. *Statutes of the Realm*, vol. ii, p. 1018.

38. D'Ewes, *The Journals of all the Parliaments*, p. 366.

39. J. E. Neale, *The Elizabethan House of Commons* [1949] (Harmondsworth: Penguin, 1963), p. 413.

40. See *ibid.*, p. 414; G. R. Elton, 'Parliament', Haigh (ed.), *The Reign of Elizabeth I*, pp. 88–9; Loach, *Parliament Under the Tudors*, pp. 40–1.

41. Foster, *Proceedings in Parliament*, vol. ii, p. 277.

42. *The Parliamentary Diary of Robert Bowyer, 1606–1607*, ed. David Harris Wilson (Minneapolis: University of Minnesota Press, 1931), p. 363.

43. Lambarde, *Notes on the procedures*, p. 66.

44. See 'Observations rules and orders collected out of diverse Journalls of the house of Commons,' British Library Egerton MS 3365, fol. 51v.

45. 'It is common policy to say upon the Wednesday that the House shall be called on Saturday, and upon Saturday to say it shall be called on Wednesday; and so from day to day by fear thereof to keep the company together' (Lambarde, *Notes on the procedures*, p. 90).

46. D'Ewes, *The Journals of all the Parliaments*, p. 283.

47. Hartley, *Proceedings in the Parliaments of Elizabeth I*, p. 546.

48. *Parliamentary Diary of Robert Bowyer*, pp. 96–7.

49. *Commons Journals*, vol. i, p. 291. In 1610, an anonymous MP was similarly outraged that only 100 MPs were present but 'moved that it might nowhere be recorded that there was so great a neglect'.

50. See *Parliamentary Diary of Robert Bowyer*, p. 97. Bills were frequently enacted when only a small percentage of the House was sitting. According to Loach, during the parliament of 1601 there was not a single division – i.e., a counted vote – in which more than half the members participated (*Parliament Under the Tudors*, pp. 40–1). This figure is all the more striking because divisions were conducted only when important and potentially controversial legislation was at issue.

51. *Parliamentary Diary of Robert Bowyer*, p. 97.

52. *Ibid.* Bowyer's account of the Commons' representativeness is quasi-mystical in part because the vehicle of representation is not a collection of agents but instead a mythic institution. Gadamer argues that similarly deconstructionist notions of representation begin to emerge when 'in light of the Christian idea of the incarnation and the mystical body [representation] acquired a completely new meaning. Representation now no longer means "copy" or "representation in a picture" ... but "replacement" ... what is

represented is present in the copy' (*Truth and Method* [1960], trans. Garrett Barden and John Cumming (New York: Crossroad, 1988), pp. 513n14, 53). MPs and parliamentary theorists, moreover, directly and indirectly borrowed their figurations of the body politic from the theological discourses.

53. Bowyer's elaboration of representation, precisely because of this deconstructionist turn, suggests some of the problems that might attend a deconstructionist critique of political representation.

54. Hooker, *The Order and usage*, p. 192.

55. Quoted in J. P. Kenyon (ed.), *The Stuart Constitution, 1603–1688* (Cambridge University Press, 1966), p. 21.

56. Hartley, *Proceedings in the Parliaments of Elizabeth I*, p. 222.

57. *Ibid.*, pp. 220–1.

58. See Michael Fried, *Absorption and Theatricality: Painting and Beholder in the Age of Diderot* (University of Chicago Press, 1980), pp. 1–70.

CHAPTER 2

A map of Greater Cambria

Philip Schwyzer

At the dawn of the eleventh century BC, Brutus, great-grandson of Aeneas and first king of the island of Britain, lay dying. Like his famous but less fortunate descendant King Lear, Brutus decided to divide the island between his three children. To his eldest son Locrine, he bequeathed the fertile region east of the river Severn and south of the Humber; the portion west of the Severn he gave to his second son, Camber, and the northern remnant to the youngest, Albanactus. The map of Britain as Brutus drew it presents to modern eyes a truncated version of England, known then as Loegria, a gigantic Scotland, called Albania, and a somewhat distended Wales: Cambria.

This is the story told in Geoffrey of Monmouth's *Historia Regum Britanniae* (c. 1136). Needless to say, the political map of Britain in Geoffrey's day did not resemble the one drawn by old king Brutus. The age when the Severn had marked the boundary between Saxon and British kingdoms, between Old English and early Welsh, was already five centuries past. But the division did to a degree reflect administrative realities and political aspirations. Geoffrey of Monmouth was certainly no Welsh nationalist, but his allegiances were Cambro-Norman and Breton, not English. His patron was the Marcher Lord Robert Earl of Gloucester who, in common with his fellow regional warlords, had every interest in resisting the incursion of English monarchical authority over the Severn into the Welsh Marches.

Perhaps because it had never reflected anything so mundane as established fact in the first place, Geoffrey's claim that the Severn marked the original – and, by implication, essential and inalienable – border between England and Wales remained current for centuries. Even after the domains of the old Marcher Lords had been extinguished forever by the Union of England and Wales under Henry VIII, chroniclers and chorographers continued to take the old claim seriously. Then as today, the Severn rose on the slopes of Plynlimon in Wales and crossed into England north of Welshpool, the greater part of its course to the sea running through the apparently English counties of Shropshire, Worcestershire and Gloucestershire. Nevertheless, William Harrison, taking it as his brief in *The Description of Britain* to record the true facts rather than ever-shifting political realities, insisted that the Severn marked the boundary between England and Wales.[1] Harrison and those of his contemporaries who stuck by the borders decreed by the first king of Britain were tracing the river to its 'source', in the sense explored by David Quint: if the physical source of the Severn lay in Montgomeryshire, its source as a border lay at the outset of history and outside of it, in a moment of transcendent authority and 'timeless, originary truth'.[2] To fly in the face of such authority was no light matter, even when that authority flew in the face of contemporary fact; John Stow clearly knew what was at stake when he declared that the river Wye was the correct border of Wales, '*although* it be new'.[3]

Those with no faith in the fables of Geoffrey of Monmouth had of course no reason to worry about his version of Britain's original divisions. William Camden was a pronounced sceptic, and he wrote of the Severn and the Wye alike as temporarily convenient markers to be discarded in the face of altered realities: '*Athelstan* thrust out the Welsh Britans from hence ... And where as before his time, Severn was the bound between the English and the Welshmen, he appointed Wye to be the limit confining them both'.[4] By the same token, however, Wales and England were to Camden little more than recent and fleeting political constructs, superimposed on the essential map of the island. Camden's *Britannia* is organised along the lines of what he called 'the ancient divisions of these kingdoms', meaning the boundaries already in place when Caesar came to Britain. For Camden, the real significance of the Severn would always be that it marked the extent of the domain of the Silures.

While large swathes of territory on the west bank of the Severn lay technically within England, the counties of Shropshire, Worcestershire, Herefordshire, and Gloucestershire fell under the jurisdiction of the Council in the Marches of Wales, based in Ludlow. The significance of the river in determining the extent of the Council's authority is indicated by the fact that while Cheshire and the city of Bristol won their freedom from Ludlow's jurisdiction in the 1560s, the counties embraced or crossed by the Severn had to wait for their release until the sitting of the

Long Parliament. The aggrieved English gentry of these counties, known in the early seventeenth century as the 'gentleman opposers', complained bitterly in parliament and the courts that they were being denied their rights as freeborn Englishmen. But James I insisted that all four transSevernian English counties should continue to be ruled by the same body that governed Wales. His inflexibility on this question of royal prerogative was enough to reduce Chief Justice Coke to tears.[5]

If the 'gentlemen opposers' suspected that in the eyes of the world and of Westminster they were not counted as Englishmen, they had only to look to the atlas for cartographic confirmation of their fears. The supplement to Ortelius' *Theatrum Orbis Terrarum* published in 1573 included a map drawn by the Welsh physician, philologist and antiquarian Humphrey Llwyd (Figure 4). Here Wales, or Cambria, is divided into its three traditional regions, Gwynedd, Deheubarth, and Powys – none of which had possessed a political existence for several centuries – and the eastern border of Powys is the river Severn. Through this audacious cartographical land-grab, Wales is made to extend as far as Worcester and Tewkesbury, at some points more than doubling in width. While the representation of physical geography is faulty in many respects – particularly in the depiction of the cartographer's native North Wales – and the delineation of boundaries apparently anachronistic and fanciful, there is no denying the enduring appeal of Llwyd's map, which was reprinted nearly fifty times in continental and English editions of the atlases of Ortelius, Mercator, Jannson and Horn, including cheap epitomes. It last appeared in 1741, a life in print of almost 170 years.[6]

Llwyd set out his principles very clearly in his *Commentarioli Brittanicae descriptionis Fragmentum*, which appeared in English as *The Breviary of Britain*:

Let us now proceed to Wales, the third part of Britain. The same is now divided from Lhoëgr, that is England, by the Rivers Severn & Dee, and on every other side is environed by Vergivian, or Irish, Ocean. And it was called Cambria, as our chronicles do report, of Camber, the third son of Brutus, like as Lhoëgr of Locrinus, and Albania of Albanactus his other sons also. This same only, with Cornwall, a most ancient country of Britons, enjoyeth as yet the old inhabitants. The Welshmen use the British tongue and are the very true Britons by birth. And although some do write that Wales doth not stretch forth on this side the River Vaga, or Wye, this can be no fraud to us. For we have taken in hand to describe Cambria, and not Wallia, Wales, as it is now called by a new name, and unacquainted to the Welshmen. In Northwales, the Welshmen keep their old bounds. But in Southwales the Englishmen are come over Severn, and have

Figure 4 Humphrey Llwyd, *Cambriae Typus* (1573)

possessed all the land between it and Wye. So that all Herefordshire, & the Forest of Dean, and Gloucestershire, & a great part of Worcestershire, & Shropshire on this side Severn are inhabited by Englishmen at this day.[7]

For Llwyd and his colleague Sir John Price, co-author of *A Description of Cambria*, the seizure of the west bank by the Saxons was a historical crime of a different order from the loss of England to those Germanic invaders; whereas the latter had been ordained by heaven and might, at least partially, be redressed by the return of a Welsh dynasty to the throne in the form of the Tudors, the loss to Cambria of 'the plain and champion country over the rivers' was a violation of the island's essential geography not to be countenanced.[8] That Lloegr could no longer be enjoyed by its old British inhabitants was a misfortune; but to say that Cambria stopped anywhere short of the Severn was simply a lie. Reminiscent as it is of the maps of Greater Serbia, Greater Albania, Greater Bulgaria, etc., produced in recent years, Llwyd's depiction of a Greater Cambria should not perhaps be accused of full-fledged irredentism; the cartographer is careful, at least intermittently, to draw a distinction between Cambria, the eternal and immutable entity, and Wales, the temporal and temporary political construct. But if, as I have suggested, Llwyd's map and the ideology underlying and promoted by it contributed to the maintenance of the jurisdiction of the Council in the Marches over the border counties, then it was certainly not without political implications. Conversely, the dissolution of the council seems to have dealt a fatal blow to Llwyd's claims to represent a timeless geography; although the map continued to be reprinted for another century, after the 1640s it no longer appeared in atlases representing contemporary geography, but only in George Horn's *Accuratissima Orbis Antiqui Delineatio*, a collection of maps of the ancient world.

For more than half a century following the initial publication of the map, references to the Severn as border abound in poetry and prose. Thomas Churchyard's *The Worthines of Wales* (1587) includes the entire west bank within its survey, with more attention paid to the author's native Shrewsbury than to any part of Wales as we know it. Christopher Ockland wrote of 'Wales on part of Albion land, which doth on Severn bound, / (Severn a mighty flood, which twixt the borders, sliding flows) . . .'[9] In the next century, John Stradling's adoration of Charles I emanated 'from Sabrine's farthest shore, / (The semicircling bound of that dominion, / Where hardy Britons your great name adore)'; and William Slatyer in his *Palae-Albion* gave praise to '[t]he sandy stream that

Sea-like flows, / And Wales, and England's parting shows'.[10] Such references are particularly prominent in the early years of the reign of James I, regarded by some as a second Brutus destined to repair the division of the island made by the first. Anthony Munday's *The Triumphs of Re-United Britannia* is one of several works in which the Severn is made to celebrate its demise as a border. In fact, of course, James was the strongest supporter of the continued authority of the Council of the Marches over transSevernian England.

The significance of the Severn in Michael Drayton's *Poly-Olbion*, in part a celebration of the union of Britain, requires special consideration. The front-matter of the long chorographical poem includes a special message 'To My Friends the Cambro-Britons' in which Drayton describes himself as:

Striving, as my much loved (the learned) Humfrey Floyd, in his description of Cambria to Abraham Ortelius, to uphold her ancient bounds, Severn and Dee, and therefore have included the parts of those three English Shires of Gloster, Worster, and Sallop, that lie on the west of Severn, within their ancient mother Wales: In which if I have not done her right, the want is in my ability, not in my love.[11]

The Severn plays multiple roles in *Poly-Olbion*; as the border between England and Wales, she is queen of western Britain, reigning over her tributaries of both nations and resolving their factional disputes. This she does by prophesying that soon the island will be truly united, and her own role as border finished forever: 'Why strive ye then for that, in little time that shall / (As you are all made one) be one unto you all' (5.77–8). Yet later in the poem the river laments the theft of her west bank by the English, and she cheers the oppressed Cambrians by reminding them of their high and ancient lineage: 'My Wales, then hold thine own, and let the Britons stand / Upon their right, to be the noblest of the Land' (8.375–6). Such partisanship is hardly in keeping with her previous desire '[t]hat she would not be found t'incline to either side' (4.40), but is revealing of the extent to which Jacobean pan-Britannicism and Welsh patriotism drew on precisely the same sources and discourses – sometimes with awkward results.

It must be noted that while the Severn was widely regarded as the true border between England and Wales, the status of the river Humber, which once divided the realms of Locrine and Albanactus, was generally held to have long since lapsed. I am not aware of any map, chronicle, chorography or other work before or after 1603 which represents the Humber as the real contemporary border between England and Scotland. The implication is obvious, but we should not conclude that the Severn was allowed to retain its status simply because this was deemed to be without threatening political consequences. If it is fair to say that the fulminations of men like Llwyd were tolerated because they were regarded as harmless, it must also be acknowledged that Welsh irredentism drew on the same source which allowed the Tudors to claim descent from ancient British monarchs and James I the title of a second Brutus. It was not forgotten that, prior to the successful appropriation of Geoffrey of Monmouth by Henry Tudor and his heirs, Welsh territorial aspirations drawn from this source had posed a serious threat to the English throne.

As Shakespeare reminded his audience in *Henry IV, Part 1*, Owen Glendower had claimed the entire west bank for his enlarged and independent Cambria. The Welsh rebel's grandiose territorial ambitions spring from the same source as the prophecies of Merlin to which he is addicted. On a deeper level, they are rooted in that geographical conservatism which provokes him to bafflement at Hotspur's idea of changing the winding of the river Trent, though this would not effect his own allotted portion. 'Not wind? It shall, it must, you see it doth'.[12] To Glendower, as to many in Shakespeare's audience, political and natural geography are essentially the same subject; that the ancient borders of the island should ever be altered is as unthinkable as that the rivers themselves should change course. Shakespeare seems to have been at least intrigued, if not altogether swayed by this point of view. The Severn attains a symbolic status early on in the play when the blood of the English Mortimer mingles in its waters with that of the Welsh rebel, as it will shortly be mingled again through Mortimer's marriage to Glendower's daughter. There is as well the strange moment in *Cymbeline* when the king commands his men to escort the Roman ambassador as far as the Severn – strange in that the Roman has just requested conduct as far as Milford Haven, and we had thought Cymbeline was king of all Britain.[13] The river clearly has border significance here, though whether it marks the limit of Geoffrey of Monmouth's Cambria or of William Camden's Silures, we are not quite sure. Similarly ambiguous and intriguing references occur in other Jacobean plays set in Roman-era Britain, notably Fisher's *True Trojans* and Rowley's *A Shoe-maker, a Gentleman*, in which the Welshman Sir Hugh displays his patriotism, proclaiming 'There's not a crag beyond the Severn flood, / But I have held against the Roman Foes'.[14]

The role of the Severn and of the nymph Sabrina in Milton's *Masque*

Presented at Ludlow Castle, aka *Comus,* is well known. The masque was presented before the Earl of Bridgewater, Lord President of the Council in the Marches, and starred several of his children. *Comus* has been read by some as calling for greater sympathy for the Welsh and their traditions, by others as recommending a firmer English hand. I incline to the latter view, but the point I would make here is simply that Wales, as we know it, does not figure in the masque at all. The children are travelling west towards Ludlow and have just crossed the Severn when the trouble starts, putting them probably more than thirty miles from the nearest Welsh county. They are in a part of Britain which is at once beyond and before the Welsh border, and the hybrid nature of the monsters they have to deal with – human beings with the heads of beasts – is suggestive of a region whose inhabitants Humphrey Llwyd called Englishmen, while slyly adding that they 'are taken almost everywhere of all other Englishmen for Welshmen.'[15] The 'barbarous dissonance' these creatures use for speech is reminiscent of those inhabitants of the border counties of whom the Welsh grammarian Gruffudd Robert complained: 'so soon as they see the river Severn . . . begin to put their Welsh out of mind and to speak it in most corrupt fashion. Their Welsh will be of an English cut, and their English (God knows) too much after the Welsh fashion.'[16] Neither truly Welsh nor properly English, the border-dwellers in Robert's imagination and in Milton's are hybrids, grotesques – monsters. Insofar as the danger threatening the Lord President's children takes the form of cultural hybridity on the west bank, Milton's masque endorses the old idea of the Severn as true border, and hence of the Council's continued jurisdiction over the four restless English counties situated partly or wholly in TransSevernia.[17]

As I have mentioned, the Council was abolished by the Long Parliament just a few years after *Comus* was performed, and, when briefly revived after the Restoration, its authority was limited to Wales as we know it. Although Humphrey Llwyd's map continued to be reprinted into the 1740s, there was no longer any administrative correlative to the idea that Cambria in its essential and immutable form extended as far as the Severn. Today, the idea must certainly be regarded as defunct, but it seems we have not quite abandoned the notion that Britain's 'real', original and eternal internal borders persist like unfading palimpsests beneath the arbitrary lines superimposed by later generations. After all, Powys and Gwynedd, names long out of use and largely forgotten when Llwyd put them on his map, were revived as recently as 1974 and are with us today, albeit diminished in extent. The Border Reforms in

Wales invite us to believe in the essential reality of certain places – to believe in a timeless Powys more 'real' than the three counties it replaced – counties whose extinction need not be mourned because they were 'really' Powys all along. Powys is to Montgomeryshire, Radnorshire, and Breconshire, as Llwyd's Cambria is to Wallia, transhistorical entity to temporary political construct. From this point of view, the re-emergence of Powys is at once a resurrection and an apocalypse – an apocalypse in the root sense of an unveiling, revealing the truth that had lain hid.

Few if any of us, of course, are prepared to count a place called Powys among the eternal verities. Many, myself included, are sceptical as to whether places on maps can ever be 'real' in the sense that Humphrey Llwyd wanted them to be, essential entities with immutable borders. But this seems to leave us with the alternative Llwyd saw all too clearly and, I cannot help feeling, was right to reject: that the strongest will always make the rules, and draw the boundaries, and cross them when they are ready, to draw new ones further on. Remember Camden's King Athelstan: 'And where as before his time, Severn was the bound between the English and the Welshmen, he appointed Wye to be the limit confining them both.' We recoil from the idea that borders can be redrawn in an instant by such swift and brutal acts of what we have learned to call ethnic cleansing. Yet we can hardly accept the notion that nations retain an inalienable right to territories which changed hands 500 or 1000 years ago – a notion which frequently provides the justification for ethnic cleansing. But what about 100 years ago? Fifty? Or in the last generation? Finding some reasonable middle ground between the idealistic irredentism of a Humphrey Llwyd and the harsh pragmatism of a King Athelstan would require us to tackle the painful question of time. At what point in time is it just, decent and right to redraw the maps? How long does it take for the real borders to change?[18]

NOTES

1. *Holinshed's Chronicles*, 5 vols., ed. Henry Ellis (London: J. Johnson *et al.*, 1807), vol. I, p. 117.
2. David Quint, *Origin and Originality in Renaissance Literature: Versions of the Source* (New Haven: Yale University Press, 1983), p. 23.
3. John Stow, *The Chronicles of England* (London: R. Newberie, 1580), p. 10 (italics mine).
4. William Camden, *Britain*, trans. Philemon Holland (London: George

Bishop and John Norton, 1610), p. 358.

5. See Penry Williams, 'The Attack on the Council in the Marches, 1603–1642', *Transactions of the Honourable Society of Cymmrodorion* (1961), part 1, 1–22; and R. E. Ham, 'The Four Shire Controversy', *Welsh History Review* 8 (1977), 381–400.

6. See F. J. North, *Humphrey Llwyd's Maps of England and of Wales* (Cardiff: National Museum of Wales, 1937).

7. Humphrey Llwyd, *The Breviary of Britain*, trans. Thomas Twyne (London: R. Johnes, 1573), fols. 49v–50r.

8. John Price and Humphrey Llwyd, *A Description of Cambria, Now Called Wales*, in David Powel, *A Historie of Cambria Now Called Wales* (London: R. Newberie and H. Denham, 1584), p. 5.

9. John Sharrock, *The Valiant Actes and Victorious Battles* (London: R. Waldgraue, 1585), translating the Latin verses of Christopher Ockland which appear in *Holinshed's Chronicles*, vol. IV, p. 879.

10. Sir John Stradling, 'To the Sacred Maiestie of My Dread Soveraigne Lord the King', *Divine Poems* (London: W. Stansby, 1625); William Slatyer, *The History of Great Britain [Palae-Albion]* (London: R. Meighen, 1621), p. 93.

11. Michael Drayton, *Poly-Olbion* [1612], J. W. Hebel *et al.* eds., *The Works of Michael Drayton*, vol. IV (Oxford: Basil, Blackwell and Mott, 1961), p. *vii.

12. William Shakespeare, *1 Henry IV*, 3.1.103, *The Norton Shakespeare*, ed. Stephen Greenblatt *et al.* (New York: Norton, 1997).

13. See William Shakespeare, *Cymbeline*, 3.5.7–17, *The Norton Shakespeare*.

14. William Rowley, *A Shoo-Maker, A Gentleman* (London: J. Okes, 1638), sig. F3r.

15. Llwyd, *Breviary*, fol. 13v.

16. John Milton, *Comus*, line 549, *John Milton: Complete Shorter Poems*, ed. John Carey (London: Longman, 2nd edn 1997); Robert quoted in J. Gwynfor Jones, *Wales and the Tudor State* (Cardiff: University of Wales Press, 1989), p. 160.

17. For an extended discussion, see Philip Schwyzer, 'Purity and Danger on the West Bank of the Severn: The Cultural Geography of *A Masque Presented at Ludlow Castle, 1634*', *Representations* 60 (1997), 22–48.

18. I am grateful to Anna Brown and Clare Harraway for their comments and advice.

CHAPTER 3

Britannia rules the waves?: images of empire in Elizabethan England

Lesley B. Cormack

In a proposal written for Elizabeth's Privy Council in 1577,[1] John Dee stressed the potential power and supremacy of England, as well as her ability to achieve a great and lasting empire.

No King, nor Kingdome, hath, by Nature and Humayn Industry (to be used) any, more LAWFULL, and more Peaceable Means (made evident) wherby, to become In wealth, far passing all other: In Strength, and Force, INVINCIBLE: and in Honorable estimation, Triumphantly Famous, over all, and above all other.[2]

Elizabethan geographers and cartographers, led by such important and influential men as Dee, helped develop a set of attitudes and assumptions that encouraged them to view the English as separate from and superior to the rest of the world. Geography supplied the many students and politicians who studied it with a belief in their own inherent superiority and their ability to control the world they now understood.[3] Indeed, the study of geography helped the English develop an imperial world view based on three underlying assumptions: a belief that the world could be measured, named and therefore controlled; a sense of the superiority of the English over peoples and nations and thus the right of the English nation to exploit other areas of the globe; and a self-definition that gave these English students a sense of themselves and their nation.[4] This message of superiority and the possibility of imperial expansion was aided by the iconographic images present in many geographical works. Through the constant repetition of such messages, students of geography began to envisage a world open to the exploration and exploitation of the English.

Historians looking for the origins of the English and British empires have long examined theoretical tracts emanating from such moments as the Union of Crowns of 1603.[5] These have yielded much valuable information, but do not give a wider sense of the cultural interest in or proclivity towards these ideas. In order to understand the underlying attitudes towards ideas of empire, we must examine alternative discursive sites, for example, court masques, street processions and illustrated frontispieces.[6] As historians such as Steven Shapin and Paula Findlen have shown, these cultural analytic spaces often provide a clearer sense of the interplay between intellectual ideas and their cultural and political applications.[7] In this essay, I will examine the imperial messages of popular geographical texts, most particularly their illustrated frontispieces, in order to assess these underlying imperial assumptions.[8] While these frontispieces should not be seen as complete in themselves, they demonstrate the widespread interest in and acceptance of these imperial images.

The empire imagined in these geographical books and frontispieces, however, did not have a single focus or direction. While the Spanish had established a form of world dominion through conquest and the resulting mineral wealth, the English were less sure of their method of expansion, or the desired results. Thus the message of England's ability to venture forth, for profit, power and fame, as Dee had maintained, was troubled by uncertainty as to just who should venture, what their goal should be and what profit would accrue. The iconographic formation of the English empire, while powerful for English readers of such geographical literature, was thus unstable and perhaps contributed to the rather erratic development of empire that was to follow.

The concept of empire can be traced back to the Roman Empire. Anthony Pagden has identified three different usages of the term empire, all with classical roots and all current in sixteenth-century Europe.[9] An empire could in the first instance refer to a self-sufficient and omni-competent state, the concept first articulated in England in Thomas Cromwell's famous phrase, 'this realm of England is an empire', in the Act in Restraint of Appeals of 1533.[10] Secondly, the empire could refer to the monarch who exercised *imperium* or command over an area. Finally, and most significantly for sixteenth-century Europe, empire referred to the extended control, usually of a Christian monarch, over more than one geographical area.[11] This last meaning, of course, encompassed the empire Spain claimed to have created and thus the empire that most interested geographical writers in late sixteenth- and early seventeenth-century England. And yet, the images of empire developed by those most interested in promoting the creation of an English empire were ambiguous in relation to this meaning. Many saw

Elizabeth or James as integral to any imperial adventure, but the underlying message of these texts and images was much more haphazard and personal than monarchical. Merchants and trade seemed just as if not more important than conquest and glory. The creation of an English empire, while clearly arguing for England's ability to achieve supremacy in the geopolitical struggle, would not place Britannia on the ship of power and control. Rather merchants and personal adventurers were to gain by this venture.[12] As well, the tangible results of these early propaganda campaigns were less than nothing, since all the expeditions potentially inspired by the images and ideas I will discuss were unmitigated disasters.[13] Perhaps this was partly due to the very ambiguity of these images, which encouraged men in various governance and mercantile positions to think of empire, but did not give them a clear sense of what this meant. This troubled concept of empire would have far-reaching ramifications in the creation of the actual empire of the next two centuries.[14]

I

The most overt iconographic example of imperial thinking came from Dr John Dee. Dee, a Master of Arts from Cambridge, was a mathematician, astronomer, geographer and on occasion necromancer. Though in recent years Dee's name has become synonymous with occultist practices and Hermeticism, in his own time he was much better known as a learned and practical geographer.[15] His interest in astronomy, astrology and geography was established while a student, and it was this initial spark that sent him on to Louvain to study with those great mathematicians and geographers, Gemma Frisius and Gerard Mercator, among others.[16] He later returned to England, where he set himself up as an astrologer and geographical advisor, becoming astrologer to Elizabeth (in which capacity he advised her on hydrographical and geographical matters) and advising the Muscovy Company, Humphrey Gilbert, and numerous other practical geographers.[17] He was equally an overt promoter of English imperialism, especially although not exclusively in *General and Rare Memorials Pertayning to the Perfect Arte of Navigation* (1577).[18] Responding to a series of serious threats to maritime security, Dee proposed that Elizabeth establish a Royal Navy to protect England from pirates, the English fishery from incursions, and to aid in the establishment of a British maritime empire. Dee directed to the politically powerful men surrounding Elizabeth an overt message of imperialism and of the necessity of using scholarly knowledge for the good of the common weal. In less overt terms, these were the lessons to be gained from a variety of geography books and from the study of geography itself.[19] The illustrated title page to Dee's book provides a visual representation of this message of power and hegemonic potential, while at the same time warning the English of the danger of ignoring this opportunity (Figure 5). While some title-pages may reflect the printer's aesthetic or practical concerns (as we shall see, some title-pages were used for a variety of books), this title-page, present in both manuscript and printed copies, bears Dee's unmistakable imprint.[20] In this engraving, Elizabeth commands the ship of state, labelled Europa. The Royal coat of arms on the rudder indicates Dee's prophesy (and present claim) of England's supremacy and leadership of Europe. Elizabeth is receiving her advisors, but she looks toward naked lady Occasion (or Fortuna), standing on the fortress to the left. Elizabeth holds out her right hand to grasp Fortune's forelock and the laurel wreath she holds – undoubtedly by founding her great Royal Navy. Britannia, kneeling on the shore, desires Elizabeth to seize her opportunity with a 'fully-equipped expeditionary force', as her scroll states.[21] This navy is to be much more than a coast guard patrolling for pirates; rather it will begin the divinely sanctioned creation of an English empire. God, Elizabeth, and St Michael on the right fight back the darkness on the left and the naval force will soon capture the foreign ships at sea. There is also a more ominous warning here, since the skull on the right acts as a *memento mori* and may be related to the ear of wheat, a Hermetic symbol for man, here somewhat inauspiciously reversed. In other words, if the readers ignore Dee's perspicacious proposal, England's end may be less than felicitous. Indeed, there are a number of hints that magic may play a part in England's greatness, from the Latin motto surrounding the title, 'Plvra: Latent: quam: Patent' (More things are concealed than are revealed),[22] to the Greek symbols in the four corners, which add up to Dee's *Monas Hieroglyphica*.[23] It is tempting to see a strong parallel between the discovery of the philosopher's stone and the creation of England as an imperial power. It is a mistake, however, to take this too far, since this text was intended for a select group of Elizabeth's advisors and some vague claim to mystical transformation would not have been particularly appropriate.[24]

If there was any doubt of the imperial message on this title-page, Dee lays it out in the text.

Figure 5 Title page from John Dee, *General and Rare Memorials Pertayning to the Perfect Arte of Navigation* (1577)

Why should not we HOPE, that, RES-PVBL. BRYTANICA, on her knees, very Humbly, and ernestly Soliciting the most Excellent Royall Maiesty, of our ELIZABETH (Sitting at the HELM of this Imperiall Monarchy: or, rather, at the Helm of the IMPERIALL SHIP, of the most parte of Christendome: if so, it be her Graces Pleasure) shall obteyn, (or Perfect Policie, may perswade her Highnes,) that, which is the Pyth, or Intent of RES-PVBL. BRYTANICA, Her Supplication? Which is, That, ΣΤΟΛΟΣ ΕΞΩΠΛΙΣΜΕΝΟΣ [a fully equipped expeditionary force], may helpe vs, not onley, to ΦΡΟΥΡΙΟΝ ΤΗΣ ΑΣΦΑΛΕΙΑΣ [a citadel of safety, such as Fortune stands on]: But make vs, also, Partakers of Publik Commodities Innumerable, and (as yet) Incredible.

Thus Elizabeth, already commanding the imperial ship as a leader of Christendom, can employ this new *Navy Royall* both to defend the autonomy of England and, more importantly, to achieve wealth, power, and hegemony. Elizabeth's location in this picture is extremely telling. Dee first places her in charge of the ship as an 'Imperiall Monarchy', an important position implying dominion over more than one country, both legislatively and spiritually.[25] He then corrects this to claim her greater place at the helm 'of the most parte of Christendome'. This implies an eschatological role as the Protestant saviour of Europeans and the newly discovered peoples alike.[26] Britannia herself, of course, kneels in a much more subsidiary position, clearly beholden to this monarch, rather than in any way defining her. It is Elizabeth, not Britannia, who will make possible the safety of the country, and even more important, in the perhaps unconscious echo of the communion prayer of consecration, it is Elizabeth who will allow the development of new mercantile endeavours. Dee goes on to place divine sanction on these expansionist and mercantilist ambitions by continuing:

Vnto which, the HEAVENLY KING, for these many yeres last past, hath, by MANIFEST OCCASION, most Graciously, not only inuited vs: but also, hath made, EVEN NOW, the Way and Means, most euident, easie, and Compendious: In-asmuch as, (besides all our own sufficient Furniture, Hability, Industry, Skill, and Courage) our Freends are become strong: and our Enemies, sufficiently weake, and nothing Royally furnished, or of Hability, for Open Violence Vsing: Though their accustomed Confidence, in Treason, Trechery, and Disloyall Dealings, be very great. Wherein, we beseche our HEAVENLY PROTECTOR, with his GOOD ANGELL to Garde vs, with SHIELD AND SWORD, now, and euer. Amen.[27]

According to Dee, God takes up the cause of the expansionist English, through the intervention of his sword-wielding angel, Michael. By weakening its enemies and strengthening its friends, God has shown England that it is now time to act.

Dee's book provided a strong pronouncement of the imperial ideology present in geographical discourse, both in the imagery of the title-page and in the message of the text. The audience for *General and Rare Memorials* was undoubtedly small, but included some of the most influential privy councillors of the day.[28] Although the navy was never established, several of Elizabeth's key advisors appreciated and shared this imperial vision for England. Dee's picture of empire was a complex one, with Britannia subservient to Elizabeth's dominion, and Elizabeth herself supplying the wherewithal for private profit as well as national glory. For all its peculiarities, however, Dee's work shared with many other geographical treatises an overt desire for an imperial future for England.

These imperial messages, as well as geographical information about the wider world more generally, were read by a large group of men, some the principal politicians and investors of early modern England, and others destined for lesser political, judicial or church careers. This study of geography, often at university, provided them with a sense of English superiority and potential hegemony, as well as with examples of the heroic feats of those champions of English expansion who had gone before.[29] The vision of geography informed these men that England stood poised on the brink of a great imperial adventure, in which they could and should participate.

II

Many of the geography books popular with university scholars in the period after Dee's book was published contained this message of English power and potential. The images of empire they conveyed, like Dee's, were multi-faceted, and many asked similar questions as to the real source of power, and the recipients of wealth. At the same time, they stressed the potential for England to achieve a greater empire, both materially and spiritually, than Spain or any other rival European power. Richard Hakluyt, for example, in a widely read compilation of travel narratives and geographical descriptions published in 1598–1600, declared through the narrative of Richard Willes, that the English were most suited to explore and control the eastern trade.

The rude Indian Canoa halleth those seas, the Portingals, the Saracenes, and Moores travaile continually up and downe that reach from Japan to China, from China to Malacca, from Malacca to the Moluccaes: and shall an Englishman, better appointed than any of them all (that I say no more of our Navie) feare to saile in that Ocean: What seas at all doe want piracie: What Navigation is there voyde of perill?[30]

Hakluyt's massive collection proved a very important source for English pride and imperial hope. Hakluyt perused historical sources to find long-forgotten English voyages in order to argue that the English had the right to foreign lands through first discovery.[31] He also included many modern voyages by the English (and others) and in this contemporary reportage he used the words of people who had been there, a style of reporting that lent great verisimilitude to his stories and allowed his readers to see the real passion and poetry, as well as hard-nosed business sense, of England's travellers.[32] His book let the English mariner or merchant develop a self-consciousness of his role in the world and so Hakluyt's book encouraged a view of a very personal and trade-oriented empire. There was no doubt that this would be an empire for the glory of Queen and country, but exactly who would have dominion was rather less clear.

John Wolfe also supplied an imperial message when he published a translated version of Jan Huygen van Linschoten's *Discours of Voyages* in 1598. Linschoten, a Dutch adventurer, had written a book describing Dutch and Portuguese voyages to distant locations, including a description of the Congo by a Portuguese explorer and an analysis of the Spanish tax system, as well as his own travels to the East Indies. Wolfe had Linschoten's book translated by W. P[hillips], at the behest of Richard Hakluyt.[33] It was one of a number of geographical descriptions published by Wolfe, sometimes in Italian and often translated into English at Hakluyt's suggestion.[34] Little is known of Wolfe's motivations in publishing these books (aside from a shrewd assessment of the market), although when placed with his early struggles against the Stationers' Company over their monopoly on printing lucrative texts,[35] one is left with an impression of entrepreneurial savvy. By the time he published Linschoten's voyages, he was a successful senior member of the Stationers' Company and had achieved the prestigious title of Printer for the City of London, as the Linschoten title-page proclaimed. Near the end of his successful career, Wolfe exhorted the English in the introduction of the translation to take their rightful place as an ocean-going, imperial nation, both for the riches such action would bring to England and for the civility they would return to inferior parts of the world. Although Linschoten's *Discours* ostensibly talks of the imperial growth of other nations, Wolfe here reconfigures the book as a story to construct an English imperial identity.

I doo not doubt, but yet I doo most hartely pray and wish, that this poore Translation may worke in our *English Nation* a further desire and increase of Honour over all *Countreys* of the *World*, and as it hath hitherto mightily advanced the Credite of the Realme by defending the same with our *Wodden Walles* ... So it would employ the same in forraine partes, aswell for the dispersing and planting true Religion and Civill Conversation therein: as also for the further benefite and commodity of this Land by exportation of such thinges wherein we doe abound, and importation of those *Necessities* whereof we stand in Neede: as *Hercules* did, when hee fetched away the *Golden Apples* out of the *Garden* of the *Hesperides*; and *Jason*, when with his lustie troupe of couragious *Argonautes* hee atchieved the *Golden Fleece* in *Colchos*.[36]

Proven by its successful defeat of the Armada, employing its famous 'wooden walls', the English nation has here become like Hercules, the semi-divine, or Jason, with his great sea-faring abilities and divinely ordained success. These two mythic figures do seem to have been recreated as nascent mercantilists, arguing for the classical precedents of early modern plunder. Wolfe sees such unequal exchanges (Hercules and Jason, after all, did not pay for their prizes, except by personal sacrifice and hardship) as at least on a par with the need to bring true religion and civil conversation to the natives of foreign locales. Indeed, the civility and Protestantism of the English equip them particularly well to pursue the import and export trade for the further 'benefite and commodity' of England itself. This is an imperial design, arguing for England's inherent superiority and ability to achieve dominion over other parts of the world, with a clear primacy of trade and commerce over conquest.

Indeed, the English Linschoten provides another important illustration of English imperialism, while expropriating the valorous deeds of another nation. Linschoten's book, in Wolfe's edition, contains the tales of Dutch and Portuguese adventure and profit, as well as evidence of Spanish wealth and power at home. Yet, on examining the illustrated title page, a tale of English supremacy is laid before the reader (Figure 6). At the top, the Royal coat of arms with the garter motto and Elizabeth's motto, 'Semper Eadem', anchors the book firmly in an English, courtly context. The translation was dedicated to Sir Julius Caesar, Judge of the High Court of Admiralty and Master of Requests to the Queen, thus directed as Dee's work had been to the powerful patronage circles.[37] Below the title, a large and very impressive carrack rides at anchor. The prominent flag jutting into the title space indicates English ownership.[38] The coat of arms on the left belongs to the City of London, announcing that this book was directed to merchants as well as courtiers. This also

Figure 6 Title page from Jan Huygen van Linschoten, *His Discours of Voyages into ye Easte and West Indies* (1598)

reminds the viewer of Wolfe's privileged position as the Printer of London, also mentioned in the text. Thus, although the book itself described foreign exploits and enterprises, the message of the illustrated title-page and introduction show that even these were to be used to the glory of England and to aid in the creation of an English empire. Just as Hakluyt used tales of other nations' discoveries to spur on English adventuring and commerce, Wolfe too hoped that exposure to the exploration of new parts of the world would encourage the English to venture forth for glory and profit.[39] While England would certainly benefit from these potential imperial ventures, the glory and profit had personal implications as well.

Christopher Saxton's illustrated frontispiece, from his 1579 atlas, also contains an overt message of English power and the utility of the geographical sciences in achieving such power (Figure 7). Saxton's atlas was funded by government patronage in the guise of Sir Thomas Seckford, Master of Requests, and was based principally on Saxton's own surveying.[40] This atlas marks an important development in government interest in a visual representation of the country, providing as it does the first clear image of the entire span of England, county by county. Elizabeth sits enthroned in the centre of the image, patron and ruler over the men on either side of her canopy.[41] On the right stands geography with compass and globe; on the left is astronomy with his armillary sphere. The usual female personifications of these disciplines have been replaced by men in Middle Eastern garb, perhaps alluding to the two works of Ptolemy. In the cartouche above Elizabeth's head, Righteousness and Peace, both female, embrace under Elizabeth's rule. Below, the two aspects of map-making, geometric and panoramic, seem to set their sights on England and Elizabeth's patronage. Since Elizabeth's support was of utmost importance in the funding of this atlas, it makes sense that Saxton would acknowledge this on the title-page. Indeed, Saxton had received Grigston Manor in Suffolk from Elizabeth in 1574, in recognition of his work and expenses.[42] The Royal coat-of-arms crowned above confirms the importance to the Queen and her government of mapping the English counties. Elizabeth reigned over all that could be measured and such mathematical control would enable England to triumph over its enemies.

As the maps of the atlas indicate, Saxton's recording of musters, lords lieutenant and places of fortification were matters of extreme importance to the Privy Council, concerned as it was with the coming war with Spain. Lord Burghley especially had been extremely keen on Saxton's

Figure 7 Title page from Christopher Saxton's atlas (1579)

mapping of the entire country, obtaining each map as it was completed and creating his own atlas for administrative use.[43] The image of empire created by this title-page, and by the atlas it introduced, was that of a self-sufficient and omni-competent state, ruled over by the dominion of a wise monarch. While this was problematised by the increasing separation of crown and county found on the later maps of the atlas,[44] Saxton's work contributed to a growing identification with England and its sense of self-sufficiency.

III

While Saxton's title-page suggests a relatively stable view of England as an imperial nation, Sir Walter Ralegh's message in *The History of the World* (1614) is rather more complex (Figure 8). The war with Spain is apparent as an important component in English self-definition in Ralegh's self-designed frontispiece.[45] That war had been a defining moment for Ralegh himself, as well as the source of much mythologising for English imperialists. So it is perhaps no surprise that the map dominating Ralegh's frontispiece would depict a vigorous battle in the Atlantic between Spanish and English forces – except for the fact that Ralegh's book deals with the history of the world to the second century BC.[46] The map, a truncated version of Ortelius' 1570 world map, has been oriented to place England and Ireland in the centre. Ralegh's ship seems once more to be venturing forth in search of El Dorado in the South Atlantic and both it and England are under the watchful eye of providence above. This masonic symbol suggests, as with Dee, a connection between the underlying magic of the world and the geographical control of that world. History herself holds the earth up to God's gaze, so that the actions thereon can be judged to have good or evil fame. With God watching over England and English deeds, how can her future be other than magnificent?

Ralegh wrote *The History of the World* during an eleven-year imprisonment in the Tower of London. Although it deals with the history of the world from creation to just before the birth of Christ, the parallels with modern concerns were real and explicitly drawn.[47] Indeed, James' reason for suppressing its publication lay in the fact that Ralegh was 'too saucy in censuring princes.'[48] This book was written as part of a campaign by Ralegh to interest Henry, Prince of Wales, in imperial adventures in general and in supporting Ralegh's conquistadorial bid to find El Dorado in particular.[49] Unfortunately for Ralegh, Henry died before

Figure 8 Frontispiece from Sir Walter Ralegh, *History of the World* (1614)

the book was completed, accounting for its rather abrupt ending. For Ralegh, the hope of a glorious English or even British empire to rival Spain died with Henry, and although he returned once more to Guiana, it was to face ignominy and execution.[50] Thus, the message of his frontispiece is a curious mixture of bravado and fatalism. History, stamping out death and oblivion, will reveal to God and the English Ralegh's great vision of empire, first glimpsed through the victory of the 'Wodden Walles' of the Armada (echoing Wolfe's earlier claim). As Ben Jonson explained in the accompanying poem:

> From Death and darke Oblivion (neere the same)
> The Mistress of Mans life, grave Historie,
> Raising the World to good, or Evill fame,
> Doth vindicate it to Aeternitie.[51]

Magistra Vitae, with her orb above her, bears more than a passing resemblance to an older iconographic image of lady world, suggesting the vanity of all earthly ambition.[52] Ralegh, more than any other writer or explorer, represented the empire of conquest rather than commerce or settlement, although the predetermined failure of such a course must colour any viewing of this triumphal frontispiece, then or now.

IV

Were these imperial messages, with all their multiple meanings, read by men intended for public office? Elsewhere I have argued that there is much evidence that they were.[53] Many students owned and read these books and many others with underlying imperial themes; a majority of these students went on to public careers of one type or another. This attention to geographical information and its message can be illustrated graphically as well as through content by an examination of a commonplace book owned by Sir Julius Caesar. Caesar was an English-born son of the Italian doctor, Caesare Adelmare, who was physician to Elizabeth and Mary. After receiving an MA at Oxford, Sir Julius became a student at the Inner Temple and received his LLD from Paris in 1581. He became Judge of the Admiralty and Master of Chancery under Elizabeth. With James' accession, Caesar became Chancellor of the Exchequer and, in 1614, Master of the Rolls, both positions being held until his death in 1636.[54] As we saw, John Wolfe dedicated his translation of Linschoten to Caesar, believing him to be interested in geography and exploration. Wolfe claimed that Caesar, as the Judge of the Admiralty, was in a position to judge how important the information in Linschoten's book was to the promotion of the English nation in imperial ventures.[55] Here then is one of the 'new men' who achieved power in early modern English governance, aided by a university education. If images of geographical imperialism were absorbed by him, they had the potential to be translated into action.

Caesar began compiling a commonplace book at Oxford in the 1570s and continued to add to it throughout his life. The book he used was a printed commonplace book: the *Pandecte Locorum Communium*. This book, published in 1572 with an introduction by John Foxe, contains a title-page with edifying verse, running heads throughout the book, and an index at the end, while the majority of the book is left blank for the use of the owner.[56] Given John Foxe's hand in the production of this volume, it is no surprise to see the preponderance of religious and moral topics implied by the various headings. What is more interesting for our purpose is the large number of geographical headings, especially when combined with the illustrated title-page, which suggests that the *quadrivium* generally, and geography particularly, were of prime importance to the student compiling his commonplace book (Figure 9).

This title-page was first used by publisher John Day to illustrate William Cuningham's *Cosmographical Glasse* (1559) and Dee and Billingsley's 1570 English translation of *Euclid*, so had wider currency than simply this commonplace book.[57] It was relatively common for printers to re-use title-pages, since they were expensive to produce, and since Day published a lot of mathematical and scientific material, such a title-page was very useful. It is striking that John Day chose to use such a mathematically and geographically-oriented title-page for this commonplace book, emphasising the importance of these areas for all students of the commonplace. In the bottom half of the page sit the female personifications of the four mathematical arts: Geometria and Arithmetica on the left and Astronomia and Musica on the right. Each holds the instrument traditional to her art. In the absence of their sisters of the *trivium*, this certainly suggests a strong emphasis on those studies more closely identified with mathematical studies of the natural world. Mercury as the God of learning presides over their collaboration. Even more striking is the top of the page. We might expect the great classical authors, whose works the attending students would surely be recording. We are not disappointed – except that these are all *geographers*, made more evident by the instruments they hold. At the top, on either side of a terrestrial globe, centred on the Old World, stand Ptolemy and Marinus, considered to have been his predecessor. Below them are

Figure 9 Title page from *The Elements of Geometrie* (1570)

Aratus and Hipparchus on the left and Strabo and Polybius on the right. Strabo is even engaged in drawing a map, an interesting endeavour for the father of descriptive geography. Even more interesting, it is a map of England. Look at the stars, Ptolemy seems to say, but with Strabo you know where you are. This message of geographical emplacement, at the very start of an important published commonplace book, demonstrates the importance of geographical thought and study to serious students.

Caesar appears to have kept this commonplace book throughout his life; his first entry was made while at Magdalen Hall, Oxford, in 1577 at the age of nineteen, and the last entry is dated 1636, shortly before his death.[58] In it he recorded a lifetime of citations, quotations and ideas. He seems to have had relatively little to say on the pages devoted to theology and mathematics, but the sections of the notebook devoted to geography and navigation are closely filled. Indeed, he added several manuscript pages with the running heads '*Cosmographia, Geographia*'.[59] He cited all the important geographical authors, including Ptolemy, Mercator, Strabo and Pliny. He discussed navigation in terms of the care and design of ships, and included chorography in such entries as 'The Singularities of England'.[60] His descriptions of other countries were usually drawn from or referred to published authorities, although sometimes he recorded his own observations.

I was ownce in Italie my selfe: but I thanke god, my abode there was but 9. daies; and yet I sawe in that little time in the citie of Venice, more libertie to sinne, than ever I heard tell of in our noble citie of London in 9 yeare. I sawe, it was there as free to sinne, not onely without all punishment, but also without anie man's marking, as it is free in the citie of London, to chouse without all blame, whether a man hast to weare shoe or pantoche.[61]

Caesar's commonplaces, added to throughout his life, show a man of substance interested in geographical issues. He read widely from the books we have been examining and saw such information as important. This information helped him develop a notion of England as a separate and self-sufficient country (as his note on Italy suggests) and to begin to think of ways to increase the possibility of England's foray into outward imperialism.

V

From the late seventeenth century on, the English began to realise the potential of imperial thinking. The first step in such empire building was their subjugation of the Irish and union with Scotland, resulting in the creation of Britain by 1707. This was followed by a rapid expansion in influence and control over large segments of the world; the British empire was a reality by the end of the eighteenth century. But in order to conquer the world in this way, the English first needed a vision of themselves as an imperial nation. This self-image as an independent and omni-competent country, as well as one with the potential to control other countries and regions of the world, had to precede the acquisition of an empire and so the English needed an imperial ideology before they could begin to construct an empire in deed. The creation of this ideology of empire was aided by the study of geography. The images I have examined in this essay contributed to this sense of superiority and separateness, although they were not unanimous in the message they communicated. While all were agreed that England (or the English) had the right to take their place as an imperial nation, they were much less united on the means to that goal, or just what the final imperial country would look like. With the exception of Ralegh, for whom conquest was less for personal gain than for the glory of his monarch, these geographical authors sought success in trade, in some settlement and in the transmission of 'true Religion and Civil Conversation'.[62] Britannia, as some coherent entity, did not rule even the iconographic waves, though the race for exploitation and hegemony had begun.

NOTES

1. William H. Sherman establishes the audience for this book in *John Dee: The Politics of Reading and Writing in the English Renaissance* (Amherst: University of Massachusetts Press, 1995), pp. 149–52.
2. John Dee, *General and Rare Memorials Pertayning to the Perfect Arte of Navigation* (London: J. Daye, 1577), p. 63.
3. See Lesley B. Cormack, '"Good Fences Make Good Neighbors": Geography as Self-Definition in Early Modern England', *Isis* 82 (1991), 639–61, for a definition of geography in this period. I here follow David Livingstone's insistence on the 'situated messiness' of the geographical tradition, *The Geographical Tradition. Episodes in the History of a Contested Enterprise* (Oxford: Blackwell, 1992). For some interesting Scottish comparisons, see Charles Withers, 'Geography, Royalty and Empire: Scotland and the Making of Great Britain, 1603–1661', *Scottish Geographical Magazine* 113 (1997), 22–32; 'Geography, Science and National Identity in Early Modern Britain: The Case of Scotland and the Work of Sir Robert Sibbald (1641–1722)', *Annals of Science* 53 (1996), 29–73; and 'How Scotland Came to Know Itself:

Geography, National Identity and the Making of a Nation, 1680–1790', *Journal of Historical Geography* 21 (1995), 371–87.

4. Lesley B. Cormack, *Charting an Empire. Geography at the English Universities, 1580–1620* (University of Chicago Press, 1997).

5. For example, Brian Levack, *The Formation of the British State: England, Scotland and the Union 1603–1707* (Oxford: Clarendon Press, 1987); Jenny Wormald, 'The Creation of Britain: Multiple Kingdoms or Core and Colonies', *Transactions of the Royal Historical Society* 6 (1992), 175–94; and J. Robertson, 'Empire and Union: Two Concepts of the Early Modern European Political Order', Robertson (ed.), *A Union for Empire: Political Thought and the British Union of 1707* (Cambridge University Press, 1995), pp. 3–36.

6. Frances Yates, *Astraea: The Imperial Theme in the Sixteenth Century* (London: Routledge and Kegan Paul, 1975); Graham Parry, *The Golden Age Restor'd: The Culture of the Stuart Court 1603–1642* (Manchester University Press, 1971); Roy Strong, *Art and Power: Renaissance Festivals 1450–1650* (Woodbridge: Boydell, 1984); and Withers, 'Geography, Royalty and Empire'.

7. Steven Shapin, *A Social History of Truth: Civility and Science in Seventeenth-Century England* (University of Chicago Press, 1994); Paula Findlen, *Possessing Nature: Museums, Collecting, and Scientific Culture in Early Modern Italy* (Berkeley: University of California Press, 1994).

8. There is a wide literature in the emblematic analysis of frontispieces, e.g. Peter M. Daly, *Literature in the Light of the Emblem. Structural Parallels between the Emblem and Literature in the Sixteenth and Seventeenth Centuries* (University of Toronto Press, 1979). I have been most influenced by William B. Ashworth, Jr., especially 'Natural History and the Emblematic World View', David Lindberg and Robert Westman (eds.), *Reappraisals of the Scientific Revolution* (Cambridge University Press, 1990), pp. 303–32. See also Michel Foucault, *The Order of Things. An Archaeology of the Human Sciences*, trans. Alan Sheridan Smith (New York: Pantheon Books, 1970). Foucault's categorisation of the sixteenth century as the 'age of similitude' is very useful here.

9. Anthony Pagden, *Lords of All the World. Ideologies of Empire in Spain, Britain and France, c. 1500 – c. 1800* (New Haven: Yale University Press, 1995), pp. 11–28.

10. Lesley B. Cormack, 'The Fashioning of an Empire: Geography and the State in Elizabethan England', Anne Godlewska and Neil Smith (eds.), *Geography and Empire* (Oxford: Blackwell, 1994), pp. 16–17.

11. Pagden, *Lords of All the World*, p. 14.

12. Richard Helgerson, *Forms of Nationhood: The Elizabethan Writing of England* (University of Chicago Press, 1992), pp. 171–81, discusses Hakluyt's tension between mercantile practicality and royal nationalism.

13. Jeffrey Knapp, *An Empire Nowhere. England, America, and Literature from Utopia to The Tempest* (Berkeley: University of California Press, 1992), claims that by stressing England's otherworldliness and trifling with conquest, English writers idealised the colonial failures of this period.

14. Pagden, *Lords of All the World*, pp. 1–10, argues that the lessons learned by Spain, England and France during what he calls the first imperial period

changed the way that particularly England, France and the Netherlands dealt with the rather different eastern imperial expansion of the late eighteenth and early nineteenth centuries.

15. Peter French, *John Dee: The World of an Elizabethan Magus* (London: Routledge and Kegan Paul, 1972); Richard Deacon, *John Dee. Scientist, Geographer, Astrologer and Secret Agent to Elizabeth I* (London: Muller, 1968); and Frances Yates, especially *Theatre of the World* (London: Routledge and Kegan Paul, 1969), have done much to encourage this tendency to see Dee as an Elizabethan 'magus'. While it is true that Dee was very interested in alchemy, numerology, astrology, and, in the end, crystal ball gazing, most of these activities were legitimate sixteenth-century pursuits and the focus on this has obscured his important geographical work. Even historians such as Sir Roy Strong, *Henry, Prince of Wales and England's Lost Renaissance* (London: Thames and Hudson, 1986), are not immune from this tendency, claiming Prince Henry's interest in Dee was neo-Platonic rather than exploring the more obvious geographical link. Nicholas Clulee provides a much more balanced view of Dee's work, arguing in *John Dee's Natural Philosophy: Between Science and Religion* (London: Routledge, 1988), that as Dee grew more interested in natural magic, he became less concerned with natural philosophy. Sherman, *John Dee*, has begun to set the record straight on Dee, showing his close interconnection with court and government, and establishing the primacy of his geographical work.

16. Mark Curtis, *Oxford and Cambridge in Transition, 1558–1642* (Oxford: Clarendon Press, 1959), p. 242; French, *John Dee*, p. 28.

17. John Dee, *The Private Diary of Dr. John Dee, and the Catalogue of His Library Manuscripts*, ed. J. O. Halliwell (London: Camden Society, 1842; repr. New York: AMS, 1968), records many instances of these men coming to consult with Dee before undertaking hazardous voyages.

18. Sherman, *John Dee*, chap. 7, includes a close reading of *General and Rare Memorials*, as well as *Of Famous and Rich Discoveries* (MS 1577) and *Brytanici Imperii Limites* (1576–8). In so doing, he makes explicit the link between Dee, imperialism, and the Privy Council.

19. Cormack, *Charting an Empire*.

20. Bodleian Ashmole MS 1789, fols. 116–7v, provides the manuscript version in Dee's hand.

21. For standard interpretations of this illustrated title-page, see Joseph Ames, *Typographical Antiquities* [1749], enlarged by T. F. Dibdin, 4 vols. (London: W. Miller, 1810–19), vol. I, pp. 660–2; Margery Corbett and Ronald Lightbown, *The Comely Frontispiece. The Emblematic Title-Page in England, 1550–1660* (London: Routledge and Kegan Paul, 1979), pp. 49–58. French, *John Dee*, pp. 183–5, provides a Hermetic twist to this image.

22. Corbett and Lightbown, *The Comely Frontispiece*, p. 49.

23. John Dee, *Monas Hieroglyphica* (Antwerp: Gulielmus Silvius, 1564). David Livingstone, 'Science, Magic and Religion: A Contextual Reassessment of Geography in the Sixteenth and Seventeenth Centuries', *History of Science* 26

(1988), 269–94, sees a direct relationship between geography and magic, especially in Dee's work. I disagree that magic was an integral ingredient in sixteenth-century geography. In fact, even John Dee seems to have kept the two relatively separate in his dealings with geographers and navigators. Still, the symbolism of this title-page argues for a closer relationship and the use of magic for the aggrandisement of the state.

24. Sherman, *John Dee*, pp. 149–50.
25. Pagden, *Lords of All the World*, p. 43, notes that the Spanish were the first to speak of the Spanish Monarchy rather than Kingdom, to show the king of Spain as an emperor through heredity.
26. Again, Pagden demonstrates that the Spanish placed great store in the fact that the Pope had appointed them to convert the natives, a position heavily criticised by English commentators, as well as some Spaniards (Pagden, *Lords*, pp. 29–33, 44–62). See also Anthony Pagden, *The Fall of Natural Man* (Cambridge University Press, 1982).
27. Dee, *General and Rare Memorials*, p. 53.
28. Sherman, *John Dee*, pp. 166–70.
29. Cormack, *Charting an Empire*.
30. Richard Willes, 'Certain other reasons, or arguments to prove a passage by the Northwest, learnedly written by Mr. Richard Willes Gentleman', Richard Hakluyt, *Principal Navigations, Voyages, Traffiques and Discoveries of the English Nation*, 10 vols. (London: G. Bishop *et al.*, 1598–1600), vol. III, p. 28.
31. Pagden sees this as an important counter-argument to Spain's claim to empire through conquest. *Lords of All the World*, pp. 80–1.
32. Hakluyt, *Principal Navigations*, vol. I, sigs. *4r, *5r.
33. Introduction to Jan Huygen van Linschoten, *Discours of Voyages* (London: J. Wolfe, 1598), sig. AIr.
34. Clifford Chalmers Huffman, *Elizabethan Impressions. John Wolfe and His Press* (New York: AMS, 1988), pp. 36–41. Most influential was Wolfe's English edition of *The Historie of the Great and Mightie Kingdome of China, by Mendoza*, trans. R. Parke (London: E. White, 1588), which remained the standard account of China for English readers for a generation.
35. Huffman, *Elizabethan Impressions*, p. 129.
36. Introduction to Linschoten, *Discours*, sig. A4r.
37. *Ibid.*, sig. AIr.
38. Corbett and Lightbown, *The Comely Frontispiece*, pp. 81–9, describe this title-page. They claim the ship is Portuguese, but have clearly missed the significance of the flag.
39. Huffman, *Elizabethan Impressions*, p. 41, discusses Wolfe's explicit statement of this desire in many of his Italian travel books and in the Mendoza translation.
40. Sarah Tyacke and John Huddy, *Christopher Saxton and Tudor Map-Making* (London: British Library, 1980), p. 25; Ifor M. Evans and Heather Lawrence, *Christopher Saxton. Elizabethan Map-Maker* (Wakefield Historical Publications, 1979), pp. 9, 66ff. P. D. A. Harvey, *Maps in Tudor England* (University

of Chicago Press, 1993), also discusses Saxton and sees the publication of his atlas as a cause of the map-consciousness of the later Elizabethan years (p. 84). Instead, I see both caused by the shared education in geography these gentlemen received as they increasingly attended Oxford and Cambridge.

41. William Ravenhill (ed.), *Christopher Saxton's Sixteenth-Century Maps* (Shrewsbury: Chatsworth Library, 1992), introduction, p. 15.
42. Tyacke and Huddy, *Christopher Saxton*, p. 6.
43. Evans and Lawrence, *Christopher Saxton*, p. 6.
44. Richard Helgerson, 'The Land Speaks: Cartography, Chorography and Subversion in Renaissance England', *Representations* 16 (1986), 51–85.
45. C. A. Patrides, introduction to Sir Walter Ralegh, *The History of the World* (London: Macmillan, 1971), p. xv. The book was initially suppressed and on its release later in 1614, the title-page had been removed. Thus, the image presented here, with no author's name, is a frontispiece, rather than a title-page proper.
46. Sir Walter Ralegh, *The History of the World* (London: W. Burre, 1614). For a discussion of the frontispiece, see Corbett and Lightbown, *The Comely Frontispiece*, p. 134.
47. Ralegh, 'Preface', *The History of the World*, sigs. A1r-E4v. Stephen Coote, *A Play of Passion: The Life of Sir Walter Raleigh* (London: Macmillan, 1993), p. 340.
48. Quoted by Coote, *A Play of Passion*, p. 341.
49. *Ibid.*, pp. 341–3.
50. For an interesting discussion of Ralegh's earlier failure in Guiana, see Knapp, *An Empire Nowhere*; as well as Charles Nicholl, *The Creature in the Map: A Journey to El Dorado* (London: Cape, 1995), who discusses the potential Rosicrucian connections, especially with the naming of the Red Cross River (pp. 309–18).
51. Ben Jonson, 'The Minde of the Front', Ralegh, *History of the World*, facing frontispiece.
52. Richard Helgerson suggested this image in his paper, 'The Folly of Maps and Modernity', at the conference *Paper Landscapes. Maps, Texts and the Construction of Space 1500–1700*, London, July 1997. See his contribution to this volume.
53. Cormack, *Charting an Empire*, examines the geography books owned by students at Oxford and Cambridge, as well as following the public careers of those students with geographical interests.
54. See *DNB*, vol. VIII, pp. 204–7; and L. M. Hill, *Bench and Bureaucracy. The Public Career of Sir Julius Caesar, 1580–1636* (Cambridge: James Clarke, 1988).
55. John Wolfe, 'Dedication', Linschoten, *Discours of Voyages*, sig. A1r.
56. Sir Julius Caesar's Commonplace Book, BL Add. MS 6038. This is described for some political and religious detail by Hill, *Bench and Bureaucracy*. Although Ann Moss, 'Printed Commonplace Books in the Renaissance', A. Dalzell *et al.* (eds.), *Acta Conventus Neo-Latini Torontonensis* (Binghamton, New

York: Medieval and Renaissance Texts and Studies, 1991), pp. 509–18, addresses the issue of commonplace books printed in their entirety (with no blank space for personal additions), she does not mention this form, with printed running heads and most of the book left blank.

57. S. K. Heninger, Jr., *The Cosmographical Glass. Renaissance Diagrams of the Universe* (San Marino: Huntington Library, 1977), was the first to describe in detail the iconography of this title-page (pp. 1–3).

58. Hill, *Bench and Bureaucracy*, p. 6.

59. BL Add. MS 6038, fol. 348r.

60. *Ibid.*, fols. 409v, 250r.

61. *Ibid.*, fol. 250r.

62. Introduction to Linschoten, *Discours*, sig. A4r.

CHAPTER 4

Performing London: the map and the city in ceremony

Andrew Gordon

I

Perspective vision and prospective vision constitute the twofold projection of an opaque past and an uncertain future onto a surface that can be dealt with. They inaugurate (in the sixteenth century?) the transformation of the urban *fact* into the *concept* of a city.[1]

When Michel de Certeau ascended the World Trade Center the view from the top provided an insight into the alienation inherent in the activity of mapping and viewing the city. De Certeau suggests that this privileged vantage point on high affords a totalising vision of the city as a text to be read, one analogous to the theoretical visions of the 'space planner urbanist, city planner or cartographer'. Both of these viewing practices construct an image of the city which remains oblivious to the activities of those on the ground, indeed is predicated upon a distantiation from the operations of the city's 'practitioners' at street level. The concern of de Certeau is with these spatial practices – the walkers whose movements enact an unauthored, unseen spatial inscription of the city – and the resistance they offer to the mechanisms of 'observational organisation' or the operational concept of a city that derives from the textualising eye, producing disciplinary spaces which correspond to an urbanistic rationale that, by the latter part of the twentieth century, was falling into decay.

This study looks in another direction. It seeks to return to the birth of that totalising moment which de Certeau speculatively locates in the sixteenth century, attempting to show how the imaging of the city from above was itself marked by the performance of a city going on down below. For if it is this moment which sees, in the construction of views of the city, the translation of the experience of the city into its conceptualisation, as de Certeau argues, then I hope to demonstrate that this process brought with it a belief in the city as an inherently spatially performed entity. The city was enacted before it was visualised, it walked before it was drawn, and the early modern viewer or imager pictured a city in terms of the organised spatial practices which were the first statement of the city as concept. This essay thus explores the relationship between two operations for whom space is the raw material in the production of representations of the city: civic ceremony and city mapping. Taking the case of early modern London it is my intention to show how the spatialising practices of the former, in which temporary configurations of the city unfold in text and performance, provide a model for the representational strategies of the latter.

II

As a way of bringing the issue of civic representation into focus I want to begin with a passage from *Coriolanus* where the Senators challenge the inflammatory rhetoric of the Tribunes that seems likely to arouse a restless populace.

MENENIUS: Fie, fie, fie!
                         This is the way to kindle, not to quench.
FIRST SENATOR: To unbuild the city and to lay all flat.
SICINIUS: What is the city but the people?
ALL PLEBEIANS: True,
                         The people are the city.[2]

This exchange offers us two opposed readings of the city of Rome. The first affords a view of the city as a constructed entity; a threat to the constitutional settlement is here a threat to the physical articulation of that idea in the civic environment. The Senators, as a representative body named for the representative space of the Senate, identify with the architectural fabric of the city. The second reading, posited by the Tribunes, maintains that civic identity resides in the social body rather than the structures which house it.[3] But these two readings of the city are not exclusive; they are interpretative strategies which can and do, at least on other occasions, engage in a dialogue with each other. Neither an uninhabited settlement, nor a simple congregation of people can by itself claim the title of city. Rather they make up a dialectical method of reading cities and what we are witnessing here is a breakdown in the dynamic of their interaction.

In *Coriolanus* this division is precipitated by a failure in the performance of civic ceremony.[4] The ritual of asking for the people's voices would enact the legitimation of the new social order in the market-place, but here it goes awry, the protagonist's ingracious and perfunctory execution of the rite resulting in what Richard Wilson has described as 'literally a crisis of representation in the marketplace'.[5] This key site in the civic topography is temporarily transformed into a space of representation in order for the fiction of plebeian political influence to be performed in a ceremonial election which inscribes the will of the people within the structures of patrician authority.[6]

The hopes which the Senators attach to the election of Coriolanus depend upon a certain conception of the function of civic ceremony. Its role in this context would have been to bring into correspondence the two readings of the city voiced above, to enact a conception of the city as both social body and representative space. It is precisely this understanding of civic ceremony as engaged in the production of spatially performed consensual images of the city which this paper looks to uncover. Yet, if the notion of performed space is central to ceremonial constructions of the city, it is equally vital to the reading of visual images of the city produced in maps and views and in their borders. Indeed the passage from *Coriolanus* seems almost to invite consideration of the relation between the city's performance in ceremony and its description in maps and views. If one transposes these lines to a treatment of the operation of city mapping it can be seen that each side of the dispute between Senator and Tribune articulates an entrenched resistance to the representation of the city in map form. The idea of reducing the city to a two-dimensional ground plan, an abstract network of lines on the page, cannot be reconciled with either half of the dialectic of civic self-imaging which a right performance of civic ceremony sets out to resolve.

The words of the First Senator 'To unbuild the city and to lay all flat' present an implicit obstacle to the notion that the city can be translated into a representational code which would, to borrow the phrase of another of the Senators, 'bring the roof to the foundation' (3.1.203). A flat city and a city without buildings are unrecognisable *qua* cities; lacking one of the defining properties of 'citiness'. Similarly, the Tribune's rejoinder posits another area in which mapping can fail to reproduce adequately the nature of civic self-identification since a strictly geometric conception of mapping constructs an unpeopled landscape in which the inhabitants, the social body of the city, play no part.

The irreducibility of the city played out here in the terms of these two

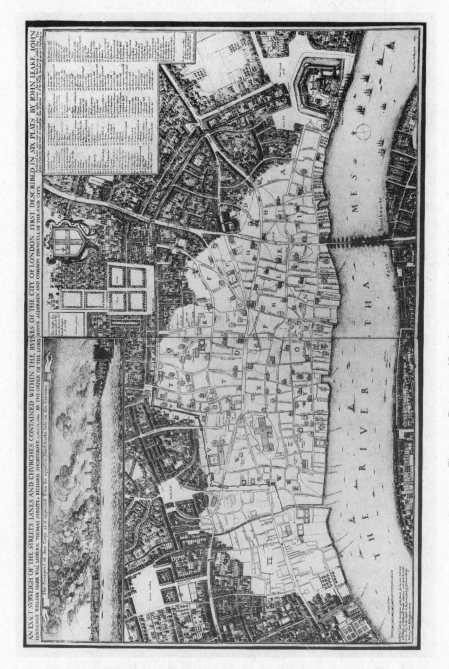

Figure 10 Prospect of London, engraving (1667)

positions appears to be borne out by the evidence of London's mapping in the early modern period. The first published maps to represent the city in the form of a linear ground plan – without people or buildings added in perspective – appeared in the aftermath of the Great Fire in 1666. Yet these publications portray in this manner only that part of the city which was destroyed by fire; the title of one underlining the significance of this representational strategy: *A Map or Groundplot of the Citty of London . . . by which is exactly demonstrated the present condition of it, since the last sad accident of fire, the blanke space signifiing the burnt part, & where the houses be those places yet standing.*[7] Here the extent to which geometric delineation in purely diagrammatic form challenged contemporary conceptions of the city is suggested by the fact that the area depicted in ground plan is explicitly described as a 'blank space' signifying, in place of the physically articulated presence of London, precisely the absence of the city.[8]

Commenting upon the mapping of Paris in the seventeenth century, Louis Marin has traced the movement from the reproduction of a 'topographic image and a geographic orientation' to a situation where '[t]he representation ceases functioning as the mimesis of a spectacle to be viewed and as the representation of an appearance. It turns into a geometric schema and analogic model'.[9] Elsewhere Marin suggests that in a 1652 map this abrupt transformation in conceptual practice is mediated by the appearance of two inserted views so that '[o]ne image is presented as what is represented, the other as representing, and the one in the other as representation.'[10] In several of the London maps engraved after the Fire this mediation of the geometric by the mimetic is developed in the context of the destruction of the city wrought by the blaze. Thus in a 1667 engraving (Figure 10) we find an inserted image based upon the numerous published views of the city from south of the river, here bearing the legend 'The Prospect of the Citty as it appeared from the opposite Southwarke side in the fire time'.[11]

The resulting vision of the city in the process of being unbuilt performs simultaneously the destruction of that representational icon from which its mimetic signification is derived; London loses its recognisable shape to become a city without a scape. It is this destruction of the city's iconic representational form, indeed of the very possibility of a mimetic representational space, which paves the way for the production of a geometric space in the depiction of the city. The unbuilding of the city creates a representational vacuum, a 'blank space' whose very lack of citiness is the precondition permitting the geometric space of the linear ground plan to enter the heart of the urban terrain.

An insight into the resistance of the city map to this new geometric space is provided by the earliest dated example to be published in England. This occurs in William Cuningham's *The Cosmographical Glasse* in the course of a dialogue between two fictional protagonists which seeks to establish the mathematical authority of cosmography over geography and chorography. The practice of chorography is defined in this context as consisting 'rather in describyng the qualitie and figure, then the bignes, and quantitie of any thinge' and this re-statement of the Ptolemaic definition is illustrated with an elaborate fold-out map of Norwich.[12]

Cuningham's choice of the city map to exemplify chorography provides the perfect foil to the construction of cosmography as a purely mathematical pursuit by foregrounding its treatment of the unabstractable city as a subject of (mimetic) representation. In the map-view of Norwich the spectator is situated within the terms of a visually recognisable construction of the city; presented with a realised civic space which offers the possibility of a potential engagement. The foreground features two figures, one with callipers, the other holding a pointer, who turn from a divided circle and gesture towards the city before them.[13] These two figures occupy a pictorial space continuous with the representation of the city. Their actions demonstrate the inhabitability of the mimetic space of the image by deictically signalling its veracity; look, there is the mill to the east, they might be saying. Yet at the same time as their presence performs a potential reality, it also underlines the constructed nature of the space which they inhabit. Their performance of the city's reality is equally a demonstration of its status as a subject within representation; their interaction with that subject foregrounding the act of reading the city's spaces in which they are engaged. As such Cuningham's map of Norwich is suggestive of the possibility of a debate over the aims of representing civic space; the city in representation becomes a site for the production of more than one view of the city.

III

That city maps were understood as representational artefacts capable of promoting certain readings of the city is suggested by the investments in particular conceptions of the city which close study can reveal. When James I granted a patent for the production of city maps, having observed the manner in which these images 'are dispersed and sent abroad into all partes, to the greate honor and renowne of those princes in whose domynions they are', he did so in anticipation that the civic sign would signify as an index of the munificence of Jacobean rule.[14] Certainly the period's most widely disseminated image of London, the well known Braun and Hogenberg map view, used its title to situate the city as part of an abundant sovereign domain: *Londinum Feracissimi Angliae Regni Metropolis* (London capital of the most fertile kingdom of England).[15] More specific interpretative strategies for the reading of the city might be produced by the relatively simple expedient of altering the text within the cartouches, a transformation which could be effected without the need for the image to be re-engraved or cut.[16] Hence the three surviving impressions of the woodcut map of London once attributed to Ralph Agas include an inscription that dates them to 1633 although the image appears from internal evidence to have been produced between 1561 and 1570.[17] The inserted text cites the founding of London by Brutus as taking place in 1130 [BC] and informs the reader that 2763 years have elapsed since then – the figure appears to be an updating of a 1603 impression that gave the latter number as 2733.[18] In each case the mathematical puzzle here accentuates a date notable for the expectation that a monarch of the House of Stuart, who celebrated descent from the Trojan Brutus, would make a royal entry into the city of London.[19] We shall return in due course to the entry of James, postponed until 1604. Of his successor Charles I it should be noted that the coronation and state entry into Edinburgh of 1633 gave rise to public expectations recorded by the Venetian ambassador that 'as the crowned king of Scotland he will have to make a public state entry here also.'[20]

The second cartouche text restates the Trojan theme and further situates the city of London within a specifically monarchic framework.

> Sith Lud my Lord, my King and Lover dear,
> Encrease my bounds: and London (far that rings
> Through Regions large) he called then my name
> How famous since (I stately seat of Kings)
> Have flourish'd aye: let others that proclaim.
> And let me joy thus happy still to see
> This vertuous Peer my Soveraign King to be.

The London produced by this operation is a locus of majesty, the 'seat of Kings' that derives both its title and its spatial determination from the action of monarchs, in its final lines proceeding to acclaim its allegiance to the sovereign. The woodcut map furnished with an appropriate text and re-issued in anticipation of a state entry would thus represent a reframing of the city for the monarch to coincide with the expected refashioning of its civic spaces to greet his arrival.

It is not the text alone, however, which produces this reading of the city in relation to the monarch as 'head and chief Chamber of the whole Realm'. The textual positioning of the image serves rather to reinforce and build upon the significance of features within the map itself which figure the city in these terms. Of these the most important is the royal barge bearing the Tudor arms depicted to the west of London Bridge, a version of which also appears in the Braun and Hogenberg map. The recent chance discovery of an additional plate belonging to the copper-plate map upon which both the former images are modelled has shown that this detail also derives from thence.[21] In the copper-plate fragment the barge is depicted without a coat of arms but with the caption 'Cymbula Regia' (The Royal Standard) that signals an unambiguous inscription of monarchic presence onto the surface of the map. The narrowest dating of the copper-plate map, to 1557–9, would make possible a reading of the presence of the royal barge in reference to the coronation of Elizabeth – both Holinshed and Stow record the ceremonial activities on the Thames attending the monarch's journey up river to the Tower.[22] However, the significance of this detail is not to locate the map as a direct record of the coronation of Elizabeth, but to establish the reference within the map to the city as a space for the performance of ceremonial authority; a space constructed in reference to the monarchic actor.[23] It is this visually accessible form of ceremonial performance enacted in the spectacle of floating royalty which the presence of the royal barge on the map of London makes reference to. As such it posits within the space of the map the terms of its own reading of the city in relation to the monarch; describing not 'what the spectator *should* see, but *how* to see.'[24]

In addition to the textual framing and the presence of the royal barge, the drawing of the boundaries of the representational field also supports an interpretation of the city under the sign of a ceremonial monarchic authority through the very determination of what constitutes the city. The woodcut map depicts an expanse from Westminster through to just east of the Tower. In so doing the space of the map frames the area of civic autonomy within the twin poles of monarchic authority – the royal palace of Whitehall and the Tower of London, symbol of royal authority within the city. These are precisely the terms of reference for the ceremonial monarchic city constructed by the royal entry in what may be called the spatial narrative of the sovereign's procession. The two focal points of royal power enclosing the *passage* of the monarch become the reference points for a signification of monarchic authority in which the appropriated places signify as royal spaces.[25] This circumscription of civic authority within the monarchic was itself enacted in the procession through the Lord Mayor's exchange of his sword of office before the Tower for the royal sceptre which he carried as far as the boundary of civic jurisdiction at Temple Bar.

The ceremonial city, the temporary product of the techniques of royal entry ritual, is thus inscribed within the woodcut map of London, lending it a permanence far in advance of the event itself. The representation of this image in anticipation of the entry of Charles or his predecessor is able to draw upon these elements in its own production of the city as a monarchic entity linked to the representational strategies of Stuart rule. If, however, the ceremonial city is present in the map as the civic sign becomes a subject of cartographic representation, then a contrary process is also observable in ceremonial practice as a form of cartographic discourse infiltrates the accounts of the ceremonial city. Hence Thomas Dekker describes preparations for the entry of James I in the following terms:

The Streets are surveyed; heigthes, breadths, and distances taken, as it were to make *Fortifications*, for the *Solemnities*. Seaven pieces of ground, (like so many fieldes for a battaile) are plotted foorth, uppon which these Arches of Triumph must shew themselves in their glorie . . .[26]

The survey undertaken here is performed prior to the transformation of the city in ceremony; it lays the groundwork for the production of a Borgesian map, a representational surface overlaying the urban terrain itself.[27] The displacement of the city beneath the monarchic map is figured in the military vocabulary of fortification and battle which emphasise the occupation of civic space by this monarchic construction. The erection of the triumphal arches, the new monuments of this temporary metropolis, constitutes only one aspect of the monarchic city's reconstruction of the urban fabric. An account of the passage of James I and Christian IV of Denmark into London in 1606 demonstrates the full extent of the transformation undergone by the capital.

Within . . . double Rayles . . . sate the Maisters, Wardens, and whole Livereys of everie severall Companie through the Cittie of London which companyes extended their length from Tower-streete to Temple Barre, . . . alongest thes Rayles cleane through out, were fastened Banners, Cornets, Flagges, Bandrels, Ensignes, and Pendants . . . [with] all the Armes, Devises, and Honors . . . of the same severall Companies: all the houses in everie streete, through which the two Maiesties did passe, had their Penthouses and Walles covered, some with Arrasse, some with other Ornaments . . .[28]

The ceremonial city is constructed as a surface, a monarchic map produced by a twofold lining of the city in which the local activity of civic life disappears beneath a mass of tapestries and hangings to be replaced by the members of the Livery Companies who themselves form part of the displayed surface directed towards the presence of the monarch. Not participating in the procession, these static figures are inscribed within a monarchic viewing of the city which receives the tribute of civic authority. This production of the ceremonial city in relation to the presence of the monarch is a central interpretative theme in Dekker's 1604 entry text where London is figured as *Camera Regia*, the King's Chamber, and each of the seven triumphal arches identified as a room within this Court Royal. From the 'with-drawing chamber' of the Tower, the King progresses through the Entrance, Great Hall, Presence chamber, Privy chamber, and finally the 'beauteous gallery' from which he emerges outside the city limits.

Dekker's text reads the city's temporary ceremonial topography in precise terms, transposing a network of spatial relations that describe degrees of proximity to the monarch onto the urban spaces of London. Just as the map inscribes the spatial narrative of the ceremony in the framing of civic authority within the monarchic, producing a ceremonial city which derives its signification from the sovereign, so the printed account goes on to locate the capital as a closed, internal space. In doing so text, map and performance combine in occluding both commercial and communal conceptions of the city; the social body becomes a static surface reflecting royal authority, whilst all traces of mercantile activity are swept beneath the red carpet which converts places of exchange into spaces within the court. The ultimate statement of this transformation comes in the verses recited by the children of St Paul's:

> *Troynovant* is now no more a Citie;
> O great pittie! is't not pittie?
> And yet her towers on tiptoe stand,
> Like Pageants built on Fairie land,
> And her Marble armes,
> Like to Magicke charmes,
> Binde thousands fast unto her,
> That for her wealth and beauty daily wooe her.[29]

In these lines the ceremonial city literally dis-places its more mundane counterpart; not only are its spaces and its representative authority appropriated to a celebration of monarchic authority, it also loses here the very right to be called a city. Dekker explains the device by inform-ing the reader that 'London . . . makes no acount for the present of her ancient title to be called a Citie, because during these tryumphes, shee puts off her formall habite of Trade and Commerce'.[30] The description of the city's transformation in these terms reveals a central opposition between this monarchic entity and the conception of the city outlined in the ceremonies of the civic authorities, for the 'formall habite of Trade and Commerce' so notably absent here is precisely what characterises readings of civic space in the annual pageants which celebrated the inauguration of a new Lord Mayor. In these events the focus was upon the civic constitution and a celebration of the trade of the Lord Mayor's Livery Company. Thus when Anthony Munday was designing the pageant in honour of the draper Sir Thomas Hayes in 1614, that meant representing London through applying the trade of clothing to the interpretation of civic space.

The walles of any Citty, were termed by the *Grecians*, according as we title our instant discourse, *Himatia Poleos*, The Cloathing or garments of the Cittie. Intimating thereby, that as garments and cloathing doe ingirt the body, defend-ing it continually from the extremities of colde and heat: so walles, being the best garments of any Citie, do preserve it from all dangerous annoyances. Here on we lay the foundation of our devise, in the honour of *Draperie* the rich Clothing of *England*.[31]

Munday, himself a member of the Drapers Company, restores to the reading of civic space the trade context which was the founding or-ganisational principle of the structures of civic authority.[32] Yet this habit of trade and commerce adopted by the city to perform its own version of London was also a formal one and as well as imaging the city in terms of a particular Livery Company, the pageant sought to solemnise the operation of the civic constitution which accorded him that office. The ever-available Thomas Dekker in the dedication of his 1612 pageant addresses the newly sworn-in Mayor thus:

Honor (this day) takes you by the Hand, and gives you welcomes into your New-Office of Pretorship . . . You have it with the Harts of many people, Voices and Held-up hands: they know it is a Roabe fit for you, and therefore have clothed you in it. May the Last-day of your wearing the same, yeeld to your Selfe as much Ioy, as to Others does this First-day of your putting it on.[33]

The Lord Mayor's office is here identified with the robe of office first worn in the ceremony of inauguration. The costume itself is a signifier of

Figure 11 John Norden, *Civitas Londini* (1600)

the performed civic constitution, the people bestowing the robe with their voices of assent. Where the monarchic city had been variously figured as the seat of kings and the *Camera Regia*, the London of the mayoral pageant is a place of political representation. The representation of the social body is structured according to the fiction of elective autonomy displayed in the formal habits of the representatives of civic authority, a fiction dependent upon repeated performance.[34]

From the monarchic conception of the city inscribed in the woodcut map of London I want now to examine how the mayoral performance of a ritual representation of the city is translated into the form of a visual artefact in another map-view of London, John Norden's *Civitas Londini* of 1600 (Figure 11). Here the central inscription situates the representation of the city within the context of the immediate structures of civic government naming both the current Sheriffs and the Lord Mayor whose arms surmount the cartouche. This emphasis on the civic constitution is underlined by the depiction of a Lord Mayor's procession beneath the main image. Here the members of the Livery Companies who had provided a static reflection of royal authority in the monarchic ceremony, find expression for their voices and their autonomy in the procession of the city's governing officials. The portrayal of representatives of civic authority provides an evident context for the understanding of the map's own representation of London in terms of mayoral autonomy. Indeed another detail seems to invite such a reading in opposition to the monarchic ceremonial city, for on the Thames to the west of London Bridge, where the copper-plate, Braun and Hogenberg and woodcut maps display a royal barge, the Norden map includes a boat labelled 'the gally fuste'. This distinctive triple-masted vessel denotes the ceremonial craft used by the Lord Mayor on such occasions as the journey to Westminster for the oath of office, and its appearance here suggests a deliberate displacement of the monarchic presence in favour of a reference to the mayoral representation of an autonomous mercantile civic space.

The *Civitas Londini* proves equally provocative in its treatment of the area depicted, focusing on the city itself in a manner unlike the maps dealt with thus far. Westminster proper is almost a casualty of the curious wide angle of description in which the curvature of the earth is wildly exaggerated, heightening the centrality of the city of London at the expense of its courtly neighbour whose position is in every sense marginalised. There is also a parallel here with the spatial narrative of the Lord Mayor's Procession which focused attention on a circulation of the key sites of the city, neglecting to traverse the walls – Munday's protective clothing of the city – and instead making the journey to Westminster for the oath in the galley foist.

The separation of London from Westminster in the long view is repeated in the insertion of two map-views which interrupt the surface of the main image but present their respective subjects in markedly different fashion.[35] That of London is framed by an ornamental cartouche featuring a title legend and an index of churches, markets, gates and streets beneath the image. The independent, titled city reproduced here enables the viewer to identify and locate via the key sites within its bounds, yet this apparent subjection to a totalising spatial order is mediated by the placement of the smaller map within the context of the larger view of London. The emphasis upon the city's constitution as enacted, and its spaces as inhabited, proclaims its continued performability.

By contrast, the map of Westminster is introduced via an unusual visual device in which the surface of the view is peeled back to reveal the map beneath. Where the map of London was superimposed onto the long view, its ornamental strapwork enabling it to stand out from the picture surface, Westminster is secreted beneath the level of the mimetic representation and the map-view. How are we to read this striking representation of the royal seat? Should its presence beneath the surface of the view be taken as a demonstration of the inherent priority of the royal presence over the artificial construction of the city; an image of the underlying and absolute nature of monarchic authority? In the light of the conception of the city as a product of performance revealed in the representational strategy of this image, an alternative suggests itself. The Westminster map has no index of key sites and the few places captioned, with the exception of some of the landing stages and the monument at Charing Cross, describe closed spaces such as the houses of the nobility and the walled 'Saint Jeames parke'. The effect of this is to situate Westminster, in contrast to the city of London, as a place of exclusive, internal spaces. Yet whereas a monarchic reading of civic space as an interior was produced in the text of James I's entry in relation to the presence of the monarch, here there is no such royal presence to authorise a like reading; even the Palace of Whitehall gets no mention. Instead of a monarchic framing of the image of Westminster, the seat of royalty is defined in opposition to the independent, self-articulating capital, as a non-city, unable to perform its own image.

IV

The Norden view, then, intervenes in a struggle to appropriate the civic sign, displacing the monarchic ceremonial city from the map, and relegating royal authority to an isolated compound from which all indication of the sovereign presence is nevertheless absent. In its place it offers an alternative ceremonial model for the reading of the city, one concerned not with a series of static devices, but governed rather by the principle of circulation. The Lord Mayor's pageants perform their version of London within the space of the city itself with the pageant floats carried through the city streets. The members of the Livery Companies and the civic officials circulate within the city of which they are themselves the representatives, performing the constitution of which they are a part. The mayoral conception of the city thus preserves the conjunction of representative spaces and the social body which together constitute the notion of a city performed in ceremony and it is this we find inscribed within the Norden image of London.

With the entry of James I we move away from the spatially performed conception of the city towards a spatially ordered viewing of one. Where descriptions of his predecessor's entry into the capital are rich in references to her ability to play her part in the ceremony, the distaste of the first Stuart monarch for the proceedings led one chronicler to comment wryly that '[h]e endured this days brunt with patience, being assured he should never have such another.'[36] No consummate public performer this. Another account records how, having heard talk of the preparations for the entry, 'our heroicke King . . . was desirous privately at his owne pleasure to visit them' and sought to gain a sneak preview.[37] In the event the desire for a private viewing of the foundations of the monarchic city was thwarted by the 'wylie multitude' who caught wind of the surreptitious presence of their sovereign. The excitement of his subjects was so great that the heroic figure was forced to take refuge within the Exchange whose gates were shut fast behind him. It was here, in this enclosed space shut off from the still operative city, that the monarch encountered a vision more to his taste:

When his Highness had beheld the Marchantes from a Windowe all below in the walkes not thinking of his comming, whose presence else would have binne more, they like so many pictures civilly seeming all bare, stood silent, modestie commanding them so to doe, which sight so delighted the King, that he greatly commended them.[38]

The contrast could not be greater between the press of enthusiastic subjects and the reverent, silenced (and no doubt awkwardly surprised) merchants within the precinct of the Exchange. That the monarch retiring behind closed doors should take pleasure in the sight of these frozen subjects arranged beneath him 'like so many pictures' is symptomatic both of his inclination towards spatial ordering and away from spatial performance and, at the same time, of the difficulties of imposing such controlled readings upon the space of the city. The concern of James with the appearance of the city, and his determination to claim authority over it, translate into an urge to intervene in the regulation of the urban fabric which registers in repeated proclamations on the subject of its size and construction.

[H]ow much it would grace and beautifie the said Cities . . . for the resort and intertainment of forreine Princes . . . if an Uniformitie were kept in the sayd Buildings, and the foreparts or forefronts of the houses, standing and looking towards the Streets, were all builded with Bricke and Stone.[39]

The preoccupation with producing an ordered surface is here directly linked to the construction of a monarchic view of the city for other privileged viewers. As such it recalls de Certeau's spectator raised to the top of the World Trade Center whose disengagement from the spatial practices of the urban morass is the precondition for an ordering of space according to a detached, ideal conception of the city. However, as I have sought to show, the early modern city held no vantage point sufficiently privileged that it could avoid altogether the intrusion of the city down below. A fact perfectly illustrated by the occasion on which James' royal visitor Christian IV scaled London's highest point to take the view:

[T]his Royall King . . . came to St. Paule's Church, where he walked and viewed the same, and from thence to the top of the steeple, where he tooke much delight to behold the beautious scituation of London, the pleasant gardens and fields adjoyning, the richnes of the Thames, so furnished with ships of great countenance and worth as he graciously applauded the excellency thereof. But amongst all the other things he admired most, when the Noblemen accompanying him did report the being of a horse upon that place, comming up such a way of great danger and so hye, that he tooke very good notice thereof, and wonderfully did admire the same.[40]

NOTES

1. Michel de Certeau, 'Walking in the City', *The Practice of Everyday Life*, trans. Steven Rendall (Berkeley: University of California Press, 1984), pp. 93–4.
2. *The Tragedy of Coriolanus*, Arden Edition (London: Methuen, 1976), 3.1.194–8. All further references to the play are to this edition.

3. On Renaissance distinctions between *urbs* and *civitas*, for which the principal precedent occurs in Book 15 of Isidore of Seville's *Etymologies*, see the recent article by Richard L. Kagan, '*Urbs* and *Civitas* in Sixteenth- and Seventeenth-Century Spain', David Buisseret (ed.), *Envisioning the City: Six Studies in Urban Cartography* (University of Chicago Press, 1998), pp. 75–108.

4. For a recent treatment of this failure and the decisive role played by Coriolanus' 'impersonation of national identity' in the disruption of relations between patrician and plebeian, see Francis Barker, 'Nationalism, Nomadism and Belonging in Europe: *Coriolanus*', John Joughin (ed.), *Shakespeare and National Culture* (Manchester University Press, 1997), pp. 233–65.

5. Richard Wilson, 'Against the Grain: Representing the Market in *Coriolanus*', *Will Power. Essays on Shakespearean Authority* (London: Harvester Wheatsheaf, 1993), p. 107. See also G. K. Paster, '"To Starve with Feeding": The City in *Coriolanus*', *Shakespeare Studies* 11 (1978), 123–44.

6. On the fictionality of this political influence see the parallels detected by Mark Kishlansky with what he terms 'parliamentary selection' during the period. *Parliamentary Selection: Social and Political Choice in Early Modern England* (Cambridge University Press, 1986), pp. 4–7.

7. This map is no. 20 in James Howgego, *Printed Maps of London circa 1553–1850* (Folkestone: Dawson, 1978).

8. In a recent study of the Great Fire's impact on Restoration culture in London, Cynthia Wall has argued that the impetus for cartographic precision derived from the need 'to explore and make known the lost, the destroyed, the rearranged.' *The Literary and Cultural Spaces of Restoration London* (Cambridge University Press, 1998), p. 83.

9. Louis Marin, *Utopics: The Semiological Play of Textual Spaces*, trans. R. A. Vollrath (Atlantic Highlands, New Jersey: Humanities Press, 1990), pp. 209, 217.

10. 'The Frame of Representation and Some of Its Figures', trans. Wendy Waring, Paul Duro (ed.), *The Rhetoric of the Frame: Essays on the Boundaries of the Artwork* (Cambridge University Press, 1996), p. 85.

11. *An Exact Surveigh of the Streets Lanes and Churches contained within the Ruines of the City of London* (Howgego, *Printed Maps of London*, no. 21). Other examples include those printed in Amsterdam by Frederick de Wit, Marcus Doornick and Jacob Venkel (Howgego, *Printed Maps of London*, nos. 16, 17 and 24). On the development of engraved views of London during this period see Irene Scouloudi, *Panoramic Views of London 1600–1666* (London: Corporation of London, 1953); and Ralph Hyde, *Gilded Scenes and Shining Prospects: Panoramic Views of British Towns 1575–1900* (New Haven, Conn.: Yale Center for British Art, 1985).

12. William Cuningham, *The Cosmographical Glasse* (London: John Day, 1559), sig. B4r.

13. For a reading of these figures which sees them as images of Cuningham at work, see Lucia Nuti, 'The Perspective Plan in the Sixteenth Century: The Invention of a Representational Language', *Art Bulletin* 76, no. 1 (1994),

105–28. See also the essay by John Gillies in this volume which discusses this map and these figures in terms of the difference between the scene of cartography – the domestic interior – and the external places of chorography's production.

14. *Patent of Aaron Rathbone and Roger Burges AD 1617 no. 1* (London: Eyre and Spottiswoode for the Great Seal Patent Office, 1857), p. 1. The patent was granted for a series of maps and descriptions of the cities of England which never materialised. I am grateful to Lawrence Worms for this reference.

15. Georg Braun and Frans Hogenberg, *Civitates Orbis Terrarum*, 6 vols. (Antwerp: Filips Galle; Cologne: apud auctores, 1572–1617), vol. 1, fol. 1. On the numerous editions of this work see the introductory essay by R. A. Skelton in the facsimile edition (New York: World Publishing Co., 1966). A close copy of the image with the same title appeared in Sebastian Münster's *Cosmographey oder beschreibung aller länder* (Basle: Sebastian Henricpetri, 1598), pp. 58–9, and subsequent editions.

16. This is particularly the case with woodcut maps where cartouches were generally carved with a hole for the insertion of blocks of text. See David Woodward, 'The Manuscript, Engraved, and Typographic Traditions of Map Lettering', Woodward (ed.), *Art and Cartography. Six Historical Essays* (Chicago University Press, 1987), pp. 174–212.

17. Howgego, *Printed Maps of London*, no. 8. The dating of the original woodcut can be determined from its depiction of the spire of St Paul's which burnt down in 1561, and the evidence of alteration to show Gresham's Royal Exchange which was erected in 1566–70. This map has been suggested as 'The Carde of London' entered by Giles Godet in the Stationers' Register in 1562–3. See Stephen Powys Marks, *The Map of Mid Sixteenth Century London*, LTS publication no. 100 (London: London Topographical Society, 1964), p. 14.

18. Thomas Dodd in *The Connoisseur's Repertory* (London: Hurst, Chance, and Co., 1825), unpaginated, describes the map in a section on the work of Agas to whom the map was then attributed. He includes a full transcription of both cartouche texts which differ from the 1633 version only in giving the earlier dating, concluding that the map was produced to coincide with James' accession.

19. The descent from Brutus, who according to legend had ruled over an undivided *Britannia*, is a feature of the Londinium arch in the 1604 entry pageant and dominates Anthony Munday's *The Triumphs of Re-United Britannia* of the following year. See Graham Parry, *The Golden Age Restor'd: The Culture of the Stuart Court 1603–42* (New York: St Martin's Press, 1981), pp. 1–21.

20. Quoted in David M. Bergeron, *English Civic Pageantry 1558–1642* (Columbia: University of South Carolina Press, 1971), p. 117. The ambassador notes that arrangements are actually underway but as in 1626, when triumphal arches had been erected in anticipation, the event did not take place. Charles did eventually make a formal entry into London in 1641 but no pageant devices

or arches were constructed for the occasion.

21. The newly discovered section was displayed along with the two other extant plates in the exhibition 'London's Lost Map' at the Museum of London, March–May 1998.

22. See John Stow, *The Annales of England* (London: R. Newberry, 1600), p. 1075; and Raphael Holinshed (ed.), *The First and Second Volumes of Chronicles* (London: Iohn Harrison, 1587), vol. II, p. 1172. For the dating of the map after 1557 see *The A to Z of Elizabethan London*, LTS publication no. 122 (London: London Topographical Society, 1979), p. xi n. 4. The latest date of 1559 is adduced from the representation of the cross at St Botolph, Bishopsgate, which according to the diary of Henry Machyn, was destroyed in August of that year. Its presence in the Braun and Hogenberg map, but not the earlier woodcut map, precludes the possibility of sequential derivation, demonstrating that they were independently based upon the copperplate original. The evidence for the derivation of the two later maps from the copper-plate engraving is given in full in Marks, *The Map of Mid Sixteenth Century London*, pp. 11–18.

23. On this aspect of royal ceremonial see R. Malcolm Smuts, 'Public Ceremony and Royal Charisma: the English Royal Entry in London, 1485–1642', A. L. Beier *et al.* (eds.), *The First Modern Society. Essays in Honour of Lawrence Stone* (Cambridge University Press, 1989), pp. 65–93.

24. Marin, commenting on the function of certain figures in the work of Le Brun and Poussin, 'The Frame of Representation', p. 84.

25. The various titles of the pageant texts for both Elizabeth and James refer to the royal entry in terms of a *passage through* the city from London to Westminster. See also Lawrence Manley's reading of the 'syntax' of the ceremonial routes which focuses on the the liminal and post-liminal phases of the Lord Mayor's procession and that of the new monarch. *Literature and Culture in Early Modern London* (Cambridge University Press, 1995), pp. 221–58.

26. Thomas Dekker, *The Magnificent Entertainment* (London: T. Man Jr, 1604), sig. B3r. The same passage appears in Harrison's illustrated record, in which the arches are shown with a ground plan and scale bar beneath them, reinforcing the notion that the ceremonial city persists as a mapped entity which even outdoes the performance since 'the hand of Arte gives them here a second more perfect beeing, advanceth them higher than they were before . . . so long as the Citie shall beare a name'. Stephen Harrison, *The Arches of Triumph* (London: John Windet, 1604), sig. B1r.

27. See Jorge Luis Borges, 'Of Exactitude in Science', *A Universal History of Infamy*, trans. Norman Thomas di Giovanni (Harmondsworth: Penguin, 1975), p. 131.

28. *The King of Denmarkes welcome: Containing his arrivall, abode, and entertainment, both in the Citie and other places* (London: Edward Allde, 1606), pp. 19–20.

29. *Magnificent Entertainment*, sig. F2r.

30. *Ibid.*, sig. F2v. The explanation is necessitated by the objections of those 'to

whose settled judgement and authoritie the censure of these devices was referred, [and who] brought . . . these lines into question'. Manley discusses this passage in terms of the rival discursive claims on the segment of the processional route shared by royal entry and Lord Mayor's pageant, *Literature and Culture*, pp. 255–6.

31. Anthony Munday, *Himatia-Poleos. The Triumphs of Olde Draperie, or the rich Cloathing of England* (London: E. Allde, 1614), pp. 5–6.

32. On the broader involvement of the Livery Companies in the promotion of civic consciousness see James Knowles, 'The Spectacle of the Realm: Civic Consciousness, Rhetoric and Ritual in Early Modern London', J. R. Mulryne and Margaret Shewring (eds.), *Theatre and Government under the Early Stuarts* (Cambridge University Press, 1993), pp. 157–89.

33. Thomas Dekker, *Troia-Nove Triumphans. London Triumphing* (London: J. Wright, 1612).

34. It is important to note the distinction between the annual re-affirmation of the order of civic government in the Lord Mayor's procession and the far rarer incidence of a monarchic entry – even so celebrated an exponent of pageantry as Elizabeth made only two state visits to the city in the course of her reign.

35. The maps are copied from the first published maps to represent London and Westminster independently in Norden's own *Speculum Britanniae: The first parte. An historicall & chorographicall discription of Middlesex* (London: n.p., 1593).

36. Arthur Wilson, *The History of Great Britain being the Life and Reign of King James the First* (London: Richard Lownds, 1653), p. 13.

37. Gilbert Dugdale, *The Time Triumphant* (London: R.B., 1604), sig. BIV.

38. *Ibid.*, sigs. BIV–B2r.

39. 'A Proclamation for restraint of Building in and about London' [10 September 1611], reprinted in *Stuart Royal Proclamations: I*, ed. James Larkin and Paul Hughes (Oxford: Clarendon Press, 1973), p. 270, no. 121. For further examples see nos. 51, 78, 120, 152, 175, 186, 204 and 255 in the same volume.

40. Henry Roberts, *England's Farewell to Christian the Fourth, Famous King of Denmarke* (London: W. Welby, 1606), reprinted in John Nichols, *The Progresses, Processions and Magnificent Festivities of King James the First*, 4 vols. (London: J. Nichols, 1828), vol. II, p. 77.

CHAPTER 5

Visible bodies: cartography and anatomy

Caterina Albano

According to Gerard Mercator, the aim of geography is to enable contemplation of the magnificence of God's creation, the mark of divine perfection manifesting itself both in the configuration of the world and in the human body.[1] By inscribing his geographical project within a theological frame, Mercator's validating gesture renders the study of the world a mode of providential revelation. In a parallel move, Helkiah Crooke explains in the introduction to his *Microcosmographia* (1615) – a synopsis of earlier anatomical texts – that the body is a little world, 'an epitome of the whole creation', because its 'admirable structure and accomplished perfection . . . carrieth in it a representation of all the most glorious and perfect works of God'.[2] Crooke's deployment of the ancient *mise en abyme* of the macrocosm figured in the body, occurring within a treatise meant to popularise the achievement of anatomical studies, is a telling example of the persistence into the seventeenth century of the need to conceptualise the body in relation to the order of the universe:[3] 'in my journey', Crooke explains, 'if I have not made new discoveries; yet certainly I have sounded the depth more truly, entered farther into the continents, coasted the shores, plied up the firths, discovered the inhabitants, their qualities, their tempers'.[4]

The tendency of the early modern period to conceive of body and space in terms of an inherent correspondence manifests itself in the practice of representation. Where the dissected body was commonly visualised in the foreground of a contextualising landscape, in geographical illustrations the 'body of the map' was often framed with personifications of the continents or images of inhabitants depicted in their regional costumes.[5] Whilst a reciprocity between body and space clearly appears to have affected the development of both anatomical and cartographic representations in the sixteenth and early seventeenth centuries, we may ask what this reciprocal context implies regarding the meaning contemporaries attached to the 'scientific' projects of geography and anatomy. Central to this question is the assumption that body and space are mutually determined within culture. In epistemological terms, the body is itself a site for the recognition of spatial organisation in the distinction between surface and internal parts, and while cultural notions about embodiment and the definition of bodily boundaries may shape the relation between inside and outside, bodily positions and movements organise the space in which they exist. This points to a relative definition of space not only according to a specific body, but more generally according to the body's cultural representation.[6] Arguably, images of the body are thus linked to spatial perception by the intrinsic relation corporeality establishes with space to enable its own definition, while at the same time an awareness of space can never be completely separated from its bodily perception.[7] This complementary definition of body and space implies both a 'historical correlation' and a context of reciprocal exchange between representations of space and representations of the body,[8] thereby challenging the assumption of their objective codification. The significance of this correlation for an investigation of early modern anatomical and cartographic illustrations becomes even clearer when we consider them as 'mental maps' which have shaped ways of perceiving both body and space.

According to Denis Wood a mental map is central to the organisation of cartographic description, informing the process of inclusion and exclusion whereby a map is made to serve certain interests and ultimately to chart 'the invisible or the unattainable or the erasable'.[9] In this sense, as John Gillies has argued, early modern cartography testifies to competing conceptualisations and representations of space which foreshadow geographical desire and pleasure over the discovery and appropriation of land. For Gillies, 'desire is intrinsic to the cartographic image itself, regardless of any iconographic embellishment',[10] since it articulates the pleasure which the colonial enterprise aroused in the early modern imagination. This desire – whether in terms of the actual voyage or its inscription on maps – can be compared to the attraction felt towards dissection, itself perceived as another form of exploration. According to Valerie Traub, anatomical illustrations express an enhanced penetration through the layers of bodily parts and the appropriation of the body's interior.[11] Yet, the early modern erotic of exploration – of the body as well as of land – is also permeated by anxieties which manifest themselves, I suggest, in both anatomical and cartographic illustrations. As the iconography of anatomy, in Traub's words, 'provides a means of analyzing the politics of intelligibility that govern early modern terms of embodiment',[12] so maps offer the means of examining what could be called a politics of specialisation, suggesting the degree to which cartography and anatomy mutually enable each other. If maps and anatomical illustrations may thus be compared as products of a process of selection, they are significant not merely as representations of corporeality and geography respectively, but also as testimony to the ideas which rendered both body and space visible and, therefore, representable in early modern culture.

BODY/SPACE

In a well known illustration from his 1524 *Cosmographia*, the cartographer Pierre Apian draws a double comparison: geography, represented by a globe, is compared to the art of painting, indicated by the picture of a head, whilst the drawing of a single eye and a single ear is set against the image of a city, exemplifying chorography.[13] This illustration, derived from Ptolemy's classical model and apparently intended to confirm the analogy between microcosm and macrocosm, does not refer to an objective similarity but, rather, to an analogy of representation. Geography, like painting, deals with the rendering of a whole entity – the globe or a head – topography, on the other hand, focuses on single places 'without any apparent comparison within them . . . as if a picture was intended to reproduce a single eye and a single ear'.[14] The analogy between body and space is translated from a mode of perception, relating the whole to its parts, into a mode of representation. Yet if, as suggested above, the link between body and space is intrinsic to the historical process of enculturation which in turn redefines both elements, a question is raised as to the validity of such a shift and the extent to which in the sixteenth century the congruence of the *fabrica mundi* and the *humani corporis fabrica* still holds true to the terms of the ancient analogy.

It is usually recognised that one of the far-reaching consequences of anatomical and cartographic study in the Renaissance was the critique of the authority of the ancients resulting from the practice of direct observation.[15] What one actually saw, rather than what – according to classical tradition – one expected to see, gradually became the focus of investigation. If the practice of cartography and anatomy may be described in this sense as illustrating respectively the discovery of new lands and the more careful observation of bodily parts, both could be considered descriptive sciences for which illustrations are a pre-eminent means of explanation.[16] The frequent inclusion of classical and ornamental images is indeed a characteristic feature of both maps and anatomical tables in this period. Maps, for example, might be embellished with coats of arms; classical, biblical or historical episodes; variations on the vanitas motif; topographical views of towns; or human figures.[17] Equally, illustrations of the dissected body contain allusions to classical sculptures or religious figures, such as St Sebastian or the Virgin, and are often framed by landscapes or architectural structures.[18] This suggests that maps and anatomical tables, despite their generic differences, are rooted in a shared visual tradition which shapes their attempts at categorisation. By examining the function of body and space in both cartographic and anatomical images, I wish to show how the critical inquiry into such representational styles may draw attention to conceptual paradigms informing the scientific projects of anatomy and cartography. In choosing this approach my intention is to expose the 'mental maps' on which these projects were grounded and, in so doing, to reveal the reciprocal context that body and space offered for new modes of analysis and visualisation.

Contemporary atlases and anatomical treatises frequently resort to such generic markers as *theatrum* and *fabrica* on their title-pages, a convention that affirms the central importance accorded to techniques of representation in both anatomy and cartography – thus, the title of Ortelius' world atlas *Theatrum Orbis Terrarum* and the anatomy theatres gracing the frontispieces of numerous treatises on dissection both allude to the manner in which world and body are put on open display, whilst Mercator's *Atlas sive meditationes de fabrica mundi et fabricati figura* and Vesalius' *De humani corporis fabrica* emphasise aspects of architectural 'fabrication'. If both the body and the world can indeed be conceived of as edifices – a space and a body constituted of different parts – they may also be intended as artificial constructions: the re-presentation of their actual referents. The visibility implied here is not that of the body or of specific locations as such, rather the emphasis is on their exposition, constitution and description. For Svetlana Alpers, the intertwining, in the Renaissance, of cartography and landscape painting is evident in the etymological links that exist between the suffix *grapho* – to write, draw, or record; used in words such as geography or topography – and its early modern rendering as *picture* or *pictura*.[19] The visual registers of both paintings and maps further converge in the term *description*, 'a rhetorical term used to refer to a verbal evocation of people, places, buildings or works of art'.[20] Accordingly, 'by employing the term description, the geographical texts accepted the graphic basis of their field while at the same time they related their records to a notion of image making', in other words, to 'the inscription of the world on a surface'.[21] Maps could thus be considered as rhetorical illustrations whose spatial profiles also re-evoked aesthetic perceptions of certain lands.

In his introduction to *The Theatre of the Empire of Great Britain*, an atlas first published in 1611, John Speed uses explicit body imagery to rationalise his descriptive approach. Comparing the 'State of euery Kingdome' ruled by 'prudent gouernment' to a body controlled by the '*Reasonable Soule*',[22] Speed explains that,

> our intendment is to take a view as well of the outward Body and Lineaments of the now-flourishing British Monarchy . . . And here first wee will (by Example of best Anatomists) propose to the view the *whole Body*, and *Monarchie* intire (as far as conueniently wee could comprise it) and after will dissect and lay open the particular Members, Veines and Ioints, (I meane the Shires, Riuers, Cities, and Townes) . . . [23]

Speed's analogy between anatomy and cartography, based on the juxtaposition of body and mind, land and state, bodily parts and geographical elements, can be seen as both iterating and expanding the reciprocity between microcosm and macrocosm. For Speed, the comparison between corporeal and geographical worlds follows from the analogous organising principles which ensure their proper functioning. The body is deployed to represent the political and physical unity of the organs – or places – which constitute the state as a material and rational entity. The analogy of body and space is thus processed through an image of natural order in which single elements are perceived both functionally and hierarchically as the individual components of an ideal harmonious unity. The geographer's investigation, like that of the anatomist, is intended to confirm such an image, by first examining the 'whole Body' as the exterior appearance of the kingdom, and then cartographically displaying the internal parts which constitute its physiological form. Yet, in this process, neither body nor space – or, more specifically, the 'British' kingdom – are neutral terms of reference. The analogy between them only becomes possible when they are subjected to a systematic method of analysis which proceeds from the whole to the particular, from the external, general outline of the body/ kingdom, to its internal, specific functional parts.

In Speed's atlas this is visually achieved in four maps representing in turn Britain, England (including Wales), Scotland and Ireland. The map of Britain is framed by ornamental borders depicting Saxon heroes on the left-hand side, and the conversion of the first seven kings on the right. This reference to historical, political and religious power is sustained in the map of England[24] with a typology of contemporary social classes in the form of several portraits which present an aristocratic couple; a gentleman and a gentlewoman; a citizen's wife and a citizen; a countryman and a countrywoman (Figure 12). Scotland is framed by portraits of the royal family (King James and Prince Henry on the left, Queen Anna and Prince Charles on the right), whilst on the left-hand side of the map of Ireland, three couples are depicted – a gentleman and gentlewoman of Ireland, a 'civil' Irish woman and man, a 'wild' Irish man and woman. These figures, clearly characterised by their clothes – and hence by the appearance of their bodies and the significance attributed to them – both contextualise and condition the reading of the maps. England is glorified by its past, but even more so by the reference to an ordered contemporary society. Scotland is inscribed politically within this harmonious body, whereas the lack of an aristocracy in the Irish map and the juxtaposition of the 'wild' and 'civil' couples suggest the need to impose control on a marginal and uncivilised part of the kingdom – the lower part of its imaginative body. By way of selection and inclusion, the visual construction of this representation of the 'British' kingdom undertakes the justification of Britain's political supremacy over Ireland, but it also highlights the centrality of England in the configuration of the whole body/kingdom. In this sense, Speed's maps delineate assumptions about the political organisation of Great Britain and an ordered society.

Similar concerns are central to the representation of the dissected body, since anatomical tables also illustrate the projection onto a flat surface of the profile and interior of a 'corporeal space'. In its attempt to reveal the structure of the bodily fabric anatomy shared in the ethos of discovery characteristic of geographical explorations and cartography.[25] Andreas Vesalius' *De Humani Corporis Fabrica* (1543), an anatomical treatise amongst the most influential of its time, is indicative of the early modern 'frenzy of knowledge' and 'pleasure of looking' which 'reach into the darkest regions and unfold the interiority of bodies as surfaces laid out before our eyes'.[26] Vesalius signals the importance he attributes to both the observation and representation of the dissected body by including a range of illustrations in his treatise.[27] In images of the muscles and skeletons in particular, the flayed body is displayed in the foreground of a landscape, while a system of letters serves to cross-reference the images of various bodily parts with the accompanying textual explanations. This suggests a mediation of artistic and scientific parameters through which the body acquires visibility: just as the geographical contours of a land become apparent in a map, so the interior of the body acquires its intelligible form in anatomical tables.

Although the landscapes of Vesalian 'musclemen' are subordinate to the representation of the human figures, a distinct relation between body and landscape is established. Like the towns or ruined buildings in the background of these images, the disproportionate human figures are revealed to the eye as spaces that can be discovered and investigated. A correspondence thus becomes manifest between the sinuosities of the landscape and the complex intertwining of the muscles, as well as between the bare terrain and the exposed skeleton. Although of little practical use, these images are significant as expressions of the rhetoric which shaped corporeality as an artifice. The body is conceived of as a space not only because it reflects the structure of the cosmos, but also because it is in itself a physical place, in whose discovery the anatomist moves from the exterior outline to its internal parts. This is evident in Bartolomeus Eustachius' anatomical engravings of the 1550s where the dissected body is presented as a space and framed by compass bearings more proper to maps.[28] Although seen in isolation the body is understood in spatial terms, with an emphasis on proportion and dimension, and inscribed within a grid which defines it as a specific location.[29] Anatomical illustrations can thus function as maps of the body which, to use Apian's distinction, aim to describe both the geography and topography of physiology.

Such a correspondence is suggested in the most striking terms by the tables in Charles Estienne's *De dissectione partium corporis humani*, published in 1545, two years after Vesalius' treatise.[30] Here, skeletons are represented either in the foreground of an urban landscape or as contorted figures which imitate the perspectival views afforded by architectonic constructions. The relations of proportion between the figures and the background imagery are significantly distorted, such that the human figure, rather than emerging from its representational context, threatens almost to disappear back into it. More conspicuously than in Vesalius, the skeleton resembles a structure homologous to the intersection of arcades and colonnades through which the viewer's gaze moves as through the cavities of the bones. The intricate vertebrae of the spine overlap with the curves of a river, or the topography of the background,

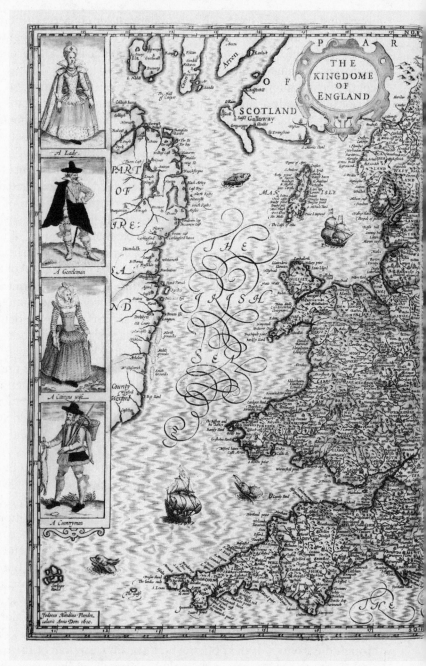

Figure 12 John Speed, *The Kingdome of England* (1611)

while numbers indicate the points at which the muscles attach to the bones, thus implying a purposefulness mirrored in the functionality of the buildings, as well as in the opulence of the landscape. Just as with maps, all the visual elements in these images are suggestive of the desire to describe the unravelled bodily interior by ordering and categorising it. The crawling figure of a man displaying his open skull is impressive for the contortion of the limbs and the indication of the nerves and arteries of the brain (Figure 13). Yet, the cavity in the skull – the detail that sparks off the anatomical inquiry – and the bulk of the body are almost indistinguishable from the ground, so assimilated is the figure into the space which contains it. The body is seen both as integral to, and evocative of, the landscape. The relation between the whole and the parts conveys the ideal order of a country and of a wholesome body in the visual congruence of civic and corporal spaces, of social and individual bodies. Just as the ruins of a building offer a glimpse of its interior space or the wide landscape renders up a distant view to the curious gaze, the dissected body displays its own dissection, and is objectified within a referential context which renders corporeality intelligible.

The continuing relevance of this reciprocity in theoretical terms is confirmed almost a century later by the Belgian anatomist Adrianus Spigelius.[31] Spigelius argues that an investigation of the body should follow the rules of cartography and move from a general outline to the particular description. In geography, the descriptions of the many and diversified regions and countries presuppose an initial presentation of the general features of these places, followed by a consideration of the single mountains, cities and rivers as well as the human activities which characterise these locations. Equally, an account of the many and different components of the human body should begin with a general *tabulam menti* of the external parts and then proceed to consider the internal ones, since a knowledge of the former is necessary in order to overcome the false assumptions which may obstruct the path of inquiry.[32] Spigelius thus asserts the necessity of a 'mental map' for the body as the enabling condition of correct knowledge, semantically validated through a visual and textual delineation, a somatographia of physicality. A correspondence is established between the whole and the parts, between the inside and outside, allowing this somatographia of corporeality to serve as a preliminary mental map of knowledge.

Such a mental projection matches Speed's imagined correspondence between a well-ordered kingdom and a balanced body. In the same way that Speed imposes on his cartographic description an organising

Entends que tout ce qui
eſtoit comprins dens les os de
la teſte/a eſté leué & nettoyé:
a ſcauoir toute la ſubſtance
du cerueau auſſy tous les nerfʒ
venes & arteres qui eſtoient
encloſes dens ladicte teſte:tãt
ſeulement reſte a voir en ce-
ſte figure/les pertuys & ſinuo
ſitez qui demeurent au dedẽs
deſdictʒ os / apres auoir leué
entierement tout le cerueau.

Figure 13 Dissected figure from Charles Estienne, *De dissectione partium corporis humani* (1589)

principle which renders the territory a state, Spigelius charts a description of corporeality onto a preconceived idea of the body. By presuppos-
ing the need for a 'mental map' in which to organise the information
gathered from dissection, Spigelius inscribes corporeality within a
framework similar to that of the cartographer, enabling him to convey
an image of the body as a 'corpus of mental categories'.[33] Like the maps
in Speed's atlas, the engravings in Spigelius' *De humani corporis fabrica*
achieve an integration of body and space, not by juxtaposing the whole
with its parts, or the outside of the body with its interior, but by the
mutual process of impingement and transmutation. In so doing, cartographic and anatomical illustrations chart the relation between outside and inside not only by delineating the contours of geographical and
physiological bodies, but also by producing an internal space subject to
systematic order and formal description. Thus, by visually rendering
corporeality a representable space, anatomical tables replicate cultural
assumptions about the body, just as maps, by inserting human figures
into the cartographic display, make possible a way of seeing which
generates a virtual image of the cultural categories defining the geographical space depicted.

GENDERED SPACES

In anatomical illustrations it is generally the male body which takes on
the role of representing the human body except where the attention
focuses on the womb and the formation of the foetus. Yet femininity
impinges on anatomy in a broader sense. Valerie Traub has read in the
gendering of the dissected body a validation of the rationality and
control that anatomy imposes on corporeality in terms of objectifica-
tion.[34] By gendering the illustration of corporeality these images reduce
the representation of the female body to the womb and, more specifically, to the pregnant womb. But in so doing these illustrations also
present us with an iteration of the process of specialisation already
uncovered in the early modern representation of the dissected body.
The female body, spatialised visually in the womb, is reduced to an
illustration of the primary social function of women. The frontispiece to
Vesalius' *Fabrica* in which the central figure is a woman with an open
womb testifies to the symbolic prominence of the dissected womb. This
might be interpreted as a disavowal of the preoccupations surrounding
procreation through the representation of the womb as a space to be
controlled by scientific discourse. Yet the significance of this specialisa-

tion appears more puzzling when considered in relation to that mutuality of space and body characteristic of anatomical illustrations, since it replicates the act of representation as an act of appropriation and control by stressing the virtuality of the image. This act of containment finds a parallel in the eroticisation of land in maps deploying allegorical female figures of the continents. An examination of the representational strategies of maps and anatomical tables in terms of desire makes possible a further exploration of the mutual contextualisation of body and space in early modern cartography and anatomical illustration.

On the title-pages of both Ortelius' *Theatrum Orbis Terrarum* and the second volume of Mercator's *Atlas* the continents are emblematically embodied by virgins alluding to the attributes ascribed to each land mass.[35] These examples of the persistence of the ancient tradition of personifications of the continents concur in showing Europe clothed and bearing signs of power – a crown and a sword–, of religious supremacy – the cross –, and of bounty – grapes, other fruit; both also picture Asia wearing fine clothing and holding a cruet of myrrh. Africa and America, by contrast, are shown as naked figures. Whilst in Ortelius America is shown as an alluring and dangerous amazon holding with one hand a severed male head, in Mercator it is suggested by the personifications of Mexicana and Peruana – two armed figures with wild animals at their side. A reference to Magellanica – a naked feminine figure in Mercator and a feminine torso in Ortelius – completes the allegorical globes. If the Eurocentric view of the cartographers is confirmed by the economic, political and religious supremacy attributed to Europe, amongst the treatment of the other continents the exotic refinement of Asia is evoked, as well as the more threatening seductive power of Africa and America. Central to this early modern personification of the continents is the identification of land with a very specific body: that of a virgin. Just as anatomical tables gender the body only in illustrating the female reproductive system, so cartography selects an image of femininity which can be conquered, subdued and handed over.

Attributes such as nudity, used to characterise America and Africa, signal the process of eroticisation of land since they accord with the descriptions of native peoples circulating in early modern Europe. Léry's account of the native Americans – which itself informed Montaigne's description of the savage – stresses the nudity and cannibalistic cravings of women;[36] here, native women represent both the fascination and the fears surrounding early modern exploration, thus creating an implicit analogy between body and space. As de Certeau has observed, in Renaissance iconography nudity could function as an attribute of innocence, as in the cases of Venus, the Virgin or Eve, symbolising the naked truth of knowledge which could be seen and apprehended:

[I]n the same way Indian women indicate the secret that knowledge transgresses and disenchants. Like the Indian women's naked body, the body of the world becomes a surface offered to the inquisition of curiosity. During Léry's time the same would hold true for the bodies of the city and the diseased which are transformed into *legible* spaces.[37]

The use of virgins in the personification of the continents can be related to classical examples of embodiment, such as that of Oeropa, and more broadly to an archetypal identification of the fertility of land with a nurturing feminine principle.[38] Yet it is difficult to avoid the recognition of a more complex context – as de Certeau suggests – for the early modern identification of land and femininity, which produces an image able to retain the pleasure of discovery and simultaneously to frame the world as a knowable and representable space. Although this process of enculturation seems principally to involve newly discovered regions, a related mode of representation can also be observed in the treatment of European countries.

To render space legible is, in fact, a political act of appropriation demonstrated by Speed's transformation of the geographical body of Britain into the kingdom of Britain as an organised and ruled space. The allegorical personification of Britain – Albion – is also a female figure: in the title-page of Michael Drayton's 1612 *Poly-Olbion* she is represented wrapped in a map holding a sceptre and cornucopia at the centre of an image framed by four male rulers of the country.[39] Similarly, a series of maps published in Germany and the Netherlands between 1537 and the early seventeenth century represent Europe in the form of an empress. In these images the profiles of the continent have been reshaped to suggest the human figure, thus allowing a significant redistribution of countries within the allegorical body of Europe. The crowned head consistently denotes Spain, the right arm Italy and the right hand holding the imperial orb Sicily – at the time under Spanish dominion –, France and Germany are situated in the upper breast, whilst Hungary, Poland and other central European countries the middle and lower parts of the body. Britain usually appears in these maps as an independent and detached island slightly above the left shoulder of Europe. Denmark, Sweden and Norway are also included near the borders of the illustrations. Yet, significantly, in two anonymous Dutch maps dating from 1598 Britain (captioned as Anglia and Scotland) is incorporated in the left arm which holds a sword in place of the royal sceptre. Here, the allusion to the defeat of the Spanish Armada in the armed arm of England appears both celebratory and threatening, as if suggesting an ambivalence towards the displacement within Europe's ordered representation.

What appears evident in these anthropomorphic images of Europe is that the traditional identification of land and virgin is here contextualised to render the geographical space of the European continent an allegorical, historical and religious place. Her geographical and imaginary bodies have been assimilated into a cultural virtuality. If we compare this to the similarly emblematic representation of the dissected womb as a locus of investigation in the title-page to Vesalius' *Fabrica*, and consider the traditional use of a female figure to personify anatomy, we find that both maps and anatomical tables testify to a re-presentation of the enculturation of space and body as a process which can be iterated through the image itself.[40] For geography the conceptualisation of land in the form of the female body suggests an attempt to exert control over de-stabilising events on the ground by reproducing in the image the potentiality of the encounter with the virgin body. In the same way for anatomy the definition of corporeality imposed upon the body by the disturbing practice of dissection is countered in the representation of the womb which functions as both the emblem and the locus of control. Thus the conceptual orders of both geography and anatomy find expression in their allegorical use of the female body.

In Spigelius' *De Formato Foetu* (1627) this process is exemplified in four plates showing the gradual uncovering of the uterus.[41] The skin of the abdomen and the placenta open to the viewer's gaze like an unfurling flower. Spigelius imagines the uterus as a field whose ground needs to be properly fertilized and irrigated: a secluded plane crossed by a large navigable river forms the background landscape to a literally and emblematically blooming womb. Indeed in the course of the four plates the more that the body is itself presented as emphatically flourishing, so the focus on the water and vegetation of the landscape is intensified, in this way literalising the idea of the uterus as a fertile ground. As Karen Newman has pointed out, 'the conventions for inscribing obstetrical knowledge ... allow for a double identificatory pleasure: identification with the immaculate, impenetrable human individual, and power/knowledge that comes of knowing the body as an object of study'.[42] This body, however, no less than the allegorical personification of the continents, is virtual. It only exists as a re-presentation; a cultural codification which, in the early modern period, was achieved through a figurative reciprocity between body and space. The eroticisation of land and the specialisation of the female body thus confirm how anatomy and geography function as reciprocal models for delineating the 'mental maps' through which both corporeality and space could be categorised and represented. By acknowledging a mutual legibility we find the pleasure of discovery implied in the unravelling and mapping of geographical or physical territories. Most significantly of all, both cartography and anatomy alert us to a process which rendered both body and space culturally visible.

NOTES

1. Gerard Mercator, *Atlas sive cosmographiae meditationes de fabrica mundi et fabricati figura* (Düsseldorf: Albert Busius, 1595), sig. A2.
2. Helkiah Crooke, *Microcosmographia* (London: W. Jaggard, 1615), p. 10.
3. This is illustrated on Crooke's titlepage. At the top of the page the depiction of the celestial spheres – further related to a scene in the Garden of Eden and to the apocalyptic consequences of the fall, on the right and left-hand sides underneath – defines the ethical and scientific realms of anatomical investigations. The in-depth knowledge gained by anatomy is illustrated by two figures standing as Adam and Eve on either side of the title. The male figure represents a pre-Harveian circulation of the blood with a lily covering his genital organs, possibly an indication of original purity, whilst the female figure shows her open womb, as an emblematic locus where the body becomes penetrable and the correlation between macrocosm and microcosm is imprinted. Since for Crooke, the purpose of anatomy is to detect and illustrate such correlations, a group of figures is presented at the bottom of the page examining a skull during a medical lecture. This depiction can be further related to the two scenes sketched at the top – one alluding to blood letting; the other to the treatment of wounds. They suggest the utilitarian aim of anatomical investigations and define distinct spheres of medical practices.
4. Crooke, *Microcosmographia*, preface to book III, p. 925.
5. Jonathan Sawday argues that the dissected human body needed this contextualisation in order to become significant: 'The dissected human body in isolation signified very little because, in terms of the paradigms of natural science, the body could not yet provide its own rationale for division. It was only after the great anatomical explorations of the late sixteenth and seventeenth centuries that it became possible to view the body in spatial isolation, with the implied context provided by the rigours of scientific investigation.' *The Body Emblazoned: Dissection and the Human Body in Renaissance Culture* (London: Routledge, 1995), p. 116.
6. For a discussion of the mutuality between body and space see Edward

Casey, *Getting Back into Place. Toward a Perceived Understanding of the Place-World* (Bloomington and Indianapolis: Indiana University Press, 1993), pp. 43–105. Casey examines how the body exists in place, while at the same time defining space itself, as in the notion of here/there, right and left.

7. Elizabeth Grosz argues that 'the lived experience of space and the spatiality of science cannot be readily separated, insofar as the "objective space" of scientific speculation can only have meaning and be transmitted according to the subject's lived experience of space.' *Space, Time, and Perversion: Essays on the Politics of Bodies* (London: Routledge, 1995), p. 92.

8. *Ibid.*, p. 97.

9. Denis Wood, *The Power of Maps* (London: Routledge, 1993), p. 5.

10. John Gillies, *Shakespeare and the Geography of Difference* (Cambridge University Press, 1994), p. 61.

11. Valerie Traub, 'Gendering Mortality in Early Modern Anatomies', Traub *et al.* (eds.), *Feminist Readings of Early Modern Culture: Emerging Subjects* (Cambridge University Press, 1996), pp. 44–92.

12. *Ibid.*, p. 44.

13. Pierre Apian, *La Cosmographie* (Paris: V. Gaultherot, 1553), fols. 3r–4v.

14. *Ibid.*, fol. 4r (my translation).

15. For a discussion of the development of cartography see Frank Lestringant, *Mapping the Renaissance World. The Geographical Imagination in the Age of Discovery*, trans. David Fausett (Cambridge: Polity Press, 1994). For a discussion of the development of anatomical studies and the importance of illustrations see K. B. Roberts and J. D. W. Tomlinson, *The Fabric of the Body: European Traditions of Anatomical Illustration* (Oxford: Clarendon Press, 1992).

16. The centrality of anatomical tables is also highlighted in Martin Kemp, '"The Mark of Truth": Looking and Learning in Some Anatomical Illustrations from the Renaissance and Eighteenth Century', W. F. Bynum and Roy Porter (eds.), *Medicine and the Five Senses* (Cambridge University Press, 1993), pp. 85–121.

17. See James A. Welu, 'The Sources and Development of Cartographic Ornamentation in the Netherlands', David Woodward (ed.), *Art and Cartography. Six Historical Essays* (University of Chicago Press, 1987), pp. 147–73.

18. See Glenn Hartcourt, 'Andreas Vesalius and the Anatomy of Antique Sculpture', *Representations* 17 (1987), 28–61; Martin Kemp, 'A Drawing for the *Fabrica* and Some Thoughts upon the Vesalius Muscle-Men', *Medical History* 14 (1970), 277–88; C. M. Saunders and Charles D. O'Malley, *The Illustrations from the Works of Andreas Vesalius of Brussels* (Cleveland: World Publishing Co., 1950).

19. Svetlana Alpers, *The Art of Describing: Dutch Art in the Seventeenth Century* (London: Penguin, 1989), pp. 133–9.

20. *Ibid.*, p. 136.

21. *Ibid.*

22. John Speed, *The Theatre of the Empire of Great Britain* (London: Iohn Sudbury and George Humble, 1611), sig. E1r.

23. *Ibid.*

24. The elision of Wales is Speed's, not mine. The title of the map in question is 'The Kingdome of England'.

25. Michael Neill, *Issues of Death: Mortality and Identity in English Renaissance Tragedy* (Oxford: Clarendon Press, 1997), pp. 128–9. Neill also refers to the frontispiece engraving of Olaus Rudbeck's *Atlantica* (Uppsala: H. Curio, 1679), in which a group of geographers is seen dissecting the globe with the assistance of Time (p. 128).

26. Michel de Certeau, 'Ethnography. Speech or the Space of the Other: Jean de Léry', de Certeau, *The Writing of History*, trans. Tom Conley (New York: Columbia University Press, 1988), p. 232.

27. Andreas Vesalius, *De Humani Corporis Fabrica* (Basel: Joannis Oporini, 1543). As Andrew Cunningham has noted, 'whether or not Vesalius was the artist for his own woodcuts, we can see that he instinctively thought in terms of pictures, diagrams and sketches'. *The Anatomical Renaissance. The Resurrection of the Anatomical Projects of the Ancients* (Aldershot: Scolar Press, 1997), p. 113.

28. On these plates, first published much later in the *Tabulae anatomica* (Rome: F. Gonzaga, 1714), see Roberts and Tomlinson, *The Fabric of the Body*, pp. 188–93.

29. Samuel Y. Edgerton, Jr., 'From Mental Matrix to *Mappamundi* to Christian Empire: The Heritage of Ptolemaic Cartography in the Renaissance', Woodward (ed.), *Art and Cartography*, p. 43. In Svetlana Alpers' essay in the same volume the author draws attention to the difference between a cartographic and perspective grid. Svetlana Alpers, 'The Mapping Impulse in Dutch Art', Woodward (ed.), *Art and Cartography*, pp. 70–2.

30. Charles Estienne, *De dissectione partium corporis humani* (Paris: S. Colinaeus, 1545).

31. Adrianus Spigelius, *De humani corporis fabrica* (Venice: n.p., 1627).

32. *Ibid.*, lib. I, chap. I, p. I.

33. Luke Wilson, 'William Harvey's *Prelectiones*: The Performance of the Body in the Renaissance Theatre of Anatomy', *Representations* 17 (1987), 63.

34. Traub, 'Gendering Mortality', pp. 53–5. See also Barbara Duden, *Disembodying Women: Perspectives on Pregnancy and the Unborn*, trans. Lee Hoinacki (Cambridge, Mass.: Harvard University Press, 1993); Karen Newman, *Fetal Positions. Individualism, Science, Visuality* (Stanford University Press, 1996).

35. Abraham Ortelius, *Theatrum Orbis Terrarum* (Antwerp: A.C. Diesth, 1570), frontispiece engraving. See also sigs. B–B2 for an explanation of the engraving. Mercator, *Atlas*, frontispiece engraving, vol. II.

36. de Certeau, 'Ethnography', pp. 232–3.

37. *Ibid.*, p. 234.

38. See Ovid, *Metamorphosis*, liber II, line 585.

39. Michael Drayton, *Poly-Olbion* (London: M. Lownes *et al.*, 1612), frontispiece engraving.

40. For representations of *Anatomia* see Sawday, *The Body Emblazoned*, pp. 183–8.

41. Adrianus Spigelius, *De formato foetu* (Venice: n.p. 1627), table IV.

42. Newman, *Fetal Positions*, pp. 96–7.

PART II

Literature and landscape

CHAPTER 6

The scene of cartography in King Lear

John Gillies

In spite of a now burgeoning critical literature, the staging of maps in the Elizabethan theatre remains fraught with mystery. What happened to a map when it became a theatre prop? Was it a hand prop or a piece of furniture (an independently readable wall map)? Did these maps speak directly to the audience, momentarily unframed and uncensored, in their own powerful cultural language? Or did the map and its culturally masterful spatial discourse defer to the stage's traditional spatiality, its time-honoured authority as the *Theatrum Mundi*? What kind of cultural transaction took place in these moments? The answers to these questions vary widely with respect to different stage maps and even to different studies of the same stage map. Here I want to focus on the deepest and most elusive moment of cartographic staging in Shakespeare: what has been called 'Lear's Map'.[1] Specifically, I wish to contextualise this stage map in relation to a prior group of stage maps, to elucidate the specific dramatic and theatrical moment of the map's existence as a stage image (a verbal *and* physical object), to track the echoes of that moment through the play's later stagings of space, and to ask what this amounts to in terms of a total cultural and ideological mediation of cartography. What is finally at issue is more than a theatricalisation of a non-theatrical discourse. As I have argued elsewhere, early modern cartography was already highly theatricalised. It staged its own relationship to the culture at large, fashioned its own cultural 'scene', and dictated its own framing in other cultural discourses (including on the stage).[2] In Lear's map however, I will suggest that the scene of cartography is imported to the stage but also dismantled and dethroned by the theatre's own more intimately bodied language of space.

I

As an image of the 'kingdom', Lear's map should be understood in the
context of Shakespeare's only other physical introduction of a map to
the stage (*1 Henry IV*, 3.1) and his only other stage image of the 'kingdom': John of Gaunt's apostrophe to England in *Richard II* (2.1.40–66).[3]
While it is true that these are images of England rather than of Britain,
they are linked to Lear's map of Britain in the sense that all are images of
the 'kingdom'. These three Shakespearean nation-scapes should be
understood in terms of a fourth: the map of England in the anonymous
Woodstock (c. 1594) which is recognised as having a clear filiation with
John of Gaunt's speech in *Richard II*, and via that with a significant
English 'landscape' in *Lear*: that of Edgar's 'itinerary' as wandering
beggar (Q: 7.179–86; F: 2.2.176–83).[4]

As images of the 'kingdom', all four of these nation-scapes operate in
broadly similar ways and within a broadly similar value-complex, and to
this extent quite distinctly from, say, the 'world' map in *2 Tamburlaine the
Great* (5.3.124–51).[5] In the first place, they are occasions of what Terence
Hawkes has – in respect of Lear's map – called 'a programme of brutal
partition'.[6] Thus, Hotspur's and Lear's maps are spoken of as being
divided into three parts. Gaunt speaks of Richard's kingdom as if 'leased
out like to a tenement or a pelting farm'. And in *Woodstock*, 4.1, the map
is exhaustively divided into four parts among four favourites.[7] In three of
these plays, moreover, the equality of the division is registered as
tendentious. Thus Hotspur carps at the equality of his 'moiety' in *1 Henry
IV*, Greene is given what is plainly the most desirable portion in
Woodstock, whereas in *Lear* Cordelia's portion is 'more ample' than those
of her sisters. Finally, in three of the four plays, the division of the
kingdom on the map signals a denaturing transition from a transcendental order of value (the mystique of kingdom or nation) to a purely
mercenary 'property' relation. Thus, in *Woodstock*, the kingdom under-
goes a double degradation: first the king is reduced to a 'landlord' who
leases his subdivided kingdom to sycophantic 'tenants' for the pecuniary
sum of £7000 per month; then the tenants sublease to subtenants who
are 'farmed', 'racked' and otherwise egregiously exploited (through, for
example, the infamously novel tax mechanism of 'blank charters',
literally blank cheques). It is just this situation that Gaunt alludes to in
Richard II, with England being leased out like 'a tenement or a pelting
farm' (in which the property is held by the tenant at the will of the
landlord, in sharp contrast to the customary Feudal 'free-hold' of the

yeoman).[8] Again, the echo of the word 'pelting' in Edgar's 'poor pelting villages' in *Lear*, signals a degraded form of land tenure in which property and tenant alike are reduced to a general paltriness ('pelting') or lowness ('low farms'). This in turn fits in with the suggestion of the brutally 'rational' style of estate management through which Goneril and Regan strip their father of the decorous extravagance of his 'one hundred knights'.

Surprisingly, in view of the elaborate triumphalism, the fetishism, of actual contemporary national maps from Saxton to Speed, the stage's version of the national map is generically grim, functional and minimal. The mere presence of such a map on the stage – invariably in a chronicle-based dramatic context – is a signal of national decay rather than the celebration of national mystique that J. B. Harley finds in Saxton's map of England ('this ethnocentric fugue of a map').[9] As well as suggesting a kind of generic critique of the national map by the stage (such maps, whatever their pretensions, have only one material function), this contradiction raises a question about the degree to which the stage map was actually visible to the audience: specifically, were these maps meant to be visually construed by the audience as well as by the characters? Were these props 'real' maps or dummy maps (effectively to be treated as stage 'letters')? We may begin by noting that (unlike the map scene in *2 Tamburlaine*) in none of these cases does the stage context *require* the map to be legible by the audience. Indeed, in the two earlier chronicle plays featuring a map (*1 Henry IV* and *Woodstock*) that possibility is all but ruled out.

In *1 Henry IV*, 3.1, a map is brought onstage at the entry of Hotspur, Worcester, Mortimer, Glendower. Hotspur asks the other three to 'sit' (4), then exclaims 'A plague upon it, I have forgot the map' (5). Glendower produces the map ('No, here it is.' [6]) and in turn asks Hotspur to 'sit'.[10] Evidently the map is to be consulted jointly with all four parties sitting. Combined with the fact that Glendower is able to so easily produce an object which Hotspur has forgotten, the joint sitting already suggests a hand prop rather than an item of furniture. Other clues also point to this conclusion. The group consultation of the map is no sooner set up than disrupted by a long and increasingly heated exchange of bragging and provocation between Glendower and Hotspur (which must eventually require each of them to stand). After some sixty lines of this, Glendower backs down: 'Come, here's the map. Shall we divide our right, / According to our threefold order ta'en?' (67–8). This is Mortimer's cue to rehearse a division by direct reference to the map on which it is evidently represented:

> The Archdeacon hath divided it
> Into three limits very equally.
> England from Trent to Severn hitherto
> By south and east is to my part assigned;
> All westward – Wales beyond the Severn shore
> And all the fertile land within that bound –
> To Owain Glyndwr; (*to Hotspur*) and, dear coz, to you
> The remnant northward lying off from Trent.   (3.1.69–76)

Along with much of the phrasing, the geographic detail here is taken straight from Holinshed.[11] Some seventeen lines later, Hotspur quibbles that his 'moiety north from Burton here / In quantity equals not one of yours' (94–5), because the river Trent 'comes me cranking in, / And cuts me from the best of all my land / A huge half-moon, a monstrous cantle out' (95–7); and then vows to make the river run straight by cutting a new channel. This leads to a territorial dispute between the neighbouring party (Mortimer), Worcester (Hotspur's uncle, who agrees with his nephew) and Glendower who refuses to think of altering Trent. Plainly the disputants are constantly making reference to the map, but equally plainly the argument is being driven by the earlier dispute between Hotspur and Glendower (who rises to Hotspur's bait a second time even though his territory is unaffected). The audience is surely not following the dispute straight from the map itself because, apart from inevitably detracting from the unhistorical rivalry between Hotspur and Glendower (the real driving force of the scene) a map would have been incapable of displaying the river to a theatre audience in anything like the detail required by the dispute.

It is equally certain that a hand prop map was used in *Woodstock*, 4.1. Unlike in *1 Henry IV*, the kingdom here is divided in exhaustive detail. After briefly bemoaning the ignominy of becoming 'a landlord to this warlike realm', who will 'rent out our kingdom like a pelting farm' (4.1.1862–3), King Richard asks Greene to 'reach me the map' (1922); then, calling his four favourites to 'come, stand by me and mark those shires assigned ye' (1925–26), he describes each portion by major geographic orientation and/or shire (thus Bushy is to have the shires 'that lie in Wales, together with our counties of Gloucester, Worcester, / Hereford, Shropshire, Staffordshire and Cheshire' [1931–32]). Clearly the favourites – each addressed personally and by turn – are being called upon to witness the divisions on the map before them. But the close character grouping (similar to the seated group in *1 Henry IV*), again suggests a hand-prop rather than a piece of furniture. A hand-prop is also suggested by the sheer exhaustiveness of the geographic detail in the dialogue. Redundancy must have been the only purpose served by the audience's seeing all this on a wall map. Finally, we should notice that, in calling for personal acts of witnessing ('See here, sweet Greene' [1943]), Richard is not making a public statement. Far from being openly displayed to the audience, this map (like that in *1 Henry IV*) is probably being seen back-on.

It would appear then there is no particular 'mystery' about the maps in *Woodstock* and *1 Henry IV*; no semiotic residue in excess of what the characters say about them. If these maps are not directly displayed to the audience, then the chances of a clash between the semiosis of the stage and the potent visual semiosis – the gaudy nationalism – of the contemporary 'nation' map, are minimised. In these two plays, the stage speaks for (and indeed over) the map. The map is denied a direct voice. In John of Gaunt's speech from *Richard II*, however (Shakespeare's redaction of the above scene in *Woodstock*) there is a difference:

> This royal throne of kings, this sceptred isle,
> This earth of majesty, this seat of Mars,
> This other Eden, demi-paradise,
> This fortress built by nature for herself
> Against infection and the hand of war,
> This happy breed of men, this little world,
> This precious stone set in the silver sea,
> Which serves it in the office of a wall,
> Or as a moat defensive to a house
> Against the envy of less happier lands;
> This blessèd plot, this earth, this realm, this England,
> This nurse, this teeming womb of royal kings . . .
> This land of such dear souls, this dear dear land,
> Dear for her reputation through the world,
> Is now leased out – I die pronouncing it –
> Like to a tenement or pelting farm.   (2.1.40–60)

Not only is a map-prop missing from this moment, but the speech itself is not significantly map-shaped.[12] The speech works by a combination of deixis ('This') and a procession of symbolic images (throne, isle, earth, seat, etc.) of the nation, all of which have no necessary implication in sixteenth-century cartographic discourse and all of which (with the possible exception of 'plot') are historically prior. While the use of deixis itself can be said to characterise the way in which maps are made to function on the Elizabethan stage, its effect here is quite different.[13]

When used in respect of an onstage map, deixis directs attention to specific geo-graphic entities on the map's surface ('See here sweet Greene'). In Gaunt's speech however, deixis is used to directly apostrophise England in terms of aggregated symbolic images. The difference is between purely functional and purely rhetorical gestures; between a cartographised anatomy and a bardic evocation of transcendent and transhistorical presence; between a single visual field and an emblematic complex. There is another difference, to which we will return shortly. Gaunt evokes the nation specifically as something indivisible and unownable; as a work of natural providence rather than a piece of property.

II

While in the same generic league as the nation-divisions in the above plays, the division of the kingdom is much more complex and elusive in *Lear*. In the first place, the map is produced in the opening moments of the play. The division of the kingdom precipitates the tragedy, it drives the plot. It is not a virtually extraneous detail as in *1 Henry IV*, or an emblematic inset as in *Richard II*, or a thematic culmination as in *Woodstock*.[14]

Secondly, while Lear's map, like its antecedent nation-scapes, signals that the kingdom is being reduced to a 'property', it is not clear what kind of reduction this is or what status it has. There is no Gaunt in this play to put a strong counter-vision of the kingdom as transcending the property relation. This does not mean that the idea of the kingdom as property is not interrogated in *Lear*, but it does mean that the interrogation is a good deal less sure of itself than Gaunt's is in *Richard II*. Thus, the 'poor pelting villages' through which Poor Tom wanders are not (like Gaunt's 'pelting farm') opposed to an unequivocal vision of national wholeness. They do represent the counterpastoral underside of Lear's map, but that cannot itself be taken as an unproblematic image of the nation. The landscape Lear imagines is clearly park-like and thus eminently within the parameters of the property relation.[15] Again, what the Fool – Gaunt's equivalent in this play – criticises Lear for is for squandering the kingdom, rather than for treating it as his personal property. Indeed, rather than denouncing the equivalence of kingdom and property, the Fool's hurtful jokes about lands and houses, snails and ants, insist on their equivalence. How do we explain the absence of the generic denunciation of the kingdom-as-property in *Lear*? One way would be to point out that in the Union controversy, James had adopted the tactic of representing himself explicitly as 'landlord' of the legally separate entities of England, Wales and Scotland.[16] To say the least, this must have complicated any attempt by Shakespeare to criticise the idea of the kingdom as the property of the King in *Lear*. At the other end of the critical spectrum are explanations which find in the play a passionate but bewildered critique of early capitalism.[17] We shall return to this discussion shortly. The point to be registered here is that the equivalence of kingdom and property is more complex in *Lear* than in the earlier plays.

A third difference between Lear's and earlier stage maps lies in the character of its 'geography'. Where the geographical outline of the divisions in the earlier plays is unambiguous (as befitting matters of recent historical record), the geography of the division in *Lear* is as hazy as its history is ancient, and also at variance with what little record exists. In Holinshed, Leir has no intention of dividing Britain between his three daughters, but of giving it whole to the daughter he expects to please him most. When Cordeilla refuses to play the game, Leir divides the kingdom between the husbands of his other two daughters more or less as in Shakespeare, with the difference that one half of the kingdom is reserved during his own lifetime. The idea of the tripartite division does not belong to the Leir story but to an earlier stage of British history – that of Brut's division of the kingdom between his three sons. It has been plausibly suggested that in altering the Leir story in this way, Shakespeare was making a complimentary allusion to James I's campaign to have England, Wales and Scotland legally united under the name of 'Britain'; by which name James explicitly recalled Brut, and the division of Britain into 'Albania' (Scotland), 'Cambria' (Wales) and 'Loegria' (England).[18] This being so, the geography of *Lear* must have had a contemporary resonance lacking in the earlier stage maps. Lear's map must have figured the contemporary geography of England, Scotland and Wales, but in a context at once ancient and prophetic.

It is just possible that these geographic divisions were visibly displayed to the audience in the form of a stage wall map. Unlike in *Woodstock*, the division of the kingdom in *Lear* takes the form of a public announcement; suggesting that when Lear identifies Goneril's portion as consisting 'of all these bounds, even from this line to this', the audience was in a position to know what he was talking about. It is possible that they would have been able to recognise that this meant Scotland simply from the name of Goneril's husband, 'Albany'. And it is likely that they would

have recognised Cordelia's portion as England for the fact of its being
'more opulent' than the other portions, and because of the etymology of
the name 'Cordelia' (Latin 'cor' or heart; Middle English 'delit').[19]
Again, if they were at all conscious of the Brutan and Stuart character of
Lear's division, they may have recognised Regan's portion as corresponding to Wales even though she is married to 'Cornwall'. Whether
or not, as Terence Hawkes claims, Cornwall is 'the old name for Wales
and the west of England', the two regions were connected in the sense
that James' son Henry was both Prince of Wales and Duke of Cornwall.[20] Yet these geographical hints are remarkably inexplicit (in view
of the geographic clarity of the previous three stage maps of the kingdom) and it is tempting therefore to think that they were made explicit
by a visible display of geographic divisions on a stage map – perhaps at a
court performance. Here however it must be said that the geography of
the division is not so coherent as has been claimed. While it is true that
there is an ancient tradition linking Cornwall with Wales, this is Roman
rather than 'British'.[21] In the chronicle history from Brut to Cordeilla,
Cornwall is clearly a dukedom within 'Loegria' (England) and is never
assimilated to Wales. Any attempt to display this visibly then could only
have compounded the confusion.[22] At the same time, a legible map
would have added nothing to the enduring tendency of the action.
While the Folio text of 1623 makes several minor changes to the Quarto
text of 1608 in respect of Lear's map (which we shall consider shortly),
none of these serve to clarify the geography of the division. In this
respect, the later text is as pointedly vague and unforthcoming as the
earlier one.

There are however distinct theatrical advantages to Shakespeare's
geographic vagueness. It has long been thought that there is an inconsistency between the trial Lear makes of his daughters' affections, and
the earlier suggestions by Gloucester (Q: 1.3–5; F: 1.1.3–5) and Lear
himself (Q: 1.38–39; F: 1.1.37–38) that the division of the kingdom has
already been made.[23] How is the trial meaningful if the division has
already been fixed? An elegant way out of this apparent difficulty, one
that makes positive sense of the vagueness of spoken geographic detail, is
to suppose that when Lear describes Goneril's portion as consisting 'of
all these bounds even from this line to this', he is in fact deciding on the
border between Scotland and England at that very moment. In this
reading, 'all these bounds' would indicate the eastern and western sea
coasts of Scotland; while 'this line' would indicate the northern sea coast
and the second line ('to this') the English border. Such a reading is more

than just convenient. In Holinshed's account of Brut's donation of 'Albania' to his youngest son 'Albanact', there is a huge grey area between ancient Scotland and England stretching from Edinburgh to Hull: '[Albania] is diuided from Lhoegres also by the Solue and the Firth, yet some doo note the Humber'.[24] A border this movable in the chronicles might well be linked to whimsicality and emotional games-manship on the stage. There is no need to suppose that the audience would need to 'read' the map themselves in order for this reading to be viable on the stage. It is more important to be reading gestures and faces. The point is that there is no inconsistency between an in-principle decision to cut the cake before the love test and actually cutting it during the love test.[25] The theatrical advantage is obvious. It explains why Goneril in particular should take the love trial so seriously. Where does Lear draw his line? Does he reward Goneril by drawing it well into 'English' territory or tease her by drawing it up near the Firth of Forth? How long does he leave Goneril in suspense before drawing the border? The theatrical possibilities are rich any way. Instead of the love test being irrelevant then (as Coleridge assumed it must be), it becomes even more outrageous. Turning Lear into a manic cartographer dynamically relates the map to the love trial in an unforgettable demonstration of the dangers of early modern cartography.[26]

The fourth and perhaps major way in which Lear's map differs from its theatrical predecessors is that Lear's dialogue evokes the visual character of the generic nation map – the iconography of the map's surface – rather than identifying or rehearsing the geography of the divisions. This is clearest in the Folio's version of his lines to Goneril:

> Of all these bounds even from this line to this,
> With shady forests and with champaigns rich'd
> With plenteous rivers and wide skirted meads,
> We make thee lady. (1.1.63–6)

The detail here is consistent with the 'landscape' effect of early modern maps as described by David Smith: 'The convention of depicting woodland by tree symbols dates from manuscript maps ... in the sixteenth and seventeenth centuries, these symbols were somewhat randomly scattered about the map'.[27] As I have argued elsewhere too, the effect here is entirely consistent with the 'landscape' effect of a Saxtonian map in which features such as 'forests', fields and rivers were represented by mimetic codes (what J. B. Harley has called 'tiny frag-ments of landscape') with a strong ambience of pastoralism.[28] It is

specifically this effect that Shakespeare chose to enhance when revising
the Quarto's,

> Of all these bounds even from this line to this,
> With shadowy forests and wide skirted meads,
> We make thee lady.   (1.58–60)

Clearly, whatever use the prop is being put to, the real energy of the
language here (its enduring tendency in performance) was invested in
creating a virtual landscape. Lear's map is essentially a stage image
compounded of a physical prop and a verbal landscape, which – for a
contemporary audience – must have inevitably evoked the Saxtonian
genre of national cartography. Of the four nation-scapes we have
considered then, this is the only one to have evoked the independent
semiotic quality – the visual rhetoric – of an Elizabethan national map,
and to have made that quality central to its purpose.

III

But to what purpose? Addressing this question will require us to turn our
attention from the moment of the map as such to its structural resonances with the rest of the play. More than this, however, we should ask
whether Lear's map engages with the immense cultural and ideological
authority of cartography in the period, and if so how it negotiates that
authority.

This question arises from the underlying relationship between theatre
and cartography in the period. Each was linked to the other through the
ancient figure of the *Theatrum Mundi* (whereby the stage was a globe and
the Globe a theatre) – in a rhetorical marriage of convenience from
which cartography achieved popularity and theatre legitimacy. In such
a context, the introduction of a map and its discourse to a play about
national history might well be taken as a bid for cultural authority; as a
sign of the stage's eagerness to stay abreast of the revolution in cartographic literacy. The price of not seeming 'mapminded' could be
high. Thus, Shakespeare was ridiculed by Jonson for giving Bohemia a
seacoast – in a romance play. For stage epics, such as *Lear*, 'mapminded-
ness' posed more serious problems. Jonson avoided the genre presumably because the attempt to stage an exemplary historical action on a
suitably epic scale seemed hopelessly at odds with geographic 'fact'.
Shakespeare was more adventurous. In *Henry V*, he famously conceded
the stage's inferiority in matters of epic and geographic scale, but defied

it by appealing to the very geographic sophistication to which he was deferring. Thus the Chorus exhorts the audience to 'scale' its imagination accordingly ('into a thousand parts divide one man') and regales it with virtual zooms from England to France.

Cartography, then, challenged the popular drama to keep up. It is perhaps no accident that the most spectacular examples of keeping up were also the first major successes of what we look back on as the 'popular' drama. Part of the appeal of the *Tamburlaine* plays (even today) is their evocation of sheer scale. Marlowe not only introduces a world map to the stage and invites the audience to read it, but he uses cartographically inspired imagery at crucial moments and lifts itineraries directly from Ortelius.[29] Cartography in these plays is not so much a setting as a structure of feeling, an ethos and a pathos. Thus, at the climax of the first play, the new geography triumphs over claims of romantic love and kinship as Tamburlaine refuses Zenocrate's request to spare Damascus. Apart from a need to keep abreast of geographic fashion ('I will confute those blind geographers / That make a triple region in the world'[30]) Tamburlaine is driven by a rage for cartographic totalisation. To his cartographically trained eye, 'peoples' blend into 'lands' and thence map-like quantities of volume, mass, scale, zone and grid co-ordinate. Battles are imagined as the clash of mobile geographic entities which overwhelm not just each other but also the natural world and the local landscape. In these plays, chorography is vanquished by geography, the human scale by the continental scale, individual persons by the impersonal sublime. If, like *Henry V*, the *Tamburlaine* plays can be taken as representing the most brilliant of the stage's answers to cartography, they also suggest the degree to which the stage is taken in and overtaken by it. By talking up to cartography but not back to it, they betray the theatre's inferiority complex and its deeper ideological complicity.

The question we must ask of Lear's map, then, is what kind of cultural negotiation is this? Is it complicit with the values and ideology of cartography, or is it a critique? These questions inform my unpacking of the map's characterological and structural resonances. We may begin by noticing the way in which the map's discursive aura – its rhetoric – is picked up in the dialogue of Lear and Goneril, the two characters who are most affected by it. Lear divides his kingdom as if it were a pastoral landscape, a seventeenth-century park as distinct from a sixteenth-century ornamental garden.[31] Compared with the transcendental imagery of nation in Gaunt's speech in *Richard II*, Lear's map figures the nation as an available object of desire. If Gaunt and Lear may both be said to fetishise the nation, they do so in different ways and to different effects. Whereas 'England' continually transcends Gaunt's attempts to imagine it – in the very plurality of its symbols – Lear's kingdom is reduced to convenient homogeneity. Where Gaunt's apostrophe to England suggests the absurdity of private possession, Lear's map suggests just the opposite. This is a delectable piece of property offered up to the desiring subject on a 'plat'. As if responding to the breeziness of a cartographic prospect, Goneril protests that she loves Lear, 'Dearer than eyesight, space, and liberty; / Beyond what can be valued, rich or rare' (F: 1.1.56–7).[32] The images of desire here seem keyed to a vision of cartographic extension, soon to be realised in the coy gamesmanship of Lear's gift 'Of all these bounds even from this line to this', and eventually persist as a kind of personal emblem for Goneril ('O indistinguished space of women's will' [F: 4.5.271]).[33] Like Tamburlaine, it seems, Goneril and Lear are intoxicated by cartography. In all three, imagined spaciousness begets a kind of *jouissance*, a specifically visual 'feeling tone'. Spatial structure, the geographer Yi Fu Tuan reminds us, is closely linked to 'perceptual equipment' and associated 'feeling tone'.[34] The space of the eye is differently structured and oriented in relation to the body, than the space of the voice or the space of touch and smell. It is also qualitatively different: being extended, imaginal, heady, relatively detached and 'elevated' (in the sense of being attuned to distance).

Goneril's 'beyond', as Garrett Sullivan has noted, contrasts with the closure and fixedness of Cordelia's 'bond'.[35] The name 'Cordelia' works to suggest the rootedness of such bonding, as of 'holy cords too intrince t'unloose'; where 'cords' might suggest anything from heartstrings to forms of familial and communal obligation emptied out from the map's landscape of pleasure. The abruptness of Cordelia's refusal to indulge her father is more easily understood if we realise the stage genealogy of her position as the favourite with the most 'opulent' of equal shares. We have already noted a structural similarity between her position at this moment and that of Greene during the division of the kingdom in *Woodstock*. But the similarity goes deeper. After having already made ample gifts of land to his other three favourites, King Richard turns the last grant into a kind of love play:

> KING: Now my Greene, what have I left for thee?
> GREENE: 'Sfoot, and you'll give me nothing, then good night landlord. Since ye have served me last, and I be not the last shall pay your rents, ne'er trust me.

KING: I kept thee last to make thy part the greatest. See here, sweet Greene,
these shires are thine, even from the Thames to Trent. Thou here shalt lie
i'th'middle of my land.
GREENE: That's best i'th'winter . . .

(4.1.1939–46)

The erotic suggestiveness of this is unmistakable in view of the fact that
Greene is the only one of the favourites to be represented as Richard's
'minion'. In terms of the generic 'division' scene, Cordelia (Cor/delit)
has been placed in a highly disreputable position. It is up to her to
redeem the 'middle lands' from the taint of desire, to restore them as a
true 'heartland'.

So far we may say that the play implicates the map not just in the
division of the kingdom, but in a suspect emotional culture in which
'space' is linked to a voyeurism with no sense of tradition or nationhood.
To be mapminded in this play is already to be licentious, materialistic
and probably amoral. Having nothing to say to the corrupt bargain
Lear offers her, Cordelia likewise has nothing to do with mappery and
the map finds no reflection in her dialogue.

IV

To this moral critique of the map, *King Lear* adds what we may call a
phenomenological critique. Phenomenology insists that space cannot
exist at all unless there is a body to perceive it.[36] Highly sophisticated
models of spatiality – such as the new cartography – cannot exist unless
the body is able to work in relative comfort. In a real sense, then, the
space of the map is underwritten by the comfort of the body. The
ultimate scene of cartography – the place in which maps are typically
read – is a domestic interior. The comfort of the map-reading body is in
fact a commonplace of early modern cartographic discourse. Maps,
William Cuningham boasted, allow one all the benefits of travel with
none of the discomfort and 'danger of enemies, losse of time, spending
of substaunce, werines of body, anguish of mind'.[37] They bring the
distant (the unknown) into the 'near' (the known); and make 'one little
room an everywhere'.[38] A phenomenological way of putting this is that
they accommodate the sphere of the eye to the spheres of the more
intimately body-bound sensorium (hearing, touch, taste, smell) within a
domestic interior. Put more simply, the map is extraordinarily commodious or accommodating: a source at once of spatial information and

intimate pleasure, a tool but also a domestic ornament. 'Some', rhapso-
dises John Dee, buy maps,

> to beautifie their Halls, Parlers, Chambers, Galeries, Studies, or Libraries with:
> other some, for thinges past, as battels fought, earthquakes, heauenly fyringes,
> & such occurentes, in histories mentioned . . . and such other circumstances.
> Some other, presently to vewe the large dominion of the Turke: the wide
> Empire of the Moschouite: and the little morsell of ground, where Christen-
> dome (by profession) is certainly knowen . . . Some, either for their owne
> iorneyes . . . some, for one purpose: and some, for an other, liketh, loueth,
> getteth, and vseth, Mappes, Chartes, & Geographicall Globes.[39]

Not least of the map's innovations would appear to be the creation of a
new experience of the bourgeois domestic interior. This could be
described as an expansive interiority ('great riches in a little room') in
which the impression of visual space and the expansive and intellective
feeling tone associated with it, permeates the more tactile and aural
feeling tones of the domestic interior without disturbing them. The
literary topos of the world-within-the-room with which we are so familiar in Marlowe, Donne and Shakespeare originates then in the writings
of cartographers such as Cuningham and Dee. Most influential of all
perhaps, was Ortelius whose *Theatrum Orbis Terrarum* (1570) Marlowe had
consulted while writing *Tamburlaine*. In the ornamental figure of the
'Theatrum' Ortelius collapsed the architectural figure of the *sala del
mappamondo*: a palatial antechamber painted with maps of the continents
and oceans.[40]

Expansive interiority is unforgettably captured in the map-lined
interiors of Vermeer. For our purposes however, Vermeer shows two
types of interior, a parlour and a study. Like the windows which they
tend to echo, the maps in Vermeer's parlours gesture toward a sublime
exteriority without ever disturbing the domestic emplacedness (and
complacency) of the oblivious (and predominantly female) occupants.
Lacking a purposive correspondence between maps and occupants,
these parlour scenes do not quite amount to a scene of cartography. In
Vermeer's matching portraits of an 'astronomer' and 'geographer',
however – portraits in which the human figure is plainly called to the
mysteries of astronomy or geography within the context of a study – the
scene of cartography is fully adverted.[41] The high cartographic vocation
of both these figures is signalled by their theatricalised scholarly robes,
their physical positions (bending over tables filled with working maps
and implements) and their farsighted gaze (divided between cartographic surfaces and a window).[42] Clearly the two figures (each posed

by the same model) are complementary. Within the scene of cartography, each plays the same role. While recalling the genre of the scholar at his desk, Vermeer's cartographers also seem to recall the vignettes of exemplary cartographers on the ornamental title-pages of cosmographic treatises.[43] Like the cloud-borne Ptolemys and Marinuses on the title-page of *The Cosmographical Glasse*,[44] Vermeer's figures are engaged in acts of dynamic observation or contemplation. Yet they differ from these figures in their naturalistic setting. Vermeer's scene of action is a domestic interior rather than an ersatz cosmos. One way to think about this wedding of cosmic/geographic space with domestic space is as a reconciliation of the antithetical spatial structuration and 'feeling tone' which the geographer Yi Fu Tuan (apparently drawing on Husserl's notions of the 'near sphere' and 'far sphere') associates respectively with the eye and the more intimate senses of touch and smell. Stretching into the distance, the space of the eye is the most attenuated and least bodied. The spaces of touch and smell, however, are strongly 'affective' and strongly bodied. Between the two is a kind of discontinuity: 'the relative importance of sight diminishes in affective space: to appreciate the objects which give it its high emotional tone our eyes may even be closed'.[45] In Vermeer's geographer and astronomer, however, the far-seeing body is comfortably at home.

In Lear's map we behold a staging of the scene of cartography in the theatre. Regardless of whether or not the opening scene takes place in an 'interior', Lear's map (his verbal landscape) is charged with the phenomenological values of interiority. Responsive to bodily manipulation, the map is equally available for emotional intimacy and emotional blackmail. This perhaps is the deeper point of its geographic vagueness. A map which is no more than its own geography cannot impress us as a cartographic artefact. Lear's map however, is above all an artefact, a fetish in which geographic values dissolve into bodily values, torrid zones into the comfort zone. What is staged in *King Lear* is not just a map-reading but the expansive interiority of early modern cartography.

The human embeddedness, the commodiousness, of Lear's map is its chief point of contact with the rest of the play. Oddly for a historical epic, the 'space' of *Lear* is defined less by geography than the primal mediacy of the body. From the moment of the map to the 'Dover cliff' scene, the major spatial idea in *Lear* is built around the bodily opposition of housedness and unhousedness, accommodation and nakedness. Lear's comment in the storm that 'when the mind's free, the body's delicate', might almost be taken as a reflection on the map-body nexus in Cuningham and Vermeer. If the scene of cartography is underwritten by mental freedom and bodily comfort, then what becomes of it once the body is assailed by all those dangers that Cuningham had imagined it as excluding? In a real way, this question is addressed by the opposition between inside and outside settings in *King Lear*.

The movement from inside to outside in *Lear* is accompanied by a stripping and abjection (and consequent foregrounding) of the body. Cast out from home, Edgar strips, degrades and mutilates his body, and imagines himself wandering with 'presented nakedness' through a landscape of 'poor pelting villages'. Similarly, Lear is ejected from a generic 'household' and stripped of his retinue in a way that anticipates the later stripping of his body, and compounds the cartographic divestments of the opening scene. A blend of the separate households of Goneril and Regan, the generic household is the site of a distinctive economy, at once 'rational' (an economy built around strictly tailoring expenditure to 'need'), and pointedly mathematised. Insistently reasoning the need, this economy counts ceremony and privilege as superfluous because in excess of what bodies rationally need. In this sense both daughters adopt a version of the landlord/tenant relationship towards their father in refusing to recognise anything about him in excess of bodily needs and his simple tenure at their own pleasure. Not unlike Richard in *Woodstock*, they

> Become a landlord to this warlike realm
> Rent out our kingdome like a pelting farm.   (1862–3)

In both plays, the change from 'warlike realm' to landlord-estate is from a ceremonious economy to an economy of the bottom line, from a roomy interiority to a shrunken one. The generic household is oddly small ('this house is little' [Q: 7.447; F: 2.2.461]) and inward looking; defined by what it cannot accommodate rather than what it can. It is in this regime that Lear's ceremonial body is whittled away to nothing.

It is significant that the action should abruptly shift from a generic 'inside' to a generic 'outside' just at the end of Lear's 'O reason not the need' speech (with the Folio's stage direction 'Storm and Tempest', and the 'exeunt Lear' of both texts). The irrelevance of the traditional geographic paradigm to this play – and its persisting grip on the critical tradition – is shown by the near universal assumption that the storm scenes must be set on a 'heath'. As Flahiff has shown however, the word 'heath' is not to be found in either the Quarto or Folio.[46] It is first introduced as an actual scenic effect in Tate's adaptation, and thereafter as a stage direction from Rowe's edition until the recent Oxford edition of the Quarto and Folio texts. What this suggests is that the 'geography' of Lear's ordeal is far less important than its 'placial' quality; a quality that has no meaning independently of the phenomenological fact that it is 'outside' the 'household' setting.[47] In both texts, Lear's exit is followed by several remarks on the growing storminess, and several to the effect that Lear is now 'outside' the house. In the last of these, Cornwall makes it clear that the stage is now to be taken as a stormy exterior:

> Shut up your doors, my lord. 'Tis a wild night.
> My Regan counsels well. Come out o'th'storm. *Exeunt*
>
> (Q: 7.465–66; F: 2.2.480–81)

During the storm scenes proper (those featuring Lear), the opposition of inside and outside (and the idea of the 'house') are continually adverted: in both of the Fool's songs and some five of his general references.[48] In all these, the inside is remembered primarily as a comfort zone of shelter, warmth and security. As another kind of 'inside', the 'hovel' is also heavily signposted. In both texts, the main storm scene ends with our being told that Lear's party is on its way to 'a hovel . . . this straw . . . your hovel . . . this hovel'; and the next storm scene opens with numerous requests for Lear to 'enter' (in all, there are six variants of this cue in Q, and eight in F).[49] Lear never does 'enter' this notional hovel (thereby exiting the stage), because Tom enters the stage from the same notional offstage direction, leaving the party yet more emphatically 'outside'.

In view of the heaviness with which the phenomenological division between insides (house and hovel) and outsides is underscored in the original texts, it is intriguing that the idea of the 'heath' should have become so deeply entrenched. Tate's adaptation introduced other settings besides a heath, but none that have been similarly canonised.[50] One explanation for the persistence of the 'heath' image, is that the 'sublime' confrontation of man and the heavens was felt to require a sublime landscape; and an unworked and uninhabited landscape (such as the 'blasted heath' in *Macbeth*) was more sublime than a humanly and socially shaped landscape. Unlike the storm in *Macbeth*, however, that in *Lear* does not 'trifle former knowings' (2.4.4). It is unremarkable. Nature is behaving normally here. Similarly, this heath is no primal wilderness, just a wasteland on the underbelly of the social world. Thus Lear explicitly links his own destitution to the social underclass of 'poor naked wretches' at the very moment that the 'hovel' setting is most insistently adverted. In the Folio, the 'poor naked wretches' speech is prefaced by a new specifically hovel-related passage:

[*To Fool*] In, boy; go first. [*Kneeling*] You houseless poverty –
Nay, get thee in. I'll pray, and then I'll sleep. *Exit* [*Fool*]   (3.4.26–7)

Whether or not Lear actually kneels at this moment, the idea that the speech is a prayer is entirely consistent with the emblematic force of the humble dwelling on the Elizabethan stage. Such virtual 'places' are commonly contrasted with palaces and indicated by gestures of humility, such as stooping or praying.[51] The point is that Shakespeare has taken some trouble to locate these scenes of Lear's abjection in the social world and to dramatise abjection as a wider social phenomenon. In this connection, we should note that Lear's evocation of poverty is uniquely authentic in early modern English theatre.[52] It is not a casual effect.

The most compelling accounts of what it means to actually live 'outside' social institutions of any kind are offered by Edgar as Poor Tom. The first of these, as we have seen, evokes a degraded rural landscape of 'poor pelting villages', which in echoing Gaunt's words in *Richard II* and Richard's words in *Woodstock*, are intimately linked with the moment of division and its instrument, the map. The second, describing Tom's diet on the road (Q: 11.117–24; F: 3.4.121–8) virtually dissolves the very ideas of landscape and geography in dismantling the relationship between observing subject and observed object. To wander a terrain aimlessly and desperately, to literally ingest it as Tom does, is to destroy its coherence as a terrain. It is no accident therefore that the major placial division between inside and outside coincides with a division between landscape as comfortably objectified and land as uncomfortably travelled. The landscape of vagrancy and madness is no longer a landscape that is primarily beheld. Lear and Tom have no 'place' from which to view the land and no particular direction to go in. It is as if in their experience, the 'commodiousness' topos of the map is deconstructed and with it the very idea of the map as a visual construction of lived space. In Gloucester this process is further emblematised. With no eyes and 'no way', he is left to steer by 'smell'.

V

Thus dissolved, landscape makes a bizarre comeback in the Dover cliff scene (Q: 20.11–24; F: 4.4.11–24), where, so to speak, the 'landscape format' of seventeenth-century Dutch painting is tipped vertically in the course of Tom's evocation of the height of Dover cliff. What is remarkable about this description is the almost pedantic use of perspective.

Crows and choughs 'that wing the midway air' look the size of beetles, a samphire gatherer at the same height seems the size of a man's head. Fishermen on the beach look the size of mice. A ship at anchor is the size of a ship's cock-boat, while the cock-boat is the size of a buoy 'almost too small for sight'. Furness relates a revealing discussion of this passage involving Dr Johnson. Finding 'the great and dreadful image of irresistible destruction . . . dissipated and enfeebled . . . [by] the observation of particulars',[53] Johnson preferred a far more generalised and monumental evocation of a high temple from Congreve's *The Mourning Bride*. To one who urged the merits of Dover cliff passage, Johnson responded:

> No, sir; it should be all precipice, – all vacuum. The crows impede your fall. The diminished appearance of the boats, and other circumstances, are all very good description, but do not impress the mind at once with the horrible idea of immense height. The impression is divided; you pass on, by computation, from one stage of the tremendous space to another. Had the girl in *The Mourning Bride* said she could not cast her shoe to the top of one of the pillars in the temple, it would not have aided the idea, but weakened it.[54]

Furness rightly objects that Johnson has taken the passage out of dramatic context. What I find interesting however, is Johnson's impatience with the advertisement of perspective as a technique. Not unlike Rowe, with his interpolation of the word 'heath' into the canon, Johnson prefers his effects sublime rather than technologised. It is not as if Johnson's visions of sublime height are without perspective, but that perspective can be occluded because it is taken for granted. Writing shortly after the first use of painted perspective on an English stage (*The Masque of Blackness*, 1605), Shakespeare does not take perspective for granted.[55]

Dover cliff, it is often forgotten, is described from two positions: above and below; each to very different effect. The view from the top (narrated by 'Poor Tom') is a virtuoso performance on a par with *Cymbeline* 1.3, a short scene constructed entirely around the idea of perspective diminution. Topping Pisanio's description of gazing after Posthumus as he sails off into the distance, Imogen protests:

> I would have broke mine eye-strings, cracked them, but
> To look upon him till the diminution
> Of space had pointed him sharp as my needle;
> Nay, followed him till he had melted from
> The smallness of a gnat to air, and then
> Have turned mine eye and wept.   (1.3.17–23)

In both cases, the 'virtuoso' element of the performance is keyed to an association of perspective with the marvellous, in the sense of dizziness or optical effects (as in the 'natural perspective' of *Twelfth Night*). The view from the bottom however (narrated by Edgar in his honest countryman guise) works in very different ways. The tone is sober, and the height actually estimated 'by computation' ('Ten masts a-length make not the altitude / Which thou hast perpendicularly fell' [Q: 20.53–4; F: 4.5.53–4]). In addition, this particular perspective view is moralised. Seen from its base, the clifftop becomes a demonic locus of despair (the equivalent of Despair's cave in *The Faerie Queene*). The lesson that Edgar wants to emerge is that despair is as relative and evanescent as viewpoint and perspective.[56]

This vertical landscape is as consciously chorographic as Lear's map is geographic. As well as calling on the technical language of perspective, Shakespeare also advertises the surveying technique of triangulation, whereby unknown dimensions are calculated by their angle of incidence with known dimensions (thus the height of a hill can be calculated by relation to a church tower once the two are plotted in a geometric relation to each other). Shakespeare does something like this when suggesting that the ship is as big as its cock-boat, or that the cliff is more than ten masts in height. While all Elizabethan maps drew on this basic surveying technique to some degree, chorographic maps relied on it absolutely. Unlike a geographic scale map which depicted an object which could not be seen, chorographic maps depicted objects which could be seen (notionally at least). This in turn meant that where geography was concerned with mass and scale and generality, chorography was concerned with particular places understood in qualitative and precisely localised detail. In *The Cosmographical Glasse* (1559), chorography is distinguished from cosmography and geography as follows:

> For lyke as Cosmographie describeth the worlde, Geographie th'earth: in lyke sorte Chorographie, sheweth the partes of th'earth, divided in them selves. And severally describeth, the portes, Rivers, Havens, Fluddes, Hilles, Mountaynes, Cities, Villages, Buildinges, Fortresses, Walles, yea and every particuler thing, in that parte conteined . . . Chorographie consisteth rather in describyng the qualitie and figure, then the bignes, and quantitie of any thinge.[57]

The distinction is driven home by the respective illustrations Cuningham supplies. The illustrations for cosmography (a generalised earthly globe set within an armillary sphere) and geography (a generalised world map) are crude and small (each roughly a sixth of a page). The illustration for chorography however is large, a double page fold-out view of the city of Norwich in the year 1558 (a year before the publication date). Unlike the previous drawings, this is the result of an actual survey made of a precise placial entity at a given moment in an ongoing history. Unlike, say Saxton's wall map, *Britannia Insularum in Oceano Maximo* (1583), which features the same generic 'landscape' composed of the same repertoire of icons as the county maps and national map in his atlas, perspective here requires an individual landscape – in this case 'Dover cliff'.[58] We might also note that chorographic literalism was also opposed to the generic requirements of 'landscape' as art, to the degree that this was (in John Peacham's words) 'not a literal prospect, but "una Maestà scenica".'[59]

The particularity of chorography is suggested by the inclusion in the foreground of Cuningham's chorographic view of a vignette of surveyors on a hilltop taking the readings on which the view itself is based. As commonly in such views, Cuningham reflexively inscribes a meta-chorographic scene within the finished chorographic product. Like cartography then – like Vermeer's cartographers and the idealised cartographer figures on the atlas frontispieces – chorography (the rendering of topography as scenery) depicts the scene of its own making. There is however a difference. Where the scene of cartography is the domestic interior or an ornamental title-page, that of chorography is a hilltop or high place. The chorographer is less a bookman or sage than a working surveyor.[60]

What kind of game does the stage play with the scene of chorography? Edgar's game is to trick his father into seeing his tragedy in a providential perspective (a variant of the game he compulsively plays with himself). In a curiously modern way, Edgar internalises the latest surveying technology as a psychological coping mechanism. If there is no disaster that is not reducible to manageable proportions by being 'put in perspective', then the psyche is theoretically able to cope with anything ('whatever doesn't kill me makes me stronger'). But if no object is too big for the psyche, then everything is relative, nothing is absolute, and tragedy cannot exist. Shakespeare's answer to Edgar's strategy is that of tragedy and the stage. Tragedy insists on the absoluteness of human suffering. The stage insists that mental perspectives are ultimately mired in human bodies. Unlike Gloucester who forgets the evidence of his remaining senses in the tortured exaltation of his imagination, the theatre forces us to attend equally to the body – a body unexalted by imaginary heights and depths, and unframed by visual illusion. When that body tumbles bathetically to the stage, a joke is played on the modernist discourse of perspective. The joke works off the contrast between speech, sublimity and perspective on the one hand, and bodies, bathos and the bare stage on the other. The humour here is more than grotesque. It is tragic. Not only is Gloucester's grand gesture (counterpart of Lear's in the storm) robbed of meaning and dignity, but the therapy itself is pointless. Gloucester dies anyway, but on the flats of insignificance and relativity ('and thats true too') rather than the heights of human defiance.

VI

What unites Gloucester's scene of chorography with the moment of Lear's map is a particular value complex and feeling tone, the origin of which lie in what I have called 'the scene of cartography': a quasi theatrical topos in which the human body (that of the cartographer) is posed in relation to the distant and sublime objects of cartographic description. Whether (as more commonly) depicted on the clouds or strapwork peaks of an ornamental atlas title-page, or within a bourgeois interior as by Vermeer, the cartographer is defined by his gaze. This, to paraphrase Yi Fu Tuan, is 'far sighted' like 'statues of eminent statesmen' who 'overlook sweeping vistas'.[61] The sublimely far seeing cartographic gaze is what unites Lear's scene of cartography with Gloucester's. In this play despair is as monumentally 'far sighted' as the cartographised vistas which so intoxicate Lear and Goneril. Farsightedness has a more sober mindset of course, as in the ingenious relativism of Edgar's internalisation of perspective (in which the body again becomes as light as air). All such attitudes however, the drama refuses, forcing the gaze back into congress with the agonised and ridiculous body. Unlike in *Tamburlaine* and *Henry V*, the stage talks back to the master discourse of cartography in *King Lear*, parading the cartographised spatial imagination only to collapse it back into the stage's own more deeply bodied spatial idiom.

NOTES

1. For earlier studies see Frederic T. Flahiff, 'Lear's Map', *Cahiers Elisabethains* (1986), 17–33; Terence Hawkes, 'Lear's Maps', *Meaning by Shakespeare* (London and New York: Routledge, 1992), pp. 121–40; Francis Barker, 'The Information of The Absolute', *The Culture Of Violence. Essays on Tragedy and History* (Manchester University Press, 1993), pp. 3–92; Bruce Avery, 'Gelded Continents and Plenteous Rivers: Cartography as Rhetoric in Shakespeare', John Gillies and Virginia Mason Vaughan (eds.), *Playing the Globe*.

Genre and Geography in English Renaissance Drama (Madison: Fairleigh Dickinson University Press, 1998), pp. 46–62; John Gillies, 'Introduction: Elizabethan Drama and the Cartographisation of Space', *Playing the Globe*, pp. 19–45. I am indebted to Garrett Sullivan for showing me a pre-publication copy of his 'Reading Shakespeare's Maps', *The Drama of Landscape: Land, Property, and Social Relations on the Early Modern Stage* (Stanford University Press, 1998), pp. 92–123; and likewise Tony Voss for showing me his 'The Lie of the Land: Some Co-ordinates of King Lear'.

2. 'Theatres of the World', *Shakespeare and the Geography of Difference* (Cambridge University Press, 1994), pp. 70–98; also, 'Posed Spaces: Framing in the Age of the World Picture', Paul Duro (ed.), *The Rhetoric of the Frame: Essays on the Boundaries of the Art Work* (Cambridge University Press, 1996), pp. 24–43.

3. All references to Shakespearean texts are to Stanley Wells and Gary Taylor (eds.), *William Shakespeare: The Complete Works* (Oxford: Clarendon Press, 1994).

4. My juxtaposition of these three theatrical map-moments is indebted to Garrett Sullivan's compelling juxtaposition of them in *The Drama of Landscape*, Section I, 'Of Landlords and Kings: The Landscapes of Estate and Nation', particularly pp. 57–123. Sullivan powerfully urges the stage's scepticism of cartographic ideology, its constitutional adherence to a more tradition-based ethic of land and land use. While in full agreement, my primary emphasis (on the function of stage maps as props) is more phenomenological than Sullivan's. I follow the Oxford edition in treating *Lear* as two different texts, the Quarto (1608) and Folio (1623). The evidence of revision in the later text is invaluable for my purposes in providing indications of enduring and / or evolving textual tendencies.

5. Christopher Marlowe, *The Complete Plays*, ed. J. B. Steane (Harmondsworth: Penguin, 1985).

6. Hawkes, 'Lear's Maps', p. 121.

7. *Thomas of Woodstock*, ed. George Parfitt and Simon Shepherd (Nottingham Drama Texts, 1977).

8. Valentine Leigh discusses a spectrum of rents from 'rentes of Lands and Tenements holden at will' to 'freehold' rents and those based on 'fealty' and 'customarie lande holden by custome called tenaunt right'. Freehold is discussed as follows: 'suche Landes and Tenementes &c thei have to them and to their heires, and the same is commonly called Freeholde, and those Tenauntes and Tenauntes for terme of life, are alwaies called Freeholders. And sometyme also, they holde by certaine Services. And every suche Tenaunt oweth fealtie to their chiefe lorde.' *The Moste Profitable And Commendable Science of Surueying* [1577] (Amsterdam: Da Capo Press; New York: Theatrum Orbis Terrarum, 1971), sigs. B3-C3.

9. J. B. Harley, 'Meaning and Ambiguity in Tudor Cartography', Sarah Tyacke (ed.), *English Map-Making, 1500–1650* (London: The British Library, 1983), pp. 22–45, esp. p. 37.

10. Chairs ('a joint stool' [2.5.381–3]) are heavily used in the previous 'tavern'

scene, so would not need to be brought onstage for this scene.

11. '[The rebels] by their deputies, in the house of the archdeacon of Bangor, divided the realme amongst them; causing a tripartite indenture to be made and sealed with their seales, by the covenants whereof, all England from Severne and Trent, south and eastward, was assigned to the earle of Marche; all Wales & the lands beyond Severne westward, were appointed to Owen Glendouer: and all the remnant from Trent northward, to the lord Persie'. *Holinshed's Chronicles of England, Scotland, and Ireland, in Six Volumes* [1577/87] (London: J. Johnson *et al.*, 1807; New York: AMS Press 1965), vol. III, p. 22.

12. Some critics tend to see this speech as map-shaped: Michael Neill, 'Broken English and Broken Irish: Nation, Language, and the Optic of Power in Shakespeare's Histories', *Shakespeare Quarterly* 45 (1994), 1–32, 15; Gillian Beer, 'The Island and the Aeroplane: the Case of Virginia Woolf', Homi Bhabha (ed.), *Nation and Narration* (London and New York: Routledge, 1991), pp. 265–90, esp. pp. 269–70; Garrett Sullivan, *The Drama of Landscape*, pp. 109–23. Phyllis Rackin thinks not, in her *Stages of History: Shakespeare's English Chronicles* (Ithaca and London: Cornell University Press, 1990), pp. 24–5.

13. See my analysis of Tamburlaine's use of deixis in relation to his stage map: 'Posed Spaces', pp. 39–40.

14. The map scene (4.1) in *Woodstock* symbolises the triumph of a mercenary culture of rack renting over Woodstock's patriotism and Richard's own conscience.

15. For Lear's park see Tony Voss, 'The Lie of the Land'.

16. For a discussion of James as landlord see Richard Halpern, *The Poetics of Primitive Accumulation: English Renaissance Culture and the Genealogy of Capital* (Ithaca and London: Cornell University Press, 1991), pp. 221–2.

17. See John F. Danby, *Shakespeare's Doctrine of Nature: A Study of King Lear* (London: Faber and Faber, 1964); Rosalie Colie, 'Reason and Need: King Lear and the "Crisis" of the Aristocracy', Rosalie Colie and F. T. Flahiff (eds.), *Some Facets of King Lear: Essays in Prismatic Criticism* (University of Toronto Press, 1974), pp. 185–219; Richard Halpern, '*Historica Passio*: King Lear's Fall into Feudalism', *The Poetics of Primitive Accumulation*, pp. 215–70.

18. Brut's division is described in *Holinshed's Chronicles*, vol. I, pp. 443–4. For the link between *Lear* and the Union controversy see John W. Draper, 'The Occasion of *King Lear*', *Studies in Philology* 34 (1937), 176–85; Marie Axton, 'The Problem of Union: King James I and *King Lear*', *The Queen's Two Bodies: Drama and the Elizabethan Succession* (London: Royal Historical Society, 1977), pp. 131–47; Richard Dutton, '*King Lear, The Triumphs of Reunited Britannia*, and "The Matter of Britain"', *Literature & History* 12, first series (1986), 139–51.

19. This suggestion would have been stronger for those audience members recalling the division of the kingdom in *Woodstock*, 4.1, where the last portion – that granted to Greene – is also the middle portion (in this case London and the English Midlands).

20. Hawkes, 'Lear's Maps', p. 125. Draper too claims that 'Cornwall in ancient times was more extensive than the modern shire' ('The Occasion of *King Lear*', 181). For Henry's identity as Duke of Cornwall see Axton, *Queen's Two Bodies*, p. 136.

21. In his *Description of Britain*, William Harrison describes how the Romans divided Britain into five portions, the fourth of which 'was surnamed Flauia Caesariensis, and conteined all the countrie which remained betweene Douer and the Sauerne, I meane south of the Thames, and whereunto (in like sort) Cornewall and Wales were orderlie assigned'. *Holinshed's Chronicles*, vol. I, pp. 30–1.

22. In the course of the many vicissitudes of 'Britain' over some dozen reigns, several Dukes of Cornwall become kings of 'Loegria' and thence of Britain.

23. See the long note on the critical history relating to this problem in Horace Howard Furness (ed.), *King Lear: A New Variorum Edition* (New York: Dover Publications, 1963), pp. 4–5.

24. *Holinshed's Chronicles*, vol. I, p. 196.

25. Gloucester's earlier remark, 'now, in the / division of the kingdom, it appears not which of the dukes / he values most' (Q: 1.3–5; F: 1.1.3–5) suggests that the division is anything but clear cut. Lear's statement, 'Know that we have divided in three our kingdom' (Q: 1.38–9; F: 1.1.37–8) says nothing about where the borders are.

26. The idea of Lear as a cartographer may seem anachronistic in a play about ancient British history, but there is strong evidence that the historiography upon which the play rests was anachronistic in just this way. *Holinshed's Chronicles* was conceived in relation to a chorography, William Harrison's *Description of Britain*. Moreover, as Edward Lynam points out, both authors viewed their project through the lens of Saxton's maps. Thus, Harrison thanks Thomas Seckford (Saxton's superior) for the loan of his 'platforms' and dedicates the 'Description of Scotland' to him. Likewise, Holinshed records his debt to 'maister Seckford's cardes' (*The Mapmaker's Art: Essays on the History of Maps* (London: Batchworth Press, 1953), p. 84). We may also note that Harrison anachronistically represents Brut making 'a generall surueie of the whole Iland from side to side, by such means to view and search out not onelie the limits and bounds of his dominions, but also what commodities this new atchiued conquest might yeeld vnto his people' (*Holinshed's Chronicles*, vol. I, p. 195). Terence Hawkes appears to be calling for something like the staging I envisage when criticising the inertness of Granville Barker's deployment of the map in his Old Vic production of 1940 ('Lear's Map', pp. 129–33).

27. *Antique Maps of the British Isles* (London: Batsford, 1982), p. 90.

28. 'Introduction', *Playing the Globe*, pp. 33–5; Harley, 'Meaning and Ambiguity', p. 25.

29. For Marlowe's debt to Ortelius see Ethel Seaton, 'Marlowe's Map', *Essays & Studies* 10 (1924), 13–35.

30. *1 Tamburlaine the Great*, 4.4.81–2.

31. For this distinction, see Francis Barker, *The Culture Of Violence*, pp. 3–4; and Garrett Sullivan, *The Drama of Landscape*, p. 105.

32. Q has 'or liberty' (1.51). Instead of implying a distinction, the Folio's 'and liberty' groups 'liberty' *with* 'eyesight' and 'space'.

33. F substitutes the word 'will' for Q's 'wit' (20.264), making Edgar's comment more about Goneril's moral character than her intelligence.

34. Yi Fu Tuan, 'Space and Place in Humanistic Perspective', S. Gale and G. Olsson (eds.), *Philosophy in Geography* (Dordrecht: G. Reidel Publishing Co., 1979), pp. 387–427, esp. pp. 398–9.

35. *The Drama of Landscape*, p.104.

36. For a convenient summary of the phenomenology of space see Edward S. Casey, *The Fate of Place: A Philosophical History* (Berkeley *et al.*: University of California Press, 1997), especially chapters 10–12.

37. William Cuningham, *The Cosmographical Glasse* [1559], The English Experience no. 44 (Amsterdam: Da Capo Press; New York: Theatrum Orbis Terrarum, 1968), fol. 120.

38. John Donne, 'The Good Morrow'. Conceits in which cartographic space is collapsed into intimate space are of course commonplace in Donne.

39. *The Elements of Geometrie of the Most AunCient Philosopher Euclide of Megara*, trans. H. Billingsley (London: John Daye, 1570), 'preface', sig. A4r.

40. See my discussion of Ortelius in *Shakespeare and the Geography of Difference*, pp. 70–98.

41. In their entry on 'The Geographer', Arthur K. Wheelock, Jr., and Ben Broos note how 'the energy in this painting is markedly different from Vermeer's quiet, contemplative images of women in interiors' (Arthur K. Wheelock, Jr. (ed.), *Johannes Vermeer* (Washington: National Gallery of Art, 1995), pp. 170–5, p. 170). For a discussion of the 'women in interiors' see my 'Posed Spaces', pp. 41–3.

42. Whereas the geographer stands and gazes into a kind of 'distance' roughly towards the window, the astronomer sits and gazes at a heavenly globe between himself and the window. Wheelock and Broos note that Vermeer appears to have revised the position of the geographer's head. Whereas he had been looking straight down at the map beneath him, with his dividers poised vertically over it, he now gazes thoughtfully into the middle distance and holds his dividers horizontally (Wheelock, *Johannes Vermeer*, p. 170). I find it significant that Vermeer should have altered the gaze from concentrated to 'farsighted'.

43. 'The scene is one that follows a tradition of scholars in their study: a rather somber room with a desk, a bureau, books, scientific instruments, and a scholar intent on his work.' (Arthur K. Wheelock, Jr., *Jan Vermeer* (London: Thames & Hudson, 1981), p. 136.) In this connection, Wheelock also notes 'the truly striking resemblance of "The Geographer" to Rembrandt's etching "Faust" of about 1652' (*Johannes Vermeer*, p. 174). This etching shows Faust bending over a table with cartographic implements, but looking towards a vision of occult learning which shines in a window.

44. See Figure 3 and Lesley Cormack's essay in this volume.
45. Tuan, 'Space and Place', p. 398.
46. Flahiff, 'Lear's Map', 21–2.
47. The only topographical detail offered is Gloucester's remark in the Quarto that 'for many miles about / There's not a bush' (Q: 7.457–8); which in the Folio becomes 'scarce a bush' (F: 2.2.473).
48. Q: 9.10–11, 25, 27, 40, 75; F: 3.2.10–11, 25, 27, 40, 74.
49. For the 'hovel' references, see: Q: 9.62, 70, 72, 79, and F: 3.2.61, 69, 71, 78. For 'enter' or 'come not in', see: Q: 11.1, 4, 21, 22, 24, 34, and F: 3.4.1, 4, 5, 23, 24, 25, 27, 39.
50. The hold of the 'heath' on editors, critics and performers since is the more remarkable if, as Flahiff suggests, the single topographical detail offered by the texts ('theres not a bush', 'scarce a bush') is actually inconsistent with heath vegetation (22).
51. In *Cymbeline* for example, Belarius 'followed by Guiderius and Arviragus' enter stooping as if from their cave:

    > A goodly day not to keep house with such
    > Whose roof's as low as ours. Stoop, boys; this gate
    > Instructs you how t'adore the heavens, and bows you
    > To a morning's holy office. The gates of monarchs
    > Are arched so high that giants may jet through
    > And keep their impious turbans on without
    > Good morrow to the sun. Hail, thou fair Heaven (3.3.1–7)

52. 'King Lear's observations on poverty and destitution in the heath (III.ii) . . . [are] unique in [their] poignant and tormented expression as well as in the authentic picture which [they give] of the state of the poor. The picture more commonly offered is a far from dismal one and is frivolous by comparison . . . it is hard to rid oneself of the impression that . . . in the majority of Elizabethan and Stuart plays the poor and vagrant are often introduced because of the eccentric, non-comformist element associated with them and because they provide excellent entertainment for spectators eager for theatrical stimulation. The fact [is] that so many beggars in these plays are bogus characters . . . by far the majority of poor and sturdy beggars appear in comedies, a genre particularly suited to the disguise convention.' Anat Feinberg, 'The Representation of the Poor in Elizabethan and Stuart Drama', *Literature & History* 12, first series (1986), 152–63, 158–9.
53. Furness, *King Lear*, p. 266.
54. *Ibid.*, p. 267.
55. See the excellent account of Inigo Jones's evolution of a visual language of 'landscape' in the masque by John Peacock in his *The Stage Designs of Inigo Jones: The European Context* (Cambridge University Press, 1995), pp. 158–207. Peacock points out that perspective in English tended to be conflated with landscape, as in the Elizabethan 'prospective', a word conflating the Italian *prospettiva* (perspective) with the English *prospect* (view) (p. 163). He also points out that it took well over a decade for Jones' audience to move beyond 'an elementary stage in their understanding of landscape' (pp. 199–200).

56. A similar moralisation of perspective is offered by Belarius in *Cymbeline*:

> Now for our mountain sport. Up to yon hill,
> Your legs are young; I'll tread these flats. Consider,
> When you above perceive me like a crow,
> That it is place which lessens and sets off,
> And you may then revolve what tales I have told you
> Of courts, of princes.   (3.2.10–15)

57. Cuningham, *Cosmographical Glasse*, fols. 6–7.

58. Why should the outlines of landscape and geography re-emerge at this point in the play? Why 'Dover'? As with the domains of 'inside' and 'outside', the text is peppered with anticipations of Dover. Cordelia's army lands there, Lear is sent there by Gloucester who is himself forced to 'smell his way to Dover'. Convenience is one answer, but one that has rarely satisfied critics who point to the oddity of emphasising this particular place in a play where conventional geography has so little meaning. Flahiff insists that Dover is important because associated with Kent, in opposition to Cornwall and Albany. In similar spirit Richard Dutton finds Dover completing the ancient British symbolism of the 'mount triangular', in which Britain is imagined as an island triangle with three 'corners'. Why, however, should Gloucester's cliff be at Dover? (In the source story from Sidney's *Arcadia*, Gloucester's counterpart plans to leap from an anonymous 'rock'.) Part of the answer may be that Shakespeare wished to put the cliff episode with the redemptive perspective attaching to Cordelia's invasion. For the rest, I should like to offer another explanation. If perspective and triangulation (the effects consciously sought in the Dover cliff passages) bespeak a consciously chorographic performance, and if chorography means the description of particular places ('describyng the qualitie and figure') rather than general regions, then we can see why this cliff has to be somewhere rather than nowhere in particular.

59. Peacock, *Stage Designs of Inigo Jones*, p. 200.

60. Chorography represents a context in which high places (cliffs) and perspective are necessarily related. Cliffs and suicide could be associated before the sixteenth century (as in the *Arcadia*), but not cliffs and perspective and hence the kind of surveying technique upon which cartographic descriptions were predicated. William Ravenhill ('Mapping a United Kingdom', *History Today* 35 (1985), 27–33) argues that the most famous map of the country in the period – Saxton's 1583 wall map of 'Britannia' – was based on topographical readings taken from high places. One of the mysteries of this map is how Saxton managed to complete a survey of the entire country within five years ('less than one month for each county', 33). The answer, argues William Ravenhill, is linked to a Welsh Privy Council letter of 10 July 1576, authorising the bearer (Christopher Saxton) to be assisted by the Justices of whatever region of Wales he happened to be in, 'to see him conducted vnto any towre Castle highe place or hill to view that countrey . . . that he may be accompanied with ii or iii honest men such as do best know the cuntrey for the better accomplishment of the service' (33). In concert with the existing

beacon system ('a nation-wide, well-organised, intervisibly-linked communication system ... a manned set of known intervisible viewpoints'), what this letter suggests, according to Ravenhill, is that Saxton could be conducted to a high place by the local beacon operators who could 'direct Saxton's theodolite open sights to a round of known places and to neighbouring beacons', all of which could then be triangulated (33).

61. Tuan, 'Space and Place', p. 400.

CHAPTER 7

Unlawful presences: the politics of military space and the problem of women in Tamburlaine

Nina Taunton

As one might expect, the sixteenth-century military camp is described by all the military treatise writers of the 1590s as a place where exclusively male identities are defined, and is visually presented as such in the numerous diagrams that illustrate the manifold possibilities for camp layout. Hence Raimond de Fourquevaux, for example, provides an image in which the centralised figure of the commander-in-chief ('the colonelle', his position at the hub of camp life fixed by symbol and script) is surrounded by protective bands of officers.[1] Other symbols within the illustration reveal that he is flanked also by horsemen carrying firearms, footmen carrying pikes and that there is enough space measured out in between these lodgings to exercise the men and range them for battle. An English treatise of the period entitled *Stratioticos* offers extensively detailed annotations accompanying its diagram of the camp, designating hierarchically ordered circles of tents from its outer to its inner reaches (Figure 14). Forming the outer (fortifying) boundaries are the heavy goods vehicles (the carters, the waggoners and their animals) which contain the rest of the camp. The paramilitary contingent (artificers, tailors, armourers, shoemakers) is also housed in the outer layers. Each pathway has a particular function; either to contain specified numbers of officers (marked G H I K) or to lead to a public gathering place to be viewed and counted (the area marked O). And Garrard marks out a special space for cattle – but not for women auxiliaries.[2] All three writers blazon the importance of the figure in command, the officers, the men and provisions for them all. Notably lacking (in these and indeed in all sixteenth-century diagrammatic representations of the military camp) is graphic and enscripted space for the women who tagged on to do the providing. This was quite simply because the presence of women in an early modern army was a punishable offence.

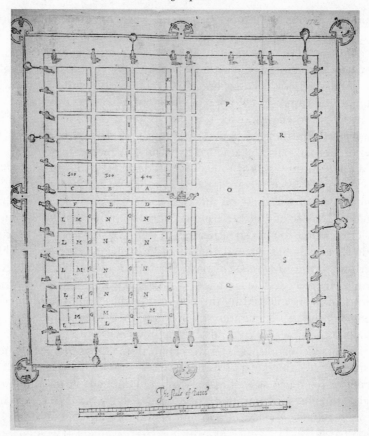

Figure 14 Military camp in Thomas Digges, *Stratioticos* (1579)

In his 1590 revised edition of his father's *Stratioticos* Thomas Digges includes Leicester's *Lawes and Ordinances Militarie for the Low Countries* which clearly states this prohibition:

And for that it often hapneth, that by permitting of many vagarant and idle women in an armie, sundry disorders and horrible abuses are committed, therefore it is ordeyned, that no man shal carry into the field, or deteine with him in the place of his garrison, any woman whatsoeuer, other then such as is knowen to be his lawfull wife, or such other women to tend the sicke, and to serue for Launders, as shalbe thought meete by the Marshall, upon paine of whipping and banishment.[3]

The opening phrase 'And for that it often hapneth' gives the clue to a problem that had to be legally defined, provided for and legislated against: the legitimate presence of 'lawfull' wives on the one hand – and on the other, the much more problematic area of the presence of sizeable numbers of women in the camps whose legitimate role as providers of comfort would include the sexual. Wives and female camp-followers were not necessarily a distinct category from women who followed the camps in the hope of eking out a living as prostitutes. All women were in effect in excess, and therefore a threat to the carefully constructed and policed boundaries built and defined by men in an environment specifically designed to exclude women.

My aim in this essay is to explore modes of spatial organisation in which women were accommodated in a hostile and exclusively male environment. I will draw on theories of spatialisation, containers and contained in looking at the troubled identity of women in a context hitherto examined almost exclusively in terms of *masculine* self-determinations. I will then extend the discussion of gendered spaces into Marlowe's two *Tamburlaine* plays. Through concepts taken from Bataille, Irigaray and de Certeau I want to show how different kinds of writing may be inflected by the notion that masculine subjecthood is predicated upon the paradox of obliteration *and* accommodation of women as occupiers of cultural space in military contexts.

Lack of places and spaces for women in all-male environments where women are legislated against is now well theorised – in psychoanalytic frames of reference as well as those of containment. From a different angle (though incorporating the social/cultural and the psychic) Georges Bataille is relevant and illuminating for any discussion of the contested spaces for women in army life. His placement of women (both whores and wives) at the centre of complex eroticised circuits of gift-giving and value-laden systems of distribution and exchange activated by male lawmakers provides a context for the denied and prohibited presence of women in the treatises and also for the women in Tamburlaine's camp. Zabina, Zenocrate and Olympia are defined against a system which does not acknowledge their being *a priori* in terms of military law and therefore fails to define or make *de facto* provision for them. These fictionalised women make a bid towards self-definition within an all-male system in which women are powerfully there, but have no rights or privileges (because they are captive) and can only accrue value through whatever they can reclaim for themselves from eroticism and class status. In order to constitute a presence in the *Tamburlaine* plays, as in Bataille's formulation, women must carve out their own territory from already measured-out excluding male space. They do this either by embracing death – or marriage.

In *The History of Eroticism*,[4] Bataille (taking as his starting-point Levi-Strauss's theories of kinship and Mauss's on potlatch gift-giving ceremonies) traces the genealogy of rules governing marriage through an archaic connection with incest taboos involving a 'double movement' which is part gift, part exchange. Women were either given away by fathers or brothers or snatched away by warring clans. These early forms are evoked in the representation of the three women in the *Tamburlaine* plays. Before Part I begins Zenocrate, an Egyptian princess, has been given to the King of Arabia. When the play opens she has just been snatched away from father and fiancé and is precipitated into an alternative circuit of value-laden exchange which does not involve reciprocity. Although Bataille discusses the value attached to women in transactions embroiled in the incestuous, where the act of giving not so much denied their value of sex with a relative as confirmed the greater value of a reciprocal act, he nevertheless places this exchange at the centre of an act of 'organic communication' in which a kinswoman is given in marriage to another man in anticipation of receiving in return the gift of a wife for the giver.[5] The position of Zenocrate and Olympia as captives (promised or married to men on the enemy side) would thus be within value-laden rules of exchange involving the 'gift' of themselves, but the position of Zabina is outside those bounds. Yet all three have been snatched, not given in exchange and therefore they are all three beyond the pale of the reciprocal generosity of gift-giving ceremonies. They have value only to the extent that they may be part of an exchange of prisoners – but this option is denied them.

Bataille goes on to describe how these archaic forms of prohibition and prescription assume women as 'precious article[s] of wealth' whose distribution was governed by rules in complex 'circuits of exchange' with 'predetermined rights'.[6] Yet the experience of transgression is present at the outset, for the rules of marriage are analogous to a transgressive act, usurping the limits of endogamy and incest. As such, these early forms of rules, limits and transgressions have an important connection with the kind of transactions involving women in the sixteenth-century military camps, where the legal and ethical boundaries are obscure and contradictory. Their doubtful position in the camps makes them the focal point of transgression (what Bataille calls that moment of 'unbridled eroticism'[7]) in the midst of circumstances in which sexuality is prohibited. Zenocrate, as a result of her privileged position as Tamburlaine's beloved is enclosed within this circuit of eroticism – a position confirmed by his paeons of Neoplatonic praise of her beauty in the midst of the carnage of the virgins of Damascus

(*1 Tamb*, 5.2.73–120).[8] Zabina too is involved in eroticised circuits of surfeit and death. In Tamburlaine's triumphal banquet she is forced to feed her husband, the defeated emperor of the Turks, scraps of meat through the bars of his cage. After the feast, Bajazeth and his queen are '[s]meared with blots of basest drudgery' (205) and 'sharp [with] hunger' (210). Yet in the midst of 'griping [their] bowels with retorqued thoughts' (174), Bajazeth finds time to think of 'words of love, whose moaning intercourse / Hath hitherto been stay'd with wrath and hate' (217–18). To illustrate such contradictions as these in cultural terms, Bataille gives the extraordinary example of the Hawaiians who rape, kill, pillage and burn down their houses on learning of the king's death – yet this deliberate breach of the most sacred laws paradoxically 'consecrates and completes an order of things based on rules; it goes against that order only temporarily'.[9] Along these lines, Tamburlaine's massacre of the virgins and his desecration of the rites of feasting may be read as a paradoxical double act of consecration. These acts of violence and slaughter serve to enshrine Zenocrate's chastity (guaranteed by the sacrifice of the virgins) in a bid to legitimise her role and also as an act of purification in a ritual move to safeguard the masculine sanctity of the camp.[10]

In psychosexual terms, the laws governing marriage and the incest taboo are part of a history of sexuality in which the negation of animal freedom brought rules to bear in a situation in which transgression was inherent. Bajazeth and Zabina affirm 'with words of love' their marriage bond in the midst of a scene in which they appear at their most abject and degraded. The experience of transgression in this scene is rendered no less fundamental to the constitution of the individual in his relation to social and psychic systems in the military camps than it is in society at large. The camp, 'gouerned by lawes as a Citie is',[11] functions as a microcosm of society. There is however a significant difference in the regulations governing sexual relations in the early modern military camp as distinct from those governing a society's sexual practices. Though Bataille goes on to state that 'the sexual act generally does not have the meaning of a crime' it takes on this meaning in the rules regulating camp behaviour, and in the banquet scene sexuality is displaced onto surfeit, where Tamburlaine and his captains gorge, with 'full bowls of wine' and fall greedily upon their food whilst Bajazeth is taunted for being too dainty to eat his own flesh, and is offered food only at the point of Tamburlaine's sword, with Zabina (and Zenocrate) looking helplessly on (4.4.37–42). When Bajazeth stamps upon this food

Usumcasane retorts that it were 'better he killed his wife, and then she shall be sure not to be starved, and he be provided for a month's victual beforehand' (48–50).

The entire business of women's involvement in scenes of war is complexly tied up with what Bataille marks out as the two areas of life which are at the edges of any social system, contributing to the frame and core of societies which are defined by the forbidden areas of sex, excreta and death.[12] The connectedness of the three zones of sex, death and the military is illustrated by such visual images as the etching by Daniel Hopfer entitled *Soldier Embracing a Young Woman* or Niklaus Manuel's drawing *Young Woman and Death as a Soldier*. The terror engendered by sex and death ('a power of annihilation, underlying a power of proliferation'[13]) at once define and undermine a person's sense of him/herself. In the banquet scene of *Tamburlaine*, part I, this disintegration of identity is expressed in the vocabulary of surfeit and cannibalism while appetite and its excess is exposed in Daniel Hopfer's etching by a dog stretching up on its hind legs to snaffle a plate of food in the background whilst in the foreground a soldier clasps the full breasts of a woman.

Genre pictures by Urs Graf and Niklaus Manuel, too, have as their subject soldiers diverted from the business of war by the distracting presence of women in war zones. Manuel's *Young Woman and Death as a Soldier* startlingly brings together images of corruption, eroticism and death that uneasily hover around the textual borders of the writings introduced so far, depicting a girl enfolded in the embrace of a skeleton. The moustachios and tatters of what remains of his soldier's garb identify him as a *Landsknecht* – a German mercenary.[14] Her consent and participation in this transgressive act is manifest in her absorption in the kiss they share and she affirms the interpenetration of the living by the dead in seeming to guide his hand. This response and gesture suggests an act of simultaneous generation and corruption. The shocking combination of death and eroticism is confirmed by the framing device, in which a cupid on the capital of a column is impaled on his own arrow. Femininity is by various devices figured as an agent of corruption as well as its victim.

An image such as this, in juxtaposition with Bataille's insight into the working of humankind, shows how prior knowledge of death and knowledge of sexuality at once go hand in hand and share a profound difference. The repulsion engendered by death has as its originating condition its opposite – consciousness of life, or of the self; and consciousness of sexuality is not entirely manifest in repulsion (this would be self-defeating from a procreative point of view) but needs eroticism as the mediator between disgust and desire.[15] There is a similar ambivalence in Daniel Hopfer's etching of a *Soldier Embracing a Young Woman*. In the foreground of the picture, the soldier's embrace is ambiguously received by the young woman whose breasts he clasps – she could be pulling him away, yet her smile seems to be welcoming. The ambivalence is reinforced by the apple tree above them, the apple of temptation poised ripe for the plucking just above her head. Bataille goes on to say that societies must address the terror of eroticism (and by implication resolve this kind of ambivalence) through their regulating laws. In a society of soldiers where women are needed yet have no place, the legislation that incurs savage penalties against sexuality takes on an intensity of meaning that is dealt with by setting up networks of taboos, prohibitions and espials which act as guarantees against the boundless horror of committing daily acts of carnage and lust.

The need for regulatory procedures against women, taken together with this experience of disgust, desire, threat and exclusion, lies at the heart of the troubled scenes in the two *Tamburlaine* plays. Zenocrate, Zabina and Olympia have to be redefined in the language of proscriptive legislation which governs their presence in enemy territory. They represent the enemy within against whom the military manual writers insistently warn. Robert Barret, for example, writing in 1598, cautions his readers that sensuality makes soldiers cowards: 'such as do carry women with them' incur shame and dishonour by a debilitating effeminacy.[16] The organisers of safety around camp parameters must be ceaselessly on guard against their corrosive presence. A temptation such as the one depicted in Urs Graf's *Death and the Soldiers*, which sees two warriors contemplating the charms of a young woman while the figure of death looks on, must not be permitted to occur. Graf's woodcut warns against succumbing to the dangerous allure of women (this one has a dog in her lap in an image of idle decadence, simultaneously suggesting the effeminisation of the soldier but also in parody of the nurturing role of a mother). The message seems to be that women emasculate and destroy in the very act of promising safety, nurture and comfort. The phallic postures of the two *Landsknechte* – their lustful intent shown in the jutting scabbard of the one and the grasping of the penis-shaped sword handle of the other – are gleefully overlooked by the mocking figure of death straddling the tree just above their heads.

The problem of women in the camps (in both Bataille and these examples from German genre pictures of the early sixteenth century) thus becomes that of the problematic presence of the 'other', or difference (i.e., that which is in excess of the given system).[17] The camps are in an important way constructed through this difference (when it is not to do with women it is to do with those other underprivileged, unnamed beings, the common soldiers) – yet the problem itself originates in the system's very organisation of difference into hierarchical distinctions of space and rank. In the *Tamburlaine* plays the symbolic order of patriarchy is predicated on the erasure of women as signifiers, so masculine identity and spaces can be said to be negatively defined against the feminine. Irigaray's analysis of a woman's role in the social 'placings' of a man at the expense of a woman's own position sheds further light on this. She explains the exclusion of women from a world created by men as a destructive process:

> If . . . traditionally, in the role of mother, woman represents a sense of place for a man, such a limit means that she becomes a thing, undergoing certain optional changes . . . the mother woman is also used as a kind of envelope by man in order to help him set limits to things . . . a woman's status as envelope and as thing(s) has not been interpreted, and so she remains inseparable from the work or act of man, notably in so far as he defines her, and creates his own identity through her or, correlatively, through this determination of her being. If, in spite of all this, woman continues to exist, she continually undoes his work, distinguishing herself from either envelope or thing, and creating an endless interval, game, agitation, or non-limit which destroys the perspectives and limits of this world.[18]

As signifiers of a limit or a boundary, then, women lose their own identity. But if this loss is only partially accomplished, they become dangerously *un*confined. In the transitory world of the sixteenth-century camp, liable to be disassembled at a moment's notice, the notion of women providing a more permanent 'place' for men on the march uncovers new sources of anxiety, some of which are reflected in the 'limits' set by the military world upon women who encroach into its precincts.[19]

John Hale and Frank Tallett both refer to the ease with which a regular whore could bypass the legal strictures against her by becoming the unofficial wife of a soldier.[20] Hale states that,

> [w]ith no marriage lines to brandish, and with the unlikelihood that these wives would have been removed from caring for a home, the chances were that 'wives' were actual, or potential whores. At a time without barbed wire or adequately trained military police, wives or 'wives' could not be kept from contact with their mates.[21]

These strictures may be understood in relation to Bataille's paradox of a lawful crime as a way of regulating sexuality: prohibitions on a crime (that of women's presence in a forbidden place) is limited (by exceptions to the rule) and its transgression occurs within the laws stating lawful instances for women's presence. There are additional anomalies, ripe with the potential for transgression. While camp prostitutes posed a danger to health and discipline, in practice few commanders excluded them from the camps altogether, even though officially their presence was punished by slit noses, burns on the right cheek and floggings.[22] Desire to limit the number of women in tow is reflected in the rules imposing fines and punishments on soldiers marrying without permission, and endeavours to sweep the camps clean of whores are reflected in edicts setting out these punishments for them.[23] However, Tallett believes that 'there is little to suggest that regulations forbidding women were being enforced with any greater vigour in 1700 than they had been one or two hundred years previously.'[24] The exceptions to the prohibition against women in camps in reality covered those women likely to be part of an army's support system. Legitimate female camp-followers, as the ordinances state, nursed, washed, cooked – but they also provided other comforts – those which increased the risk of spreading venereal diseases.[25] The problem of distinguishing between the two and of banishing the one whilst retaining the (usually unpaid) services of the other is one that is uneasily hinted at in *Tamburlaine*, Parts I and II, as I will show.

The camp as a hallowed all-male space is mapped out by Raimond de Fourquevaux, who believed that 'all things should be gouerned and moderated' in a camp, so that it 'might be the harbour of all honest men, and their refuge and Sanctuary, within which, all things ought to be as safe, as in one of our Churches'. Women (of whatever kind) have no part to play in this all-male sanctum. They are simply not mentioned in his provisions for an orderly camp since they are potential sources of disorder and causes of soldiers' neglect of duties and indiscipline.[26] A soldier's set of high personal standards should however include a prohibition not only on the robbing of a host or enemy country's churches but also on the ravishing of women.[27] Rape should be 'grievously' punished by following the example in Aurelian of tying the offender's legs to two high trees bent down and letting them go at the same time 'so that the trees springing up, pluckte him in two peeces'. Adultery with a 'hostess' (a woman in whose house soldiers were billeted) is considered just as 'reprehensible' and Fourquevaux cites Macrinus' punishment for this with some relish. The offenders were to be stitched into the bellies of 'two great Oxen' that had been 'paunched', but with their heads left sticking out, 'to the intent that they might speake eache unto other' – fixed forever in discourse at the point of an agonising death. They were to remain so until they rotted, 'and were eaten with the Vermine that engendered of the flesh, as it did corrupt: yet not so soone, but they pyned many dayes'.[28]

Taken alongside such punishments as these, Tamburlaine's ways of dealing with intransigence appear pretty restrained, and when it comes to the question of women in the camp he is confronted by the same sort of grey areas articulated by Fourquevaux and the ordinances. He too is faced with the need to distinguish between different kinds of women, the question of the propriety of their presence in a professional all-male environment and the different kinds of duties and functions in this environment that might specifically require women to perform them. When Zenocrate is first brought before Tamburlaine it is as a hostage, legitimately captured since she is carrying papers stamped by the enemy Turk's 'privy-signet' as a means of safe-conduct. His soldiers have behaved with courtesy and restraint and Tamburlaine himself is being perfectly proper when he refuses 'to enrich' his 'followers / By lawless rapine from a silly maid' (*1 Tamb*, 1.2.9–10). However the problem of how to find Zenocrate a suitable place in his entourage remains. As a prisoner and a woman she has to be strictly supervised on two counts. She is a princess and cannot therefore appropriately join the ranks of the female camp-followers (who in any case tended to travel with an army from home). And she is too high-born to be assigned to the duties of cook, laundress, mender or tender of the wounded. Tamburlaine's first expedient is to make her a 'wife'; within two minutes of meeting her he requires her 'fair face and heavenly hue' to 'grace his bed that conquers Asia' (36–7), though almost in the same breath he admits that this might not after all be appropriate and it might be best to 'invest' her 'empress of the East'. Therefore, despite her reluctance 'to live with' him Tamburlaine recommends himself to her as a legitimate partner, hoping that she will 'willingly' remain with him (85–105). The problem is finally resolved in the transformation of Zenocrate's unwillingness to go along with Tamburlaine's plans for her ('I must be pleas'd perforce' [258]) into reciprocal love, and thus from a situation in which she would be 'suppos'd his worthless concubine' (3.2.29) to one of expressed satisfaction at the prospect of being 'match'd' (55) with him. In this instance Zenocrate and Tamburlaine collude in an appropriation and re-application of the

military laws, thereby divesting them of their main constraining function. Michel de Certeau (writing on the ways in which the rules of
institutional practices are subverted by the 'users' (or consumers) of a
culture by many small, daily 'creative' reinterpretations of rules which
constitute an individual's resistance to state or institutional repression –
and which undermine and deflect the power of that state or institution)
provides an apt analogy for this process in the reception of Spanish
culture by the indigenous populations upon whom it was imposed:

Submissive, and even consenting to their subjection, the Indians nevertheless
often *made of* the rituals, representations, and laws imposed on them something
quite different from what their conquerors had in mind; they subverted them
not by rejecting or altering them, but by using them with respect to ends and
references foreign to the system they had no choice but to accept. They were
other within the very colonization that outwardly assimilated them; their use of
the dominant social order deflected its power, which they lacked the means to
challenge; they escaped it without leaving it. The strength of their difference lay
in procedures of 'consumption'.[29]

In other words, by creatively reappropriating Spanish laws, the Indians
could escape the strictures imposed upon them.

As a legitimate wife, Zenocrate has a role to play in the routine duties
of a camp commander. She is at his side (formally as his betrothed) at
official parleys with emissaries from the foe in order to enhance the
impression of a well-run camp. When for instance Tamburlaine invites
the Basso to 'view well my camp, and speak indifferently' Zenocrate's
presence suggests that he not only wants to exhibit the strength and
readiness of his army ('Do not my captains and my soldiers look / As if
they meant to conquer Africa?' [3.3.9–10]) but that he (no less than
Bajazeth) has a wife-to-be by his side of the calibre of those women who
took up arms on the field of battle beside their husbands.[30] And as
commanders' consorts both she and Zabina can actively promote a rival
cause by flyting in the camp while the husbands are fighting on the field:

Zenocrate: Ye Gods and powers that govern Persia,
             And made my lordly love her worthy king,
             Now strengthen him against the Turkish Bajazeth,
             And let his foes, like flocks of fearful roes
             Pursu'd by hunters, fly his angry looks,
             That I may see him issue conqueror!
Zabina: Now, Mahomet, solicit God himself,
             And make him rain down murdering shot from heaven,
             To dash the Scythians' brains, and strike them dead,
             That dare to manage arms with him
             That offer'd jewels to thy sacred shrine
             When first he warr'd against the Christians!   (3.3.189–200)

Even more significantly, however, and in terms of their unstable position as women in a man's world, they threaten each other with job demotion in the event of either husband's victory over the other in the field. Since neither of them have cultural spaces (both are prisoners – spoils of war) and since each is deprived of place, both 'threaten . . . by what they lack'.[31] Irigaray writes of women denied their 'place' as being 'enveloped'[32] by the confines and limits imposed upon them by men, yet which are an analogue to the limitlessness that is the outcome of men's 'nostalgia for the foetal dwelling-place'.[33] The position men construct for women as mothers but also as women is at once confining and boundless – and dangerously ambivalent, for the limits imposed by men are homocidally suffocating:

[H]e buys her a house, shuts her up in it, and places limits on her that are the counterpart of the place without limits where he unwittingly leaves her. He envelops her within these walls while he envelops himself and his things in her flesh . . . these envelopes . . . are invisibly alive, and yet have barely perceptible limits; . . . they offer a visible limit or shelter that risks imprisoning or murdering the other unless a door is left open.[34]

There are no doors left open for either Zabina or Zenocrate; neither have their own place or space and therefore both suffer loss of any identity separate from that conferred on them by Tamburlaine, the man who imprisons them both. In their state of dereliction and dependency they have no strategies available for survival other than to vie with each other. Both are bereft of the means of self-definition so they attack one another not in personally abusive epithets but by insulting the men who confer titles upon them. Zabina challenges Zenocrate in the name of her concubinage to Tamburlaine, giving herself precedence as 'empress of the mighty Turk' while Zenocrate responds not in her own name but in her role as the woman 'betroth'd / Unto the great and mighty Tamburlaine' (3.3.169–70). And they threaten each other with punishments that are domestically demeaning in the event of victory in a battle in which neither are involved. Zabina will have Zenocrate be 'laundress to [her] waiting-maid' (177) while Zenocrate will force Zabina '[t]o dress the common soldiers' meat and drink' (185). In the event Zabina ends up in an even worse position. She becomes Zenocrate's 'handmaid's slave', to be 'whipt stark nak'd' if 'abuses' continue to 'flow . . . from her tongue' (4.2.69–74) and is forced to feed her husband 'with the scraps' from Tamburlaine's 'board' (87–8). Alternatively, her standing in the camp confirmed, Zenocrate can now on occasion be permitted to give advice even though it might not be favourably received, or followed. She pleads in vain for mercy to Damascus, though as a concession to her status, her father's life is spared.

Similarly, in the second part of *Tamburlaine*, Olympia's presence in the camp has to be regularised. Since she is a captain's widow and has 'bravely' buried her husband and son, '[l]est cruel Scythians should dismember' them (*2 Tamb*, 3.4.37), she will not be hauled off as spoils of war. Techelles plans to bring her before Tamburlaine, who in recognition of her courage is sure to 'match [her] with a viceroy or a king' (41). Even though they force her against her will into accompanying them, Techelles and Theridamas are mindful of the dire consequences of rape and conduct her decorously back to camp. Olympia herself, however, is too aware of the tenuousness of her position to be able to derive much comfort from this:

Olympia: Distress'd Olympia, whose weeping eyes,
              Since thy arrival here, beheld no sun,
              But clos'd within the compass of a tent,
              Have stain'd thy cheeks and made thee look like death,
              Devise some means to rid thee of thy life,
              Rather than yield to his detested suit,
              Whose drift is only to dishonour thee.   (4.2.1–7)

Her cheek, stained by tears, evokes the punishment of branding camp whores on the cheek, and she interprets Theridamas' suit as an assault on her honour by making her a 'wife', hearing nothing that might be construed as a proposal of marriage in his promises to make her 'stately queen of fair Argier' and to have her 'cloth'd in costly cloth of massy gold' (39–40). He is, in Irigaray's terms, enveloping her in embellishments – works of artifice that have no perceptible limits yet constrict by imposing 'a visible limit or shelter that risks imprisoning or murdering the other'.[35] It is also an act Bataille associates with the useless splendour of the prostitute: 'dressed up, bejewelled bodies become objects, focal points of luxury and lust' (like the bejewelled and complacent women in Urs Graf's *Death and the Soldiers* and Daniel Hopfer's etching of a *Soldier Embracing a Young Woman*), exerting the 'dangerous fascination' of excess.[36] No exit is available for Olympia, either. Her fears for her honour turn out to be well-founded, for Theridamas cannot suffer rejection. Since he appears too impatient to obtain permission to marry through the official channels and since his bribes of opulence have not prevailed, coercion is his only remaining option:

Theridamas: I'll use some other means to make you yield.
Such is the sudden fury of my love,
I must and will be pleas'd, and you shall yield:
Come to the tent again.   (4.2.51–4)

For Olympia the choice is stark. Since she will be neither wife nor
'wife', suicide – murder of the self – is her only recourse. Theridamas, in
his desire to 'transport' Olympia from her captive status by negating her
allegiance to her dead husband and son in order to 'incorporate' her
into an alien status and environment, is courting danger. Since there is
no 'third term', that is, no visible relationship between 'the container'
(Theridamas) and the limits (social, religious, cultural) which define him
and regulate his actions, he is, in relation to Olympia, all-powerful.
Neither Zabina nor Olympia have any defining 'third term' – they
have both been ripped away from the protective bounds of their former
life – and therefore, by the rules of the kind of logic that requires the
balance of three terms in relation to each other to prove its premise
(subject, other, defining boundaries), both Olympia and Zabina become
'dangerously all-powerful' in relation to the men who have robbed them
of the freedom of self-definition. This power has emerged through a
literal imprisonment and a figurative blockading of neutral zones –
'intervals (or enter-vals)' – whose existence in the lives of men and
women is explained by Irigaray as providing points of exit or entry
which give liberty of movement, or the option of immobility without
imprisonment, which should be available to both.[37] For these two wives
of enemy leaders, this imprisonment is both literal and figurative.
Zabina resists submersion with the enemy by 'creating an endless . . .
agitation' and the only way she can put an end to the limitlessness of
her captivity is by braining herself against the bars of the cage that
imprisoned her husband. And since the confrontation between Olympia
and Theridamas takes place in another limitless space – a no-man's land
(in the tear-drenched, '[c]ontagious smells and vapours' [4.2.11] of the
gutted landscape) – and beyond the reach of any delimiting regulations,
the only means of resistance open to her, too, are murderously transgressive ones.

Written at a time when England was expensively embroiled in several
off-shore battlefronts and with home shores repeatedly threatened by
Spanish invasion, the manuals and the two *Tamburlaine* plays contribute
to a sense of alarm and a scurrying to secure boundaries found in
various literatures whose subject is to do with military matters. The

extent to which these border anxieties are expressed in simultaneously literal and figurative modes is beyond my present scope, though I think that the instability of women in the military camp is both literally and figuratively represented. My concern has been to indicate a number of ways in which diverse texts with a military theme revolve around the problems associated with lack of official provision for the presence of women in the sixteenth-century military camp. Along with the graphic images of an earlier era, these configurations accentuate the anomalous position of women in an all-male environment by simultaneously acknowledging and negating them as signifiers and functionaries. Without refuge, yet despite these prohibitions continuing to exert a dangerous allure, women were represented as defilers of the purity of the sanctum of the all-male camp.

Officially excluded yet indubitably there, women in the sixteenth-century camp occupy an uneasy and often self-cancelling space as part of gift-giving reciprocities on the one hand, and on the other as defilers of space consecrated to masculinity. This lack of recognition and therefore definition rendered women destructively aberrant in a situation which denied them legal existence. And because their actual presence exposed ambiguities in the laws which excluded them, women in military contexts are ambivalently represented as casualties of war and as helpless captives, but also as a threat to the order of the camp. But while it is true that they undermined the discipline of soldiers' daily lives in their unconfinement, yet the indeterminacy of their position opened up areas of negotiation that are hinted at in all the texts and explored in some depth in the *Tamburlaine* plays. By processes of creative re-application these plays offer further exploration of modes suggested in the genre woodcuts, etchings and drawings through which women in the sixteenth-century military camp could resist obliteration by at once affirming and sidestepping the laws that forbade their presence.

NOTES

1. The illustration is found in Raimond de Fourquevaux, *Instructions for the Warres*, trans. Paul Ive (London: T. Man and T. Cooke, 1589), p. 67; it would re-appear two years later in William Garrard, *The Art of Warre* (London: R. Warde, 1591), p. 269.
2. Garrard, *Art of Warre*, p. 270.
3. Thomas Digges, *Stratioticos* (London: R. Field, 1590 [1st edn 1579]), p. 273.
4. First published posthumously as *L'Histoire de l'erotisme*, Vol. VIII of *Oeuvres Complètes* (Paris: Gallimard, 1976).

5. Georges Bataille, *The Accursed Share*, trans. Robert Hurley, *The History of Eroticism*, Vol. II (New York: Zone Books, 1993), p. 43. See also Catherine Belsey's final chapter, 'Finding a Place', *The Subject of Tragedy* (London: Methuen, 1985), pp. 192–221.
6. Bataille, *Accursed Share*, p. 37.
7. *Ibid.*, p. 57.
8. Unless otherwise stated, all quotations are taken from Christopher Marlowe, *The Complete Plays*, ed. J. B. Steane (Harmondsworth: Penguin, 1982).
9. Bataille, *Accursed Share*, pp. 89–90.
10. More will be said about this later on.
11. Fourquevaux, *Instructions*, p. 191.
12. 'The natural domain of the prohibitions is not just that of sexuality and filth; it also includes death'. Bataille, *Accursed Share*, p. 79.
13. *Ibid.*, p. 99.
14. Created by Maximilian in 1486 as a result of urban depression and rural inflation in Germany, these mercenary companies were contracted out to governments on all continental war fronts. Armed with the pike, they were a rigorously drilled infantry unit, operating in Swiss-style heavy columns. In the genre drawings and woodcuts of (for example) Graf, Dürer, Altdorfer and Hopfer, they came to be visually stereotyped by their dress and swagger – slashed sleeves, ostrich feathers, flowing moustachios and aggressively phallic thrust of codpiece and sword-hilt. Their outsider status was accentuated by their behaviour – dangerous licence on the one hand and fierce self-discipline on the other.
15. Bataille, *Accursed Share*, p. 82.
16. Robert Barret, *The Theorike and Practike of Moderne Warres* (London: W. Ponsonby, 1598), p. 10.
17. See, for example, Belsey, *Subject of Tragedy*, p. 221. Doris Feldmann in 'The Constructions and Deconstructions of Gendered Bodies in Selected Plays by Christopher Marlowe', Nina Taunton and Darryll Grantley (eds.) *The Body in Late Medieval and Early Modern Culture* (Aldershot *et al.*: Ashgate, 2000), 23–31, discusses Tamburlaine's self-definition as producer of space (he is a user of swords and transformer of words into actions) as against the appropriation of Zenocrate's signifying spaces.
18. Margaret Whitford (ed.), *The Irigaray Reader* (Oxford: Blackwell, 1991), p. 169.
19. The rules for the regulation of women and other peripheral beings are set out in Leicester's *Ordinances* of 1586, reproduced in Digges, *Stratioticos* (1590 edn), pp. 273–84.
20. Frank Tallett, *War and Society in Early Modern Europe, 1495–1715* (London: Routledge, 1992), p. 134; J. R. Hale, *War and Society in Renaissance Europe, 1450–1620* (London: Fontana, 1985), p. 161.
21. Hale, *War and Society*, p. 161.
22. *Ibid.*, pp. 161–2; Tallett, *War and Society*, p. 132.
23. Tallett, *War and Society*, p. 132. Correspondingly, those who 'lay violent

handes upon any woman with childe, or lying in child-bed, . . . widdowes, . . . or . . . young virgins' incurred the death penalty. Digges, *Stratioticos* (1590 edn), p. 173, reiterating Leicester's edicts nos. 5 and 6 (1586). It is significant that by the time Thomas Digges came to supplement these in the 1590s he specifies vagrant women. In the earlier (1579) edition only vagabonds are mentioned. These edicts give specificity to Bataille's linkage of sex and death as dual and inseparable objects of terror. And in their provision of protection only for mothers, widows and virgins, they give point to Irigaray's perception of women as providers of a safe zone for men at the expense of her own identity – which is legally defined as a container for men, as a custodian of men's estates and as an object of value in defining men's honour.

24. Tallett, *War and Society*, p. 132.
25. Again, regulations can usefully be understood in relation to Bataille's notion of transgressions that comply with the transgressed law, where there is a zone marked off by infringement of the rules. Bataille, *The Accursed Share*, pp. 124–6.
26. Fourquevaux, *Instructions*, p. 194.
27. *Ibid.*, p. 288.
28. *Ibid.*, pp. 290–1.
29. Michel de Certeau, *The Practice of Everyday Life*, (trans.) Steven Rendall (Berkeley: University of California Press, 1987), p. xiii.
30. Such women are idealised in More's *Utopia*. At a later date Castilian soldiers paid tribute to such female courage on the real battlefront at Leucate in 1637.
31. Whitford (ed.), *Irigaray Reader*, p. 169.
32. *Ibid.*, p. 170.
33. *Ibid.*
34. *Ibid.*
35. *Ibid.*
36. Bataille, *The Accursed Share*, pp. 141–2.
37. Whitford (ed.), *Irigaray Reader*, p. 171.

CHAPTER 8

Marginal waters: Pericles and the idea of jurisdiction

Bradin Cormack

In 1577, John Dee published his *General and Rare Memorials pertayning to the Perfect Arte of Navigation*, proposing there that Queen Elizabeth establish a 'Pety-Nauy-Royall' as a means to secure the coastal seas for English merchants and fishermen, and thereby to protect the '*Publik-Weale*, of this Kingdom'.[1] Dee's arguments for English sovereignty in the northern seas resemble and probably influenced the similarly wide-ranging, even extravagant, claims made in the more politically charged atmosphere of the early seventeenth century: arguments made, for example, by Alberico Gentili in the posthumously published *Hispanicae Advocationis Libri Duo* (1613) and, most notably, by John Selden in his *Mare Clausum*, a text published late in 1635 by command of Charles I, but begun some seventeen years earlier in response to the legal and political crisis that pitted a Jacobean royal prerogative and English fishing interests against the massively successful Dutch fisheries.[2] I wish here to focus on only one, and an ancillary, facet of Dee's text. In a striking rhetorical gesture, Dee repeatedly refers to the Athenian orator Pericles and to those speeches, as reported by Plutarch and Thucydides, in which he promotes the Athenian Republic's naval power. More is at stake in Dee's text than the credit of classical authority; although at times Pericles is, in Frances Yates' formulation, simply 'quoted with approval for [his] views on the importance of sea sovereignty', Dee transforms him through a series of progressively pointed citations into an active model for Tudor England.[3] The Athenian is introduced on the first page of the treatise proper, when in an elaborate game of personae Dee cites Pericles' funeral oration to justify praising the author of the treatise, namely Dee himself;[4] thereafter, Pericles appears only as a spokesman for the advantages of marine *imperium*. In that capacity he can, as a figure from Greek history, at first be brought only hypothetically into an English present:

What wold that Noble, Valiant, and Victorious Atheniensien PERICLES, say, yf, now, he were lyuing, and a Subiect of Authority, in this Brytish Kingdom? ... Who, taught by word, and proued in effect, *Vnam Pecunia parandae rationem putandam, Naues quamplurimas habere* [that the one method of obtaining money which ought to be considered is having many ships] ... .[5]

A page later, Pericles becomes even more explicitly an exemplary model; if the dead and republican hero can be imagined as a hypothetical 'Subiect of Authority', Dee always has principally in mind living English subjects, those with authority to effect political change:

O Pericles, thy life (certainly) may be a pattern and Rule to the higher Magistrates (in very many points) most diligently, of them, to be imitated.[6]

But the Pericles transformed in this passage to exemplum is not merely a model, but already a figure belonging, at least potentially, as much to the present as to history. When Dee laments that this 'Graeke *Pericles* can not, readily, for our purpose, be found out' in England,[7] that formulation suggests that the purely hypothetical has become, if not historically probable, at least possible. Through a mixing of exemplum and exemplar, Dee is moving towards a version of Pericles which fully integrates past and present, Athenian and English; that version appears most forcefully late in the treatise, in Dee's rhetorical appeal for some 'Brytish, or English Pericles'[8] to put into effect the political platforms Dee outlines: here is a fully (re-)patriated Pericles, a Pericles typologically instantiated as Dee's hoped-for 'higher Magistrate'.[9]

The references move, we see, in closing circles around the present and the particular, which is to say that Dee uses the figure of Pericles with a political and polemical end. Dee may have intended his title for Christopher Hatton, to whom the treatise is dedicated; ultimately, of course, he was thinking not of a subject, but of the queen herself. But Elizabeth, ignoring the platform laid out in the *Memorials*, did not press a jurisdictional claim over the northern seas, probably, as T.W. Fulton suggests, because of her concern to protect her subjects' trade and fishing interests by opposing all *foreign* pretensions to *mare clausum*.[10] Dee's reference to a 'Brytish, or English' Pericles may thus seem prescient: it is James VI and I who comes most compellingly to merit Dee's title. In this paper, I will be asking what the terms are of James' claim to sea sovereignty, in order to revisit a question that J.M.S. Tompkins posed in 1952 in respect of one of Shakespeare's most puzzling plays, and which seems in the context of Dee's rhetoric to come into sharper focus. Why Pericles?[11]

Tompkins was asking two questions: why in 1608 did Shakespeare choose to dramatise a story so ill-suited to the stage; secondarily, why did Shakespeare rename a protagonist who in all his source stories is known as Apollonius of Tyre? In answer, Tompkins convincingly points to Shakespeare's thematic interest in patience, a virtue more fully embodied by his Pericles than by any of the source protagonists. Tompkins further argues that, by invoking from Plutarch a figure exemplary of patience, Shakespeare's new name, in fact, responds to his new theme. Inevitably, then, Tompkins downplays the traditional linking of Shakespeare's play and Sidney's *Arcadia*, of Pericles and Pyrocles. And justifiably so: further evidence that it is chiefly Plutarch who haunts Shakespeare's text derives, as was shown in 1975, from other names in the play: 'all six of the Greek names in *Pericles* which do not derive from Gower – Pericles, Cleon, Philemon, Escanes (or Aeschines), Simonides, and Lysimachus – are to be found in North's Plutarch, all but the last two within the Life of Pericles.'[12]

Although I accept both parts of Tompkins' argument, I have cited Dee's use of Pericles to imply a different sort of answer to his question, an answer rooted in Jacobean politics and in the kind of provisionally topical reading Leah Marcus has referred to as 'local'.[13] The most striking quality in Shakespeare's play is its awkwardly virtuosic fracturing of dramatic action across distance and national boundaries. That dispersion is thematically crucial, for in the story of Pericles Shakespeare represents the extension of authority across international distance, the agent of that extension being the sovereign himself, cast by the contingencies of romantic tragicomedy into other jurisdictions and, crucially, onto the sea, the marine distance separating his own jurisdiction from those alternative ones. It is in two senses apt, then, that the play's scene is said to be 'dispersedly in various Countries'.[14] The dramatic action is dispersed across those countries, and is also constituted by that dispersion. Like Plutarch's orator and Dee's British hero – crucially, as we shall see, like James himself – Shakespeare's protagonist uses the sea in the service of empire. The narrative progresses by means of the Mediterranean or Mediterraneans that separate the play's cities and kingdoms; the sea is the play's second protagonist, facilitator of and actor in Pericles' imperial story.

The central terms in *Pericles* are jurisdictional. At the end of Act 2, Pericles faces one in a long line of adventitious obstacles the play throws in his way. King Simonides of Pentapolis plays a trick on the recently shipwrecked prince, whom he believes to be simply a knight and gentleman of Tyre. Although, in fact, he wishes the knight and his daughter to marry, Simonides accuses Pericles of having 'bewitched' Thaisa into an inappropriate desire. Pericles protests. The terms of the following exchange between the two sovereigns embody the play's jurisdictional theme:

> *Sim.*   Traitor, thou liest!
> *Per.*   Traitor?
> *Sim.*   Ay, traitor.
> *Per.*   Even in his throat – unless it be the king –
>   That calls me traitor I return the lie.   (2.5.54–6)

Pericles' personal honour is, of course, at stake. His sword, he says, will prove that anyone who accuses him of being a 'rebel to [Thaisa's] state' is 'honour's enemy' (2.5.60–3). But, in the double meaning of 'state' and in the juxtaposition of the terms 'traitor', 'rebel' and 'enemy' we hear how the prince's honour is also broadly political. Francis Bacon would have understood Pericles' position: in his speech for the crown in the Case of the *Post-Nati* (1608), he presented the mirror-image of the same point, as one version of his argument that the infant Robert Calvin could inherit at English law. A Scotsman, he says, '*subject* to the natural person of the king, and not to the crown of England', could be by law no enemy to the king or to the subjects of England. 'Or must he not', Bacon says, 'of necessity, if he should invade England, be a rebel and no enemy.'[15] By insisting that he is no *traitor*, Pericles defines his allegiance as his own, marking his state as distinct from Simonides', and his authority as ultimately independent of the jurisdiction within which, through the accidents of Romance, he now finds himself. In this sense, Pericles' qualification, 'unless it be the king', assumes a sly second meaning. In the phrase, Pericles acknowledges the sovereign authority before which matters like private honour become necessarily negligible. But to the extent that he is himself the king referred to, Pericles is articulating the ground precisely of his public though secret resistance to that alternative authority. In a moment of high diplomacy, we might say, Pericles protects his life by saying that he is not, in this particular case, giving the lie, even as he simultaneously and secretly does give the lie, thereby preserving his own sovereign integrity.

Shakespeare's play as a whole thematises the impact of legal jurisdiction on the integrity of sovereign authority, and the status of national identity beyond national boundaries. It addresses the status of those boundaries, in part, through a sceptical and practical identification of authority and brute strength. Pericles justifies his initial flight onto the sea by subordinating jurisdiction to power: even in Tyre, he says, though Antiochus' 'arm seems far too short to hit me here', he can take no comfort in 'the other's distance' (1.2.9–11). The threat of that hypothetical conquest resonates through the play. The fishermen whom Pericles meets on the Pentapolis coast provide in their 'pretty moral' about the inhabitants of what Pericles calls the 'wat'ry empire' (2.1.35, 50) a model of human relationships grounded in force:

> *3. Fish.* Master, I marvel how the fishes live in the sea.
> *4. Fish.* Why, as men do a-land: the great ones eat up the little ones.
>
> (2.1.26–9)

And, earlier, when Cleon of Tharsus is told that ships have been sighted off the coast, he misreads the fleet as an emblem of war:

> Some neighboring nation,
> Taking advantage of our misery,
> Hath stuff'd the hollow vessels with their power,
> To beat us down . . . (1.4.65–8)

In fact, Pericles' vessels, stuffed with grain that will feed the famished population, are emblems of a different kind of international bond: on the one hand, princely beneficence; on the other, gratitude, deference, obligation.

If the play acknowledges the ultimate authority of a demystified power, of force, it simultaneously erodes the boundaries between the kinds of international relationship usually designated as political, diplomatic, economic and military. It is worth stressing, for example, that in spite of the language of princely generosity, Pericles enters with Cleon into a highly charged reciprocal relationship: it is only because of Cleon's debt to her father that Marina can, disastrously, be raised in Tharsus. As Tharsus' saviour, of course, Pericles speaks not of legal debt, but of an international relationship grounded in love and the kind of reciprocity central to natural, not artificial, law:

> We do not look for reverence, but for love
> And harbourage for ourself, our ships and men. (1.4.99–100)[16]

But when Pericles returns to Tharsus to deposit his child there, the language of love seems newly inflected. Cleon refers to his own quasi-feudal 'duty' towards Pericles, as grounded in a secondary and similarly feudal bond between Cleon and the community of Tharsus (3.3.17–22). Most crucially, Pericles commends Marina to Cleon's 'charity', where the competing meanings of that word expose the complex economic realities underlying an idealised political alliance not quite undone by those realities (3.3.12–16). In one of Shakespeare's two principal sources, Laurence Twine's *A Patterne of Painefull Aduentures* (repr. 1607), Pericles' wheat is even more narrowly implicated in the realities of exchange. There, the prince initially sells his stored wheat to the starving inhabitants for 'no more than I bought it for in mine owne Countrey, that is to say, eight peeces of brasse for euery bushell.'[17] The telling point here is surely that Apollonius can be so precise as to price. The text is elsewhere silent on whether the prince is telling the truth about that original cost, but not so on the social implications generally of introducing money into the diplomatic equation:

But Apollonius, doubting lest by this deede, hee should seeme to put off the dignity of a prince, and put on the countenaunce of a merchant, rather than a giuer, when he had receiued the price of the wheate, hee restored it backe againe to the vse and commoditie of the same Cittie.[18]

The circle of exchange disguised as non-exchange completes itself when the civic population transmutes the brass coins into a brass statue erected in the market place, and representing the prince in a military chariot, 'holding corne in his right hand, and spurning it with his left foote'. The wheat in its aspect as mercantile good and political gift is repaid literally in the same coin. And diplomacy and trade both are emblematically exposed as versions of military conquest.[19]

It seems crucial, then, to Shakespeare's consideration of international relations that Cleon's initial reading of the ships as conquest should turn out literally to be prescient: sixteen years on, at the play's conclusion. Pericles' ships are poised to launch a marine invasion of Tharsus, in order to punish Cleon's lack of gratitude and, more basely, to add Tharsus to the prince's rapidly expanding possessions (5.1.250–1). For, Pericles' fears aside, it is he, and not Antiochus, who through the play extends his arm across distance in the service of transmarine empire. At the play's conclusion, he possesses: Tyre; Pentapolis and Mytilene, which he receives through his own and Marina's marriages; by implication, Tharsus; and even, in Twine's version, Antioch, whose crown is 'reserued' to Apollonius, presumably by election.[20]

Delay and dispersion turn out, then, to be strategic. When Pericles abandons Tyre, his literal dispersion of authority to a delegate, Helicanus, is mirrored by his abandoning land and law in favour of the sea, a natural and brutal nature to which Pericles is necessarily subject: 'And I, as fits my nature, do obey you' (2.1.4). And beyond the sea are other political orders to which, potentially, Tyre is also variously subject. If the play begins with Pericles' disastrous choice to bind himself to Antiochus and to the terms of Antiochus' riddling wager, it presents thereafter a series of more subtle negotiations between the prince's authority and his subjection to the foreign. As we have seen in his exchanges both with Simonides and with Cleon, the same physical displacement that threatens to disperse his goods and his royal identity enables the repro-duction of that identity in an altered form: so the prince's spent coin, his unthrifty but naturally strategic beneficence, is repaid by Cleon's sense of feudal obligation and by the citizens' statue, which is both visible brass and a visible sign of civic deference; and when Pericles articulates his own submission to Simonides, he marks it, in part, as resistance and reconfirmation of Tyre's sovereign autonomy. And so with the sea itself: the natural sea that, off the coast of Pentapolis, bereaves Pericles 'of all his fortunes' (2.1.9) also returns to him the rusty paternal armour that admits him to Simonides' court and ultimately to a royal and interna-tional marriage. Pericles' necessary acknowledgement of alternative power consistently reinscribes the source of his own authority.

An important, even exemplary, instance of that political dynamic is found in the dinner scene at Pentapolis, when Pericles, at table, looks on King Simonides:

> Yon king's to me like to my father's picture,
> Which tells me in that glory once he was;
> Had princes sit like stars about his throne,
> And he the sun, for them to reverence.
> None that beheld him but, like lesser lights,
> Did vail their crowns to his supremacy;
> Where now his son's like a glow-worm in the night ...   (2.3.37–43)

The passage is concerned at various levels with how authorities meet one another. Pericles, named for his jousting victory 'king of this day's happiness' (2.3.11), here gazes on the picture of a real king. And yet in Pericles' meditative construction of authority, Simonides rapidly falls into the background, in favour not only of Pericles' 'father's picture', but also of Pericles himself. There is, of course, submission at Simonides' court, just not Pericles' submission: veiled in his father's armour, dressed as a mere 'gentleman of Tyre' (2.3.81), the prince vails no crown. When he speaks of the reverence paid his father by other sovereigns, we are able to hear echoed there chiefly the 'reverence' Pericles claimed not to look for from Cleon. The kind of supreme deference that Pericles describes as governing the relationship between authorities belongs, that is, supremely to his father and to himself. Even as he uses the aside to contemplate the weakness of his own position, Pericles is reinventing the national identity disrupted by his jurisdictional displacement as an imperial or transnational identity, one which he now conceives to be, no less than his father's armour, his true inheritance. The dramatic action that follows this scene will, through all of its twists and turns, see Pericles effect that transformation.

EMPIRE'S IMAGINARY LINES

Like Aeneas, Pericles imposes an imperial authority on the Mediterranean, and through similar means: by making the right kind of marriage, implicitly by conquest, chiefly by moving across the water, often with the trappings of a merchant: with wheat, as we have seen, or the 'full bags of spices' that he places in his wife's casket before consigning it to the ocean, and which seem a treasure to those in Ephesus who discover them in the chest which the sea tosses up on the shore as wreck or jetsam (3.2.67–8). In Pericles' journeys, the play represents the early modern fascination with the ocean as limit and as a visible site in which relationships between nations are forged. Like Pericles' ships off the coast of Tharsus, however, the sea was an ambiguous quantity. If, crucially, it marked jurisdictional distinction, it also enabled, as in the play, the blurring of distinction through the transformation of a national into an imperial identity. But only uneasily: the mapping of so contestable and so public a space was, for reasons both pragmatic and strategic, as fluid as the ocean itself.

In 1613, William Welwood, Professor of Civil Law at St Andrews, published his *Abridgement of all Sea-Lawes*, including there, as a response to Grotius' 1609 *Mare Liberum*, an argument in support of the traditional extension of territorial jurisdiction into coastal waters, and of James' innovative attempts to restrict Dutch fishing off the English and Scottish coasts.[21] Welwood repeats Grotius' scoffing remark that any pretence to private possession of the seas must rest, finally, on marine boundaries established neither by nature nor by the hand of man, but simply and ridiculously by 'an imaginarie or fantastik line'.[22] With such lines, Grotius hypothesises, a geometer or astronomer could lay claim to all the earth and heavens. Welwood, however, finds the imaginary more persuasive. It is true, he says, that islands like Guernsey, that sands or rocks or other 'visible marks' most explicitly designate the 'bounds (or laying-out the limits) of the diuisible parts' of the sea, and thus most efficiently enable possession. But God has also endowed men with understanding and allowed them with 'the helps of the compasse, counting of courses, sounding, and other waies, to find forth, and to designe *finitum in infinito*, so farre as is expedient, for the certain reach and bounds of seas, properly pertaining to any Prince or people'.[23]

The navigator's fantastic lines become effectual only if human intention can, of itself, generate or underwrite extension. And for Welwood, possession on both sea and land *is* sufficiently marked by entry into part of the area being claimed, if it is 'with a minde to possesse all the rest thereof euen to the due marches' or the equivalent marine limits.[24] But the obvious problem with so employing the imaginary or the intentional is that it might have, in reality, no correlative. In a response to Welwood written around 1614, but published only in 1872, Grotius would write that imaginary lines, precise though they be, cannot effect appropriation except in conjunction with a 'corporeal act' of possession: by a fleet, in other words, or in narrowly adjacent waters, by coastal guns.[25] As the truism has it, possession is nine-tenths of the law. Now, Welwood is closer to this eminently practical position than his rhetoric sometimes implies; thus, having defended a theory of intentional sovereignty, he must finally suggest what the actual limits naturally due a prince or people are. He invokes the classic formulation from the civil law: 'Wich bounds *Bartolus* hardily extends and allowes for Princes & people at the sea side, an hundreth miles of sea forth from their coasts, at least; and iustly, if they exercise a protection and conseruacie so farre'.[26] In that final qualification, we are back to Grotius' or, indeed, to Pericles' *de facto* subordination of jurisdiction to force.

Welwood's reference to the need for 'protection and conseruacie' does not undo his theoretical assertion that coastal seas pertain really to the adjacent territory, but it helps to reformulate the crucial problem for a national representation of the sea: how to designate a space that can be intended as sovereign, but which is manifestly open to the operation of alternative powers? No answer can satisfactorily exclude the primacy of force, but I am concerned here with an early modern answer grounded in a less sceptical authority: James' alternative symbolic attempt to map marine sovereignty as the natural extension or continuity of the king's natural person. From the perspective of national law, that attempt is so little surprising as to seem, in fact, necessary: given that the common law is the law of the *land*, it is only through the prerogative that national law could in the first place imagine the sea as a legal space. But the prerogative can operate on the sea in respect not only of national, but also of natural law and international law. And in that sense, the royal person and royal intention can be strategically deployed so as to circumvent the problem of alternative corporate claims on the ocean, and thus to generate a version of empire that seems really to subvert the ocean's contestability.

We can illustrate the point, first, by considering the uses to which an early and famous Jacobean chart was put. In March of 1605, the Trinity House presented to Sir Julius Caesar, Judge of the High Court of Admiralty, a map showing twenty-seven selected headlands on the English coast; printed alongside it was a textual explication, which, in order to establish 'the bounds and limits, how farre the Kings Chambers, hauens, or ports, on the Sea coasts do extend', defined those reserved waters to be 'all the Sea coasts within a streight line drawen from one Headland to the next Headland, throughout this Realme of England'.[27] James used the chart to supplement a royal proclamation of 1 March 1605, in which, in order to prevent his subjects from disrupting the peace recently negotiated with Spain in the 1604 Treaty of London, he declared that his officers should treat as a neutral and safe zone the coastal waters intercepted by lines drawn between the represented headlands.[28] Like their fantastic counterparts invoked a decade later by Welwood, these straight lines – imaginary also, even to the extent of not appearing on the Trinity House chart – mark a sovereignty, though not an innovative one. As T.W. Fulton points out, there was nothing novel in James' declaration: areas of the sea close to a country 'were recognized as belonging to it, in the sense at least that hostilities of belligerent men-of-war or the capture of prizes were forbidden within them; they were "sanctuaries" under the jurisdiction and protection of the adjoining territory'.[29]

However traditional the claim was, the terms in which that marine jurisdiction was described and defended reward a closer scrutiny, since they are crucial to James' conception of his international authority. As we have seen, some of the areas delimited by the twenty-six imaginary lines are royal ports; the others are designated by the map-makers as 'King's Chambers'; both names place the spaces within an intensely personal jurisdiction, controlled at the king's pleasure. Selden would emphasise this in his 1635 *Mare Clausum*, when he redirected British attention to James' proclamation:

Wee have very great Creeks of Sea cut off by these lines from the Sea round about, which they call *Regias Cameras* The KINGS CHAMBERS, and the Ports Roial. Even as in an hous the inner private Rooms, or Chambers, or Closets . . . are reserved for the Master . . .[30]

Now, Selden deploys his domestic metaphor in support of Charles' claims to property in the northern seas, arguing that James' invocation of the Chambers' 'more narrow title' implied 'in like manner ... his Dominion [*dominium*] over the rest of the Sea'.[31] But this was retrospectively to read James' project as more radical than it was. Lost in Selden's citation of the proclamation is an historically slippery distinction between sovereignty (*imperium*), which is concerned with jurisdiction and the exercise of legal authority, and property (*dominium*), to which pertain the most direct and absolute rights of use, including the critical right of exclusion.[32] Selden circumvented the distinction precisely in order to claim for Charles a sovereignty 'of the most absolute kind',[33] a sovereignty carrying with it the broader rights pertaining to *dominium*. The crucial point here is that, although Selden read as imperial *dominium* the chambers represented in the 1605 chart and proclamation, nowhere there had James claimed in respect of them more than imperial jurisdiction (*imperium*).

James' less direct claim was no less strategic for being modest; it can be understood, indeed, as a version of his ongoing insistence that the mystery and indirection of the prerogative be maintained. On the sea, the personalised language of royal jurisdiction exclusive of *dominium* was sufficiently flexible as instantly and incontrovertibly to include not only Spain and the United Provinces, but all the world, albeit only in a circumscribed way: so long as a ship of 'what Nation soever ... bee within those our Ports and places of our Jurisdiction, or where our Officers may prohibite violence' it shall be 'understood to bee under our protection'.[34] The potential scope of that sentiment would come clear in May 1609, when James attempted to encourage English fishing by imposing restrictions on the Dutch fishery. In his 'Proclamation touching Fishing', James required that foreigners obtain a license from him in order to fish 'upon any of our Coasts and Seas of Great Britaine, Ireland, and the rest of the Isles adjacent'.[35] Although modelled on a traditional Scottish tax, the so-called 'assize-herring', the 1609 tax was innovative in being applied to foreigners.[36] In the proclamation, James justified his action by declaring that foreign fishing had, first, encroached on his 'Prerogative Royall', his 'Regalities' and 'Right', and, second, had hurt his own 'loving Subjects, whose preservation and flourishing estate wee hold our selfe principally bound to advance before all worldly respects'.[37] Coastal jurisdiction here is marked as the extension of both the prerogative and of a personal bond between king and subject. According to the latter, James is bound by an oath of protection, in exchange for which he receives an oath of allegiance from the subject to be protected. The legal relationship articulated here, referred to elsewhere by Sir Edward Coke as '*ligatio mentium*' and a double and reciprocal 'ligamen', is one that had already served James well: in the 1606 Case of Impositions, it was seen to justify the imposition of new duties on an English merchant; in the 1608 Case of the *Post-Nati*, it grounded the rights at English law of Scottish subjects born outside of the common law but within the natural allegiance of the king.[38]

The innovation in the proclamation of 1609, however, is that the weight of James' personal bond with his subjects falls on foreign fishermen, on those who are not his subjects at all, and would thus normally be bound to him only within the geographic confines of a narrowly conceived *dominium*. Here was the crux. To make plausible a shift of obligation from subject to alien, to allow *imperium* to operate with the force of *dominium*, James emphasised in phrases like 'our Coasts and Seas'[39] the idea of a geographical limit to his claims, even as he kept the precise extent of the limit strategically vague. The proximate sea is effectively constructed as a space that enables a personal relationship independent of place to operate in an unusual way; through a delicate balancing act, a sea that is not property generates, because of the king's obligations to the subject, a further obligatory relationship between the king's person and the foreign. This is, in part, how the royal chambers operated in 1605: foreign ships, because of their geographical proximity to the coast, could be 'understood'[40] to be under the king's protection, to be within the scope of an otherwise irrelevant personal relationship. Understood or imagined to be. The geographical lines demarcating the royal chambers and, more loosely, the proximate seas, and the conceptual lines or 'strings' connecting the king's mind to other minds, jointly provided a way to think of the sea as a site where, through the operation of a personalised royal authority, obligatory international relationships could be generated as radically natural.[41]

Richard Helgerson has delineated in chorographical descriptions of England the gradual displacement of royal authority onto an idea, in Drayton's *Poly-Olbion*, for example, of Britannia as the land itself.[42] I would add to that argument that royal authority is simultaneously relocated on the sea. We might think, for example, of the frontispiece to Camden's 1607 Latin and 1610 English *Britannia*.[43] This is an imperial image: the four parts of James' British dominion, England, Scotland, Wales and Ireland, are each represented, as they are in the quarterings of his royal coat of arms. They are, moreover, materially linked through the lines extending outwards from the compass rose imposed on the North Sea (Oceanus Germanicus) at the right of the image. Such compass markings were critical to both the production and use of marine charts, since through the loxodromes or oblique windlines extending from the compass rose, mariners were able to discover for any point the available winds, and so set a course. A working chart showing the winds radiating from a group of related compasses would, in the words of one marine historian, appear 'to be covered with a medley of criss-cross lines' until it became clear that each of those lines 'was a rhumb or wind'.[44] But as a set of imaginary lines thus corresponding to a natural phenomenon, the loxodromes could also become political strategy, expressing precisely the *a priori* status of royal jurisdiction that we have briefly explored in the legal arena. It is not coincidental, then, that the compass rose on Camden's map so strongly resembles the sun, a popular symbol of James' royal and transnational authority.[45]

The point is beautifully embodied in John Speed's 1611 atlas, the *Theatre of the Empire of Great Britain*. The atlas can be read, in fact, as an instructional manual on how to read the compass rose as an emblem of royal jurisdiction or *imperium*. In the general map of James' whole kingdom (see Figure 15), Speed represents four medallions; three are manifestly imperial: in the upper left, the royal coat of arms; mid-way down, an imperial Britannia in emulation of a Roman medallion; on the right, an image taken from a coin pictured in Camden's *Britannia*, and representing Cunobilis, the original Cymbeline and the first king to unite all of Britain. Grouped as it is with these three, the fourth medallion, the compass rose, cannot but absorb their imperial significance.

In order to extend this initial association, the atlas manipulates the symbol in a variety of ways. The compass rose is shown prominently, for example, in a map of Lancashire next to the portraits of the four Lancastrian kings, themselves embedded in a rose-emblazoned frame. Above them, James' personal motto, *Beati Pacifici*, is translated into English. The compass rose can be seen here as James' version of the union of the white rose and red by Henry VII, a monarch to whom James consciously looked back as a model of kingship. In a map of Warwickshire, Speed includes in the left margin an image of the compass rose (see Figure 16) suspended from a decorative frame above a geometer's compass. In the following map of Northamptonshire, the frame and geometer's compass have stayed, but the compass rose has been replaced with what can therefore be considered to be its equivalent: the royal arms (see Figure 17). Similarly, in the map of Rutlandshire, Speed includes on the left margin a highly stylised compass rose,

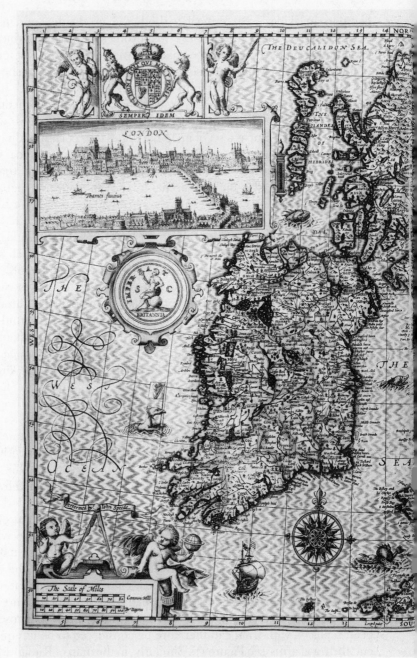

Figure 15 John Speed, *The Kingdome of Great Britaine and Ireland* (1611)

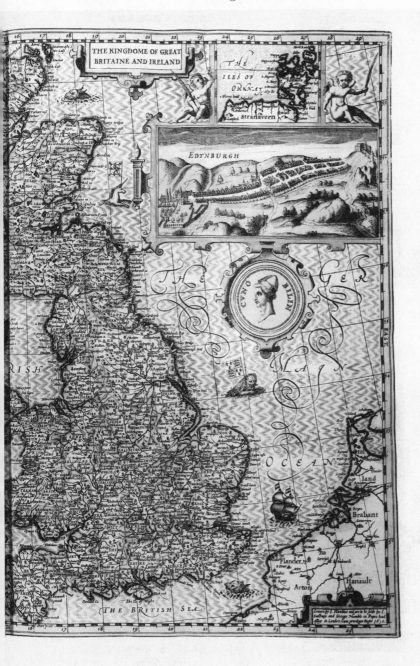

Figure 16 Detail from 'Warwickshire' in John Speed, *The Theatre of the Empire of Great Britain* (1611)

Figure 17 Detail from 'Northamptonshire' in John Speed, *The Theatre of the Empire of Great Britain* (1611)

Figure 18 Detail from 'Rutlandshire' in John Speed, *The Theatre of the Empire of Great Britain* (1611)

Figure 19 Detail from 'Rutlandshire' in John Speed, *The Theatre of the Empire of Great Britain* (1611)

recognisable through the fleur-de-lis that traditionally marked north (see Figure 18); in the right margin of the same map and in the same framing device, he substitutes the royal arms (see Figure 19). The symbolic conflation of the compass rose and the royal is firmly in place by the time we reach a quite literally dazzling example of the point in the general map of Wales (see Figure 20). Here the compass rose, void of all its traditional marks other than the loxodromic lines, has become identical with the royal arms that now occupy its gutted centre. In a convenient and strategic heraldic table printed at the beginning of the atlas, Speed designates these arms, generically identifiable as royal, as belonging specifically to the ancient Welsh Princes.[46] In a map of Cardiganshire in Wales, the same political point is made by a medallion suspended from a frame and hovering over the Irish sea (see Figure 21). Here represented is a compass rose obscured by the superimposed Welsh Crown. Since Henry had been created Prince of Wales in 1610, the year preceding the publication of the atlas, it is hard not to think of the rose's explicit symbolic value in the Welsh maps as addressing not only James' imperial authority, but Prince Henry's own widely admired commitment to the extension of British influence through exploration, trade and military force.

Speed's atlas provides the reader with a lesson in the transformation of a mariner's cartographic tool into a symbol of imperial sovereignty. That representational fluidity is wholly appropriate, since, as an imperial sign, the compass rose itself transforms the sea: symbolically, to be sure, but also to the extent that it delineates the very mechanics of early British empire, the jurisdictional strategy through which contestable space beyond the law could be structured as natural possession. It is quickly becoming a cliché to say that empire is a virtual phenomenon, but for James it was meaningfully so. As historians of early colonialism and empire, we are apt, under the influence of writers like Grotius and Selden, to think of *dominium* as the ultimate ground for international relations. But James' invocation on the sea of a jurisdiction precisely exclusive of *dominium* should not be understood as a default strategy, or as a still imperfect version of the more exacting argument made by Selden on behalf of James' son. A map from Camden's 1610 *Britannia*, his depiction of Lancashire, makes the point (see Figure 22). Here is the compass rose operating as it does in Speed. Camden's map indicates that it has been re-engraved from the original designed by Christopher Saxton for his 1579 atlas; crucially, however, that earlier map shows suspended over the Irish sea, not a compass rose, but Elizabeth's arms.

Figure 20   Detail from 'Wales' in John Speed, *The Theatre of the Empire of Great Britain* (1611)

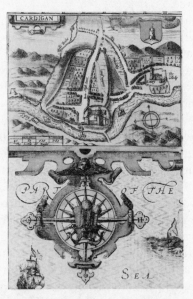

Figure 21   Detail from 'Cardiganshire' in John Speed, *The Theatre of the Empire of Great Britain* (1611)

Figure 22 Detail from 'Lancashire' in William Camden, *Britannia* (1610)

As a representation of royal authority, Camden's compass rose is both more indirect and more powerful than are Saxton's arms: more powerful, perhaps, because more indirect. The overriding fact for British imperial thinking in the period was the absence of *terra nullius*, of uninhabited territory over which, according to natural law, a discoverer could press a national claim to mere *dominium*.[47] To move out beyond national borders was necessarily to move, with Pericles, into alternative jurisdictions, or into spaces like the sea in which direct containment was *de facto* impossible. Empire was a matter always of meeting the foreign in so artificially natural a way as to accommodate it with loss of neither advantage nor prestige.

IMAGINING CONTRACTS

I have already suggested ways in which *Pericles* is concerned with just such problems of sovereign accommodation. A final striking representation of that concern highlights the play's near obsession with the alternative names available to authority: prince, king, regent, governor. At the end of the first scene in Act 5, Pericles offers Marina in marriage to Lysimachus; 'for it seems / You have been noble towards her' (5.1.260–1). Ironically elided in Pericles' formulation, of course, is Lysimachus' earlier attempt to coerce Marina into prostitution: 'Come, bring me to some private place; come, come' (4.6.89–90). It is also true that a governor may not be quite the best match for a princess. But when Pericles introduces his future son-in-law to Thaisa, he renames him: 'This prince, the fair betrothed of your daughter, / Shall marry her at Pentapolis' (5.3.71–2). Central to this deferential elevation is the nature of the contract required by Pericles to preserve his own prestige, even as he recognises and accommodates in Lysimachus a useful alternative to his own royal self. As such, the renaming is the tighter and obverse version of his earlier reference to 'inhospitable Cleon' (5.1.251), an act of naming that makes the proposed conquest of Tharsus seem merely natural. To the extent that the new designation of Lysimachus comes also to seem or be natural, it constitutes a resolution to the confusion that generates the play's action, the misnaming at the heart of Antiochus' incestuous relationship with his daughter: 'He's father, son, and husband mild; / I mother, wife, and yet his child' (1.1.69–70). Of course, Pericles rejects this initial instance of confusion, even though he embraces the second; names are to be accepted or refused, offered or withheld, but always they are strategic.

Marriage brings Pericles two of his new kingdoms. Like the *imperium* for which the republican Pericles of Athens was a spokesman, Prince Pericles' empire is generated on the sea, but a sea that persists in sending him onto land to find a friendlier version of its own hostile nature, a more stable 'ground' for sovereign extension across distance. At issue in the play's marriages and in its close concern for naming is the acknowledgement that international bonds are forged less through natural law than according to contract, whereby named parties enter into a named and stable relationship. At the same time as James was trying to exercise an innovative jurisdiction over the northern seas, England was engaging the United Provinces on the matter of access to the East Indian spice trade, over which the Dutch had a virtual monopoly. In this debate, England came to occupy a position directly opposed to the one articulated in respect of the northern fisheries. Arguing from the natural freedom of commerce, as articulated, for example, in Grotius' *Mare Liberum*, they insisted that, whatever the Dutch role in liberating the Indian seas from the Portuguese, the English were as much entitled as they to trade in the islands. At a London conference in 1613, Grotius himself answered the charge. The issue was not the natural freedom of the seas, nor the natural freedom of commerce, but rather, he said, the exclusive nature of the trading contracts that the Dutch East India Company had made with the island-sovereigns, contracts that the English could not legally impede. According to these, Grotius said, the island princes had granted exclusive trading rights in exchange for Dutch protection against the Portuguese.[48] The terms of this commercial contract, we might note, correspond closely to those of the natural bond between king and subject, as articulated by James in 1609. But the shift in emphasis from natural law toward a precise and local artificial obligation allowed the Dutch a more certain solution to the problem of competing interests than had been available to James, and a more rigid one, also, than he would have entertained.

Grotius' discursive shift to contract clarifies the importance of naming for the early trade empires. International trade depended not so much on the extension of the sovereign self as on its proliferation, the identification and designation of the alternative sovereign parties who could effect the stabilising and advantageous treaty or contract. The acts of naming in *Pericles* are contractual; but they show how the stable contract becomes the site also for the more flexible construction of relative international prestige. And that is necessarily a delicate matter. To put the problem in our cartographic terms, even if the compass rose symbolises the natural extension of national authority, it remains unclear, of course, what exactly happens when lines from two roses intersect. Partly, as a concession both of the global to the local, and of the natural to the artificial, names happen. At times they seem explicitly strategic, as in an English complaint about the Dutch republican competitors in the Indies:

[A]s they [the Hollanders] hinder our trade, so they forbeare not (which I cannot but write with stomacke) the honour of our King and kingdome, as presuming sometimes to call themselues *English*, and pretend Embassage, and presents from his Maiesty, which they did to the King of *Siam*. In other places calling the Crowne and State of *England* into comparison, which made the King of *Achem* aske captaine *Best* whether the King of *England*, or the King of *Holland* were the greater Monarke.[49]

If the point here is that the Dutch become more successful traders by becoming English, that is so because the names available to the English monarchy more effectively or efficiently mirror the King of Achem's authority than do the Dutch republican names. Not surprisingly, the meeting of nations is shaped also by the names chosen by or accorded to the East Indian sovereigns. In 1607, The English East India Company requested from James royal letters to the various island-princes, each written according to his own particular 'stile': 'The most puissant Prince . . . of Suratt'; 'The Highe and Mightie Kinge of the Molloccos'; 'The Right Honorable the Sabander of Luntor'.[50] The differences between such names mark the priority of the local for the mercantile encounter. But the concession to the local can be contained even as it is articulated. When James sent a letter in 1604 to 'the greate and mightie kinge of Bantam, & of the dominions and territories adioyning', he was acknowledging in that name a sovereignty very like his own, a royal identity necessary to his own trade empire. But James did not, as he would in the case of Spain or France, refer to this royal alternative as brother. The significance of that omission is emphasised at the bottom of a copy of the letter preserved in the first Letter Book of the East India Company: 'Note that the Kinge writeth him not brother'.[51] The familial is too prestigious, perhaps, or too dangerous a marker. Like Pericles' recognition that the names Antiochus offers him are dishonourable, and like his elevation of Lysimachus or his natural degradation of Cleon, James' linguistic negotiation establishes as favourably as it can the terms of the contractual and imaginary line whose purpose was always, after all, to preserve across distance an integrated sovereign self even as that self was dispersed.

NOTES

I am grateful to Stephen Orgel, Sean Keilen and Rebecca Weller for their comments on earlier drafts of this essay.

1. John Dee, *General and Rare Memorials Pertayning to the Perfect Arte of Navigation* (London: J. Daye, 1577), p. 4. For a recent and compelling treatment of John Dee's relationship to early English conceptions of marine empire, see William H. Sherman, *John Dee: The Politics of Reading and Writing in the English Renaissance* (Amherst: University of Massachussetts Press, 1995), especially chapter 7.

2. Gentili's argument can be found in chapter 8, *De marino territorio tuendo*, an account, as the book's general title implies, of certain Admiralty cases in which Gentili acted as advocate for the Spanish Embassy in London. See T. W. Fulton, *The Sovereignty of the Sea* (London: Blackwood, 1911), pp. 358–9. For the date of Selden's text, see Fulton, *Sovereignty of the Sea*, pp. 288, 366–7; and Richard Tuck, *Philosophy and Government 1572–1651* (Cambridge University Press, 1993), p. 212. Tuck gives the publication date as 1636; I have retained the traditional date of 1635.

3. Frances Yates, *Astraea: The Imperial Theme in the Sixteenth Century* [1975] (London: Ark, 1985), p. 48.

4. Dee, *General and Rare Memorials*, p. 1.

5. *Ibid.*, p. 11.

6. *Ibid.*, p. 12.

7. *Ibid.*

8. *Ibid.*, p. 37.

9. In a marginal note on the phrase 'Brytish, or English Pericles', however, Dee reaffirms his fears about England, and offers an exemplary figure alternative to Pericles: 'Yf Pereles *Pericles* be dead, pore *Pletho* (as a Passager in the Ship of the Common-welth) By leaue, doth vtter his Faithfull Care, to the Helm-man.' The reference is to the fifteenth-century Byzantine Gemisthus Plethon, whose orations on maintaining imperial power in the Peloponnesus Dee appends to his treatise. For Dee's use of Plethon's orations, see Yates, *Astraea*, pp. 48–50, and Sherman, *John Dee*, pp. 161–2.

10. Fulton, *The Sovereignty of the Sea*, p. 15.

11. J. M. S. Tompkins, 'Why Pericles?', *Review of English Studies* 12, no. 3 (1952), 315–24. For reasons of convenience, I have in this essay attributed authorship of *Pericles* to Shakespeare alone, even though it is clear that the text is the product of a collaboration. The question of authorship is taken up at length in the introductions to *Pericles, Prince of Tyre*, ed. J. C. Maxwell (Cambridge University Press, 1965), and *Pericles*, ed. F. D. Hoeniger, Arden Edition (London: Methuen, 1963).

12. M. P. Jackson, 'North's Plutarch and the Name "Escanes" in Shakespeare's *Pericles*', *Notes and Queries* 22 (1975), 174.

13. Leah Marcus, *Puzzling Shakespeare: Local Reading and Its Discontents* (Berkeley:

University of California Press, 1988). For two recent readings of *Pericles* in the context of Jacobean politics, see chapter 2 of Constance Jordan's excellent *Shakespeare's Monarchies: Ruler and Subject in the Romances* (Ithaca: Cornell University Press, 1997); and Constance C. Relihan, 'Liminal Geography: *Pericles* and the Politics of Place', *Philological Quarterly* 71, no. 3 (1992), 281–99.

14. William Shakespeare, *Pericles*, ed. F. D. Hoeniger, Arden Edition (London: Methuen, 1963), p. 2. All further references to the play are to this edition.

15. The quotation from Bacon is cited from T. B. Howell (ed.), *A Complete Collection of State Trials*, 33 vols (London: Longman, 1809–26), vol. II, p. 598.

16. Pericles' request for harbourage recalls an important passage in the *Aeneid*, where Ilioneus complains to Dido about her treatment of the sea-weary Trojans:

> Quod genus hoc hominum? quaeve hunc tam barbara morem
> permittit patria? hospitio prohibemur harenae.   (1. 539–40)
> (What race of men is this? What country is so barbarous as to permit this
> custom. We are denied the welcome of a dry beach.)

These lines were a *locus classicus* for early modern discussions of natural law and the *ius gentium*; in his defence of the freedom of trade and navigation, for example, Hugo Grotius turned to the passage as embodying 'that law of hospitality which is of the highest sanctity'. And he appealed, in turn, to that hospitality as evidence that all nations hold the seas in common. When Pericles asks for harbourage, he is asking for something that is already naturally his; in a real sense, then, Cleon's favour is no favour at all, and so generates no obligation in the receiving party. As in his verbal exchange with Simonides, Pericles remains free even as he enters into a political union. For Grotius' citation of Virgil, see his *Mare Liberum / The Freedom of the Seas*, ed. Ralph Van Deman Magoffin (New York: Oxford University Press, 1916), p. 9.

17. Laurence Twine, *The Patterne of Painefull Aduentures* [1594] (London: V. Sims, 1607), sig. C2r.

18. *Ibid.*

19. For a similar analysis of Pericles' gift, see Steven Mullaney, *The Place of the Stage* (University of Chicago Press, 1988), p. 138.

20. Twine, *Patterne*, sig. E2v.

21. For a general account of the exchange between Grotius and Welwood, see Fulton, *Sovereignty of the Sea*, pp. 338–58.

22. William Welwood, *An Abridgement of all Sea-Lawes* (London: T. Man, 1613), p. 68. The Grotian passage quoted by Welwood can be found in Grotius, *Mare Liberum / The Freedom of the Seas*, p. 39.

23. Welwood, *An Abridgement of all Sea-Lawes*, p. 68.

24. *Ibid.*, p. 67.

25. Fulton, *Sovereignty of the Sea*, pp. 356, 349. For the date of Grotius' response to Welwood, the *Defensio Capitis quinti Maris liberi*, see Fulton, *Sovereignty of the Sea*, p. 343. For an account of the development of Grotius' thought that

takes full account of the *Defensio* see J. K. Oudendijk, *Status and Extent of Adjacent Waters: A Historical Orientation* (Leiden: Sijthoff, 1970), pp. 15–33.

26. Welwood, *An Abridgement of all Sea-Lawes*, p. 69.

27. *A Note of the Head-lands of England* (London: R. Barker, 1605). STC 10019 and 17940. The chart is reproduced in Fulton, *Sovereignty of the Sea*, p. 121, and in John Selden, *Of the Dominion, or Ownership of the Sea* [1652], trans. Marchamount Nedham (New York: Arno, 1972), p. 366. Slightly different versions of the text can be found in Selden, *Of the Dominion, or Ownership of the Sea*, pp. 369–70; and in Fulton, *Sovereignty of the Sea*, pp. 753–4.

28. *A Proclamation for revocation of Mariners from forreine Services* in James Larkin and Paul Hughes (eds.), *Stuart Royal Proclamations* (Oxford: Clarendon Press, 1973), vol. I, pp. 108–11. For an extended account of the implications for marine sovereignty of the proclamations I discuss here, see Fulton, *Sovereignty of the Sea*, pp. 118–64.

29. Fulton, *Sovereignty of the Sea*, p. 119.

30. Selden, *Of the Dominion, or Ownership of the Sea*, p. 365. Nedham's 1652 English translation of Selden's text is largely sufficient for my purposes in this essay. Where the Latin term has seemed important, I have enclosed in square brackets the Latin original.

31. Selden, *Of the Dominion, or Ownership of the Sea*, pp. 366–7.

32. An excellent account of the complex history of *dominium* and *imperium*, is J. H. Burns, *Lordship, Kingship, and Empire: The Idea of Monarchy 1400–1525* (Oxford: Clarendon Press, 1992). For the equally complex relationship between *dominium* and *ius* (right), see also Richard Tuck, *Natural Rights Theories: Their Origin and Development* (Cambridge University Press, 1979).

33. Fulton, *Sovereignty of the Sea*, p. 373.

34. Larkin/Hughes, *Stuart Royal Proclamations*, vol. I, p. 109.

35. *Ibid.*, p. 219.

36. Fulton, *Sovereignty of the Sea*, pp. 124, 148–53.

37. Larkin/Hughes, *Stuart Royal Proclamations*, vol. I, p. 218.

38. For Coke's definition of allegiance as 'duplex et reciprocum ligamen' see the account of Calvin's Case in Howell, *Complete Collection of State Trials*, vol. II, pp. 613–14.

39. Larkin/Hughes, *Stuart Royal Proclamations*, vol. I, p. 219.

40. *Ibid.*, p. 109.

41. I am not claiming, of course, that the strategy convinced those who did not want to be so convinced. Unsurprisingly, Grotius focused on the distinction between *dominium* and *imperium* in his answer to the claim that James could exclude foreigners from his coasts as from his land. Grotius was determined to define fishing rights as a matter not of *imperium*, but solely of *dominium*, and thereby expose the pretentions of the English claim in the North Sea. See Oudendijk, *Status and Extent of Adjacent Waters*, pp. 27–31. In the context of the operative legal distinction, however, James' invocation of a geographically charged *imperium* seems, politically, remarkably astute.

42. Richard Helgerson, *Forms of Nationhood: The Elizabethan Writing of England*

(University of Chicago Press, 1992), especially chapter 3.

43. The frontispiece is reproduced in Helgerson, *Forms of Nationhood*, p. 121.

44. David A. Waters, *The Art of Navigation in England in Elizabethan and Early Stuart Times*, 3 vols (Greenwich: Maritime Museum, 2nd edn 1978), vol. 1, p. 63. Waters has an excellent description of how the central or 'mother' compass on a chart was related to the sixteen or thirty-two subsidiary compasses.

45. In his 1604 treatise on the union, Sir Henry Spelman designates James as 'the greate sonne of our Brytish orbe'. His use of the metaphor is notably darker than might appear, however, since James' removal from Scotland to London in 1603 is compared to the sun's movement toward the equator, a change that brings the southern kingdom 'the springe of a . . . florishing government' but necessarily leaves the northern one in 'the winter of a desolate state'. See Sir Henry Spelman, 'Of the Union', *The Jacobean Union: Six Tracts of 1604*, ed. Bruce Galloway and Brian Levack (Edinburgh: Scottish History Society, 1985), pp. 178–9.

46. The table, printed opposite Speed's dedication to James, is entitled 'THE ACHIEVEMENTS OF OUR SOVERAIGNE KING IAMES AS HE NOWE BEARETH With the ARMES of the Severall kings that have aunciently raigned within his nowe Dominions.'

47. Exceptionally, in 1613, James claimed in support of the Muscovy Company that Spitzbergen was, by reason of discovery, English dominium, arguing thence for an English monopoly on whaling in the seas around that distant island. See Fulton, *Sovereignty of the Sea*, pp. 181–3, and Oudendijk, *Status and Extent of Adjacent Waters*, pp. 36–7.

48. G. N. Clark and J. W. J. M. Van Eysinga, *The Colonial Conferences Between England and the Netherlands in 1613 and 1615, Part II* (Leiden: Brill, 1951), pp. 59–81. See also Oudendijk, *Status and Extent of Adjacent Waters*, pp. 37–40.

49. IR [Robert Keale], *The Trades Increase* (London: W. Burre, 1615), p. 48. Captain Best had returned in 1614 from the tenth voyage undertaken by the East India Company. See *The Voyage of Thomas Best to the East Indies, 1612–1614*, ed. William Foster, WHS, 2nd ser., LXXV (London: Hakluyt Society, 1934).

50. George Birdwood and William Foster (eds.), *The First Letter Book of the East India Company* (London: Quaritch, 1893), pp. 103–10.

51. *Ibid.*, p. 48.

CHAPTER 9

'On the Famous Voyage': Ben Jonson and civic space

Andrew McRae

Readers of Ben Jonson have long appreciated the significance of his representations of social space. 'To Penshurst' is commonly placed at the forefront of the Jonson canon, seen to typify his preoccupation with the 'centred self' of the pre-modern subject, and the location of that subject within a physical and psychological 'home'.[1] His satiric verse and city comedies have likewise attracted attention, for their disturbing appreciation of the ways in which social and spatial structures in London corrode human values. Jonson's most sustained non-dramatic engagement with his city, however, has received relatively little notice. 'On the Famous Voyage', which narrates a journey up the polluted Fleet Ditch from Bridewell to Holborn, is by far the longest poem in Jonson's *Epigrammes*, and almost twice the length of the famous country-house poem, yet only one critic has considered it worthy of a research article.[2] Recent studies of literary constructions of the city have also dodged the text: Lawrence Manley's *Literature and Culture in Early Modern London* accords it only passing references; Steven Mullaney, whose exploration of marginal spaces parallels in important ways Jonson's poetic navigation, does not mention the piece.[3]

This history of neglect can largely be attributed to queasiness in the face of the poem's subject matter. Swinburne famously dismissed the 'Famous Voyage' as out of tune with English sensibilities. 'Coprology', he suggested, 'should be left to the Frenchmen . . . It is nothing less than lamentable that so great an English writer as Ben Jonson should ever have taken the plunge of a Parisian diver into the cesspool'.[4] More recently, Richard Helgerson has placed the text 'among the filthiest, the most deliberately and insistently disgusting poems in the language'.[5] Beyond this prevalent discomfort, however, critical opinion has diverged, and the disagreements raise important questions about the significance of the poem. Most notably, 'On the Famous Voyage' has been interpreted as 'a typical Renaissance parody',[6] a studied 'satire on the age'[7] and as burlesque underpinned by Rabelaisian humour.[8] J. G. Nichols' assessment is less definitive, but by consequence manages to accommodate several of the predominant strategies in the multivalent poem; he adopts a 'distinction between "mock-heroic, where the treatment is grandiose; and burlesque, where the treatment is low"', and describes the 'Famous Voyage' as 'a mixture of mock-heroic and burlesque with incidental contemporary satire'.[9]

In this essay I want to contextualize Jonson's troublesome poem, situating it within the physical and cultural environment of early modern London. This aim undersets a combination of literary and spatial interpretation. As postmodern geographers and social theorists have demonstrated, space demands analysis not merely as a neutral container but as itself a product.[10] Moreover, the production of space implies not only the drive of economic power across the land, but an interrelated cultural fashioning of meaning and consciousness. At a time of unsettling change in London, characterised by rapid population growth, the movement of commercial and industrial practices towards capitalist structures, and devastating outbreaks of dearth and plague, cultural products played a crucial role in shaping the spatiality of urban life.[11] 'On the Famous Voyage' emerges within this context as an ironic commentary on, and disruptive intervention in contemporary constructions of space. The poem interweaves strains of satire and saturnalia, as Jonson maps a journey through a grotesque urban body.[12]

My discussion will consequently look first at the construction of this body, through the poem's use of a journey along a waterway as a means of spatial cognition, and through Jonson's overt gendering of the city. This will involve a consideration of the cultural meanings attached to voyages and voyagers, a survey of the route of these voyagers, and an analysis of the cultural associations of women with water which Jonson exploits. Once the men enter this feminized body, the focus of the poem shifts to the city's excretion and consumption. My second section will thus consider the predominantly satiric strategies in these passages of the poem, as Jonson glances at various aspects of corruption, yet modulates his tone with strains of a markedly popular vitality. The infamously morose insistence on human excrement, I will argue, is enlivened by carnivalesque humour.[13] In its conception of the city, therefore, Jonson's poem may be seen to undermine orthodox practices and discourses of civic space, allowing a glimpse of a vitally alternative spatiality.

I

At the outset of the seventeenth century the predominant conceptions of space in London were torn between tradition and nascent modernity. The demands of the former constructed spatiality upon accretions of memory and localised mythologies, while the latter suggested rather the abstract and homogeneous space which would become characteristic of the modern capitalist city. Early maps of London combined these ways of perceiving the city, introducing the concept of a cartographic guide, but also focusing on traditional landmarks and incorporating civic iconography. For the non-elite, however, London was still a city without maps, largely opaque to the outsider. Literature of the period affords countless examples of countrymen and women baffled by their first experiences of the city. As demographic, social and economic changes presented fundamental challenges to the city and its inhabitants, civic space was therefore at once a stable home and an alienating conglomeration of confusion. It was a site steeped in history, being reshaped by perplexing forces. These conditions necessitated new mentalities of settlement and innovative constructions of social space, as English men and women reassessed the functions and structures of their capital.[14]

The journey, particularly in an age before the street-map, offered a preeminent form of spatial cognition and articulation. Notably, the main section of John Stow's *Survey of London* (1598, 1603) is structured in the form of a perambulation of the city, ward by ward and street by street. Like any journey, Stow's is an exercise in definition and placement, as he records the history and social functions of the myriad sites of London. Stow perceives change but defers to local tradition; he records alterations to the physical landscape but endorses attempts to fix his own citizen's ethos upon the city. Tellingly, he rarely ventures into the alleys that housed large populations of immigrant poor, preferring to notice government attempts to 'stop up' such sites of disorder.[15] Formal processions similarly offered a mechanism for imprinting a model of social order onto civic space. The annual lord mayor's procession – the most important of a range of ceremonial passages through London's streets – at once asserted principles of social order and shaped civic mythologies. In Manley's evaluation, such ceremonies fashioned the city as 'a sacral space, a physical embodiment of ceremonial tradition and community spirit'; customary processional routes 'helped to link the city's open, outdoor public spaces, forming a single interior of contiguous ritual zones'.[16]

If the orderly movement of Stow and the ceremonial procession of the civic elite participated in the construction of urban space, however, so too did countless quotidian journeys. While ceremonial movement fashions a spatiality enriched by tradition and enforced by the disciplinary mechanisms of government, the manifold itineraries of individuals suggest rather the 'procedures of everyday creativity' analysed by Michel de Certeau.[17] Such paths through the city construct a spatiality of encounter and immediacy, opposed at once to the abstraction of geometry and the tradition of ceremony. 'The moving about that the city multiplies and concentrates', according to de Certeau, 'makes the city itself an immense social experience of lacking a place.'[18] Significantly, the governors of London sought to control civic space by controlling movement: by restricting entry to the city for potential provincial and continental immigrants; by limiting access to public sites; and through the imposition of curfews. The constant struggle for spatial discipline is highlighted by anxiety surrounding 'nightwalking', a crime which at this time denoted prostitution when attached to women and the threat of disorder and property crime when attached to men.[19] Bridewell, which Jonson notes 'may, in time, concerne us / All, that are readers' (lines 42–3), stood as the central institution for the enforcement of that discipline.

Many works of popular literature explore the contours of spatial order. Several of the jest books which flourished from the latter sixteenth century centre on peripatetic figures exploiting the opportunities of urban space. *The Merrie Conceited Jests: Of George Peele* (1607), for example, delineates an individual who moves most comfortably through alleys and alehouses, cheating companions and dodging the law.[20] Similarly, many ballads represent acts which flouted spatial discipline, occasionally in unsettling ways. In one text, 'Shameless Joan' of Finsbury is said to have crawled backwards 'through the City ... with a lighted Candle in her Back-side, and scar'd the Watch who was amaz'd at that dismal sight'.[21] This poem narrates a journey which originated in an alehouse wager, not dissimilar to that made by Jonson's heroes in the 'Famous Voyage'. When all the city was asleep:

> Accordingly away she went,
> And in her brawny Fundament,
> A lighted Candle plac'd must be,
> Which was a dreadful sight to see.

The watchman is understandably disconcerted, but does not prevent the traveller, who fulfils the terms of the bet, then 'turn'd about / And fairly blew the Candle out'. Joan's project, which may or may not have a basis in fact, is represented by the balladeer as a singular exercise in spatial transgression, setting against popular appreciations of civic procession across the city the image of a huge, drunken, self-sodomised woman moving on her knees at night. Figures of disorderly and grotesque female bodies, I will suggest below, resonate similarly, albeit more subtly, through Jonson's images of his native city.

Shameless Joan was probably not available to Jonson as a source, but claims a place within the literature of outlandish peripatetic feats which he invokes in the 'Famous Voyage'. His heroes, Shelton and Heyden, set forth

> (in worthy scorne
> Of those, that put out moneyes, on returne
> From *Venice, Paris*, or some in-land passage
> Of sixe times to, and fro, without embassage,
> Or him that backward went to *Berwicke*, or which
> Did dance the famous Morrisse, unto *Norwich*).   (lines 31–6)

These topical references are well known. From the late sixteenth century, a number of men had undertaken travels on the strength of wagers, and several had returned to publish accounts of their adventures. Richard Ferris rowed by sea from London to Bristol; Will Kemp, Shakespeare's first stage clown, morris-danced from London to Norwich; and at the time Jonson was writing, the long career of John Taylor, whose feats included a 'pennyless pilgrimage' in the steps of Jonson from London to Edinburgh and an unsurprisingly abortive attempt to row a brown-paper boat up the Thames from London to Kent, was just beginning.[22] These travellers, of middling and lower social origins, seized on the economic opportunities of fantastic voyages. In a manner typical of the genre, Kemp's morris dance transforms a cultural form of rural festivity into a commercial venture, while his subsequent pamphlet translates the exercise in self-promotion into the realm of literary culture.[23]

Such practices violated principles around which Jonson struggled to define his own work and values. In contrast to the energetic opportunism of these travellers and their social milieu, Jonson typically valorises images of circularity and 'rooted stability'.[24] Travel, if it is to be endorsed, must therefore be represented in accordance with this controlling ethos. For example, in the eulogistic 'To William Roe' (*Epigrammes* 128), which invites many points of comparison with the 'Famous Voyage', the commercial interests of the mercantile adventurer are sup-

pressed beneath Jonson's established moral vocabulary. Roe's 'begin-
nings here, prove purely sweet, / And perfect in a circle alwayes meet'
(l. 7–8). Instead of highlighting the physical rigours and concrete accomplishments of England's 'good ÆNEAS' (l. 12), Jonson fixes on his travel
as circular, looking to the time 'when we, blest with thy returne, shall see
/ Thy selfe, with thy first thoughts, brought home by thee' (lines 9–10).
'Returne', a word of financial significance for the merchant adventurer,
is here loaded with ethical value, as the traveller carries only his 'first
thoughts' back to the 'home' of his family and nation. Roe assimilates
his experiences into a form of social enrichment; 'he changes his travels,
into nourishment and profit'.[25]

But while it is a relatively straightforward matter to contrast Jonson's
attitudes towards William Roe and William Kemp, his representation of
Shelton and Heyden is more complex. The introduction of the pair is
not entirely satiric, as he holds them at parenthesis' length from the
other voyagers, and infuses the passage with a convivial humour. The
two men conceive of their act, moreover, at '*Bread-streets* Mermaid' (l.
37), a tavern with which Jonson was associated, and which he mentions
elsewhere in the *Epigrammes* as a source of wine which will 'take my *Muse*,
and mee'.[26] A key to interpreting the authorial attitude towards Shelton
and Heyden is Jonson's representation elsewhere of another traveller
closely associated with the Mermaid. Thomas Coryate's *Crudities* (1611),
perhaps the most capacious of English Renaissance travel texts, is a
careful description of continental cities, written by a man of independent means and considerable learning. Jonson, though, was a central
figure in the project of packaging the *Crudities* as carnivalesque, and
presenting Coryate as a buffoon. Against the wishes of the author, but
under the auspices of Prince Henry, the literary community poured
forth prefatory poems on a travel book many knew only by its fabricated
reputation.[27] Jonson's contributions included verses on the frontispiece.
Of one image, in which a tablet portrait of the author is surrounded by
three female figures (one of whom is clearly unwell), Jonson juxtaposes
contrasting perceptions of Coryate's travels:

> These be the three countries with their *Cornu-copia*
> That make him as famous, as Moore his *Utopia*.
> *Or,*
> Here France gives him scabs, Venice a hot Sunne,
> And Germanie spewes on him out of her Tunne.[28]

Coryate clearly hoped for fame and reward. Jonson's efforts to belittle
the author and his work in this respect are therefore cruel, but not

without a personable humour, which Coryate himself appears to have accepted.[29] Jonson is concerned to situate a peer within the London literary community, depicting a potential rival as a figure of rough fun.

'On the Famous Voyage' similarly claims a community of readers, which Jonson binds together with a mesh of puns and topical allusions. There is no reason to believe that the voyagers were not themselves members of this community. Peter Medine identifies 'Shelton' not as the Sir Ralph Shelton lauded in *Epigrammes* 119, but rather Thomas Shelton, translator of *Don Quixote*; and 'Heyden', he determines, is Sir Christopher Heydon, a prominent defender of astrology.[30] These two men, Medine argues, Jonson would have despised for their respective literary and intellectual endeavours.[31] But while this argument is attractive, he can find no evidence for the identifications, beyond the suitability of the pair for his reading of the poem as 'a serious indictment of the times'.[32] He appears to assume that the incident has no basis in fact, and that Jonson rather 'selected' figures 'who would have served a particular satiric purpose'.[33] Without further evidence this is a dangerous assumption, which may distort a reading of the poem. Instead, given the number of other topical referents in the poem, it seems reasonable to suggest that the voyagers were personally known to the poet (and Sir Ralph Shelton might well have been one of them), although their exact identification is not essential to an understanding of the poem. The narrative might be based on a failed search for prostitutes, which might also have been linked to a tavern wager.[34] Consequently, the poem might be approached similarly to Jonson's representation of Coryate: as an act of refashioning and comic embellishment. Hercules is a suitable tutelary deity, as he was associated not only with physical heroism but also with gargantuan sexual labours.[35] Like Aeneas, Hercules also travelled to 'hell': a word which affords Jonson a pun, suggesting both a brothel-district and the vagina.[36]

The route of the journey, whether concocted or merely retold by Jonson, is exploited for its conjunction of institutions of civic discipline with emanations of disorder. The men begin their trip along the outside of the city wall at Bridewell, a former royal palace which was handed to the City of London by Edward VI and used thereafter, according to Stow's early eighteenth-century successor, as 'a Place where all Strumpets, Night-walkers, Pick-pockets, vagrant and idle Persons, that are taken up for their ill Lives . . . are forced to beat Hemp in publick View, with due Correction of whipping'.[37] The Fleet prison, from which 'out-cryes of the damned' subsequently assail the voyagers (l. 172), housed debtors as well as prisoners convicted by the Star Chamber. Holborn, the men's destination, was associated with both punishment and transgression. The journeys of the condemned to Tyburn executions passed through Holborn, and its thoroughfare was often used for the public carting and flogging of criminals. Its concurrent reputation for crime and prostitution, upon which Jonson draws more explicitly, is illustrated by contemporary literary references; for instance, in *A Fair Quarrel*, by Middleton and Rowley, those seeking instruction in the art of roaring are advised to 'repair into Holborn at the sign of the Cheat-Loaf'.[38]

The journey is also a 'liquid deed' (l. 193), by water rather than by land. The poem's emphasis on the groggy flow of fluids through the body of the city explores the significance of the liquid in London. For Stow, the waters of the city were a source of civic pride, and claimed a place at the front of his *Survey*.[39] He celebrates particularly the controlled flow of water, issuing from conduits which themselves stand as civic monuments. In West Cheap the monument was gendered and classicised; there, Stow records, 'was set up a curious wrought tabernacle of gray Marble, and in the same an Alabaster Image of *Diana*, and water convayed from the Thames, prilling from her naked breast'.[40] Nature, figured in the flowing water and nurturing female form, is thereby fused with the culture of a city capable of engineering and classical appropriation. The conduits, the principal source of water for Londoners, were also important stations in the lord mayors' processions. 'At these stations', Lawrence Manley comments, 'where normally the city's life welled up to be gathered by apprentices of a morning, and where water turned to wine during entries – nature, culture, and grace converged in pageant form.'[41]

As Jonathan Gil Harris has demonstrated, however, representations of the flow of water into London were always equivocal, as civic pride was shadowed by associations of fluidity with bodily incontinence. One of the major sources of water for Londoners was popularly known as 'pissing conduit', while many other conduit buildings were variously 'identified ... with the body's orifices'.[42] More importantly, in the present context, the flow of fluids through both civic and human bodies was appreciated as a disturbingly murky process. Notably, Stow's typically sanguine representation of the 'watering' of the city is undermined by notes of anxiety concerning pollution in the waterways.[43] Houndsditch, he claims, takes its name 'for that in olde time when the same lay open, much filth ... especially dead Dogges were there layd or cast'.[44] The Fleet Ditch, once better known as the Fleet River, had suffered a similar fate. Stow laments the failure of attempts to 'cleanse' the stream, which have left it 'woorse cloyed ... then ever it was before'.[45] But despite his concern with the provision of fresh water to Londoners, Stow generally shuns any mention of the attendant flow of sewage out of the city. He wants to see the Fleet Ditch cleansed, but does not acknowledge its vital role in the discharge of filth. His city consumes openly, but excretes discreetly; its pissing alleys, similarly, receive no mention in the *Survey*.[46] Nor does Stow discuss proposals to replenish London's water supplies, which were actually in a parlous state.[47] The original plans for the New River, an artificial waterway which drew water to the capital from Hertfordshire, intended that it would flush out all polluted ditches around the city, while also bringing water to individual houses. Until shortly before its 1613 opening, however, the work was mired in controversy, surrounding funding, the rights of landowners along the route, and the transformation of water into a private commodity.[48]

For all the civic pride attached to the supply of water, then, the cultural status of London's liquid remained problematic. Channels of water tend to collapse troublingly into flows of filth; the careful civic control over nature is undermined by the unsteady passage of matter through body and city alike. This ambivalence towards the fluid was evident in the lord mayors' processions, which moved to the celebratory pageants at central conduits only after more unruly scenes by the Thames. Manley notes that the water pageant which marked the lord mayor's landing by barge was typically 'the roughest and most boisterous' of the day, adorned with 'amphibian mascots, pagan gods, giants, and heroes', and exposing the porous boundaries between nature and culture.[49] While the procession on land is carefully linked to civic monuments and tradition, the flow of water threatens to dissolve such aggrandizing strategies. Jonson plays on the attempts to manipulate images of order in the lord mayor's arrival when he suggests of the putrid barge which passes the famous voyagers, that 'one day in the yeere, for sweet 'tis voyc't, / And that is when it is the Lord *Maiors* foist' (lines 119–20). The word 'foist' admits useful puns, meaning a barge, but also a fart or a cheating rogue.[50]

The image of civic ceremony which collapses in a scatological pun is paradigmatic of the poem's strategy of setting bodily ferment against discourses of spatial and social stability. Crucially, the sewer which should be a river, encumbered with the stench of excrement and disorder when civic pride requires purity and consistency, is mapped as a path through a seething body. As the heroes move upstream through the 'dire passage' (l. 59), the poem moves haltingly through images of excretion to images of the preparation and consumption of food. The 'passage' thus crudely mirrors the function of the alimentary canal, understood in Renaissance medical theory to be a single channel winding through the body, which received and digested food, and subsequently ejected excrement. Theorists exercised their minds, as Gail Kern Paster notes, to separate the processes of the canal, but failed to dispel completely the 'specter of monstrous appetite, of ingestion and excretion in endless, horrible simultaneity'.[51] As I will consider further in the second section, Jonson's wilful confusion of these processes exploits the attendant anxieties, suggesting at once a social and spatial corruption in the body of the city.

The heroes' 'entry / To this dire pasage' through 'A dock ... that called is Avernus' is also, more emphatically, figured as sexual penetration (lines 58–9). 'Dock' is a suitably confused pun, suggesting the vagina but also the anus.[52] The entrance is degraded and exhausted, like the imagined genitalia of the prostitutes who may be the object of the voyage, and who are an underlying figure throughout the poem. The men are motivated to visit Holborn in part because 'the powerfull *Moone*' has made 'the poore *Banck-side* creature wet it' shoone' (lines 29–30). This is probably a reference to an exceptional tide which has flooded the major city brothels on the south bank of the Thames, but also invokes associations of women with water and incontinence, in both senses of the word. In predominant cultural constructions, the compelling excess of the female body was seen to be evident at once in uncontrollable sexuality and unquenchable flows of fluids.[53] The attendant association of whores and water was underlined by the principal site of the city's brothels, and cruelly exploited in an Elizabethan punishment, recommended by William Harrison, which involved 'dragging ... them over the Thames betwene Lambeth and Westminster at the tail of a boat'.[54]

The poem's grotesque exposition of female excess continues as the men move upstream:

> Thorough her wombe they make their famous road,
> Betweene two walls; where, on one side, to scar men,
> Were seene your ugly *Centaures*, yee call *Car-men*,
> *Gorgonian* scolds, and *Harpyes*: on the other
> Hung stench, diseases, and old filth, their mother,
> With famine, wants, and sorrowes many a dosen,
> The least of which was to the plague a cosen.
> But they unfrighted passe, though many a privie

Spake to 'hem louder, then the oxe in LIVIE;
And many a sinke pour'd out her rage anenst 'hem;
But still their valour, and their vertue fenc't 'hem.   (lines 66–76)

In the 'wombe' of the city-whore, conventional images of generation
and familial identity undergo a sea-change. The 'mother' of 'stench' and
'diseases' is merely 'old filth'; 'famine, wants, and sorrowes' are
'cosen[s]' to the plague. At the end of the section, Jonson exploits a pun
on 'sink', which is a receptacle for waste or sewage, and in the body an
organ of digestion and excretion. In the female body, the signification of
'a place where things are swallowed up or lost' extends to the vagina (a
sense exploited in *The Faerie Queene*); and this usage aligns with instances
of 'sink' denoting a whore or brothel.[55] An implicit threat throughout
the journey is the pox, which was itself perceived as 'flowing matter'
which could move around the body.[56] At the entrance to the 'passage',
Jonson plays on the corruption of the site in the injunction to 'stop thy
nose', for 'this *Dock*'s no rose' (lines 59–60). As editors have noted, the
sentence appropriates a botanical proverb concerning a common weed;
but it suggests also the long-lost 'rose' of maidenhead, and perhaps also
glances towards the colloquial nomination of syphilitic sores as 'roses'.[57]
The nose is a common euphemism for the penis, the feared 'light pains'
of which shade from the wanton pleasures of copulation to the pains
which might result from sexual lightness. Hercules' sore 'backe, and
bones' similarly combine intimations of sexual exhaustion and venereal
infection.[58]

The feminised civic body crudely shaped through these lines is best
understood in terms of the Renaissance grotesque, which is typically
derived from 'the unstable coalescence of contrary images of the flesh:
indulged, abused, purged, damned'.[59] Jonson consistently couples dis-
figurement with bawdy word-play, disease with pleasure. The grotesque
body of his city accords with Bakhtin's 'unfinished and open body
(dying, bringing forth and being born)', which 'is an incarnation of this
world at the absolute lower stratum'.[60] It explosively disrupts the order
of civic panegyric, which shapes a closed and monumental spatiality,
comparable to the body of classical statuary. Jonson rather figures the
civic body as gross and misshapen, entered through the polluted orifice
of the ditch at Bridewell Dock.[61] This strategy is compounded in the
classical grotesquerie which embellishes the poem. Centaurs, harpies, a
chimera, Briareus and Hydra all combine human and animal features
(lines 68, 69, 80, 81, 83). Moreover, Jonson's mock-heroic apparatus
relentlessly domesticates, fusing grotesque embellishment and topical
referent. The warrior Briareus is aligned with a randy beadle '(Who

hath the hundred hands when he doth meddle)' (l. 82); and centaurs are 'Car-men' (l. 67), bringing their nightly loads to the Ditch. The body of the city is thereby mirrored in the bodies of its inhabitants, comically misshapen civic functionaries who highlight the city's insistent sexual and excretory energies.

II

After the early imagery of degraded sexuality, the 'Famous Voyage' in fact moves insistently towards a concentration on the city's processes of excretion and consumption. In accordance with the materialising strat-egy of the poem, Jonson roughly equates the 'filth, stench, noyse' of the classical underworld (l. 9), with the unsanitary condition of the Fleet. In the *Aeneid* VI, the most important classical subtext for the poem, Aeneas encounters within the jaws of the underworld 'Grief', 'Cares', 'Dis-eases', 'Age', 'Want', 'Death' and 'Distress'.[62] Jonson's parallel passage offers the similarly abstract 'diseases', 'famine', 'wants', 'sorrowes', but also 'old filth, their mother' (lines 70–1). Further, as he claims at the outset, 'what was there / Subtly distinguish'd, was confused here' (lines 9–10). The prevailing material and categorical confusion admits an essential connection between dirt and disorder. 'Reflection on dirt', according to Mary Douglas, 'involves reflection on the relation of order to disorder, being to non-being, form to formlessness, life to death.'[63] Jonson's insistence on filth, which underpinned Edmund Wilson's analysis of the poet as anal-erotic, might thus be appreciated as a valuable poetic strategy.[64] The poem's mobilisation of the grotesque, within the civic body, facilitates a strain of satire remarkable for its understated sense of vitality and regeneration.

The quintessential manifestation of filth in the poem is shit, variously precipitated into the Fleet Ditch and coagulating as 'Mud' at its mouth (l. 62). The use of the city ditches as sewers was a point of common knowledge, but one sidestepped by those influenced by new ideas of bodily and spatial civility.[65] In the final line of his poem, Jonson invokes the precedent of Sir John Harington's mix of scurrility and lavatory design in *The Metamorphosis of Ajax* (1596). But while Jonson's spirited appropriation of classicism is similar to that upon which Harington bases his text, his underlying purpose is markedly different. The turd in the 'Famous Voyage' is basically a satiric device. Lying 'heap'd like an userers masse' (l. 139), it recalls Jonson's characteristic disgust for wealth hoarded rather than employed for the public good.[66] Shit 'languishing stucke upon the wall' sets the stubbornly recumbent human excrement against the ostensibly solid achievements of human architecture (l. 136). Itself caught between categories of fluid and solid, shit threatens at once to clog waterways and corrode buildings. In Jonson's moral satire, by extension, it serves to undermine the achievements of culture, mocking human pride and ambition.

Jonson exploits the satiric potential of the turd most remarkably as the voyagers are forced to row close to the walls and thus risk injury from the privies above:

> At this a loud
> Crack did report it selfe, as if a cloud
> Had burst with storme, and downe fell, *ab excelsis*,
> Poore MERCURY, crying out on PARACELSUS,
> And all his followers, that had so abus'd him:
> And, in so shitten sort, so long had us'd him:
> For (where he was the god of eloquence,
> And subtiltie of mettalls) they dispense
> His spirits, now, in pills, and eeke in potions,
> Suppositories, cataplasmes, and lotions.
> But many Moones there shall not wane (quoth hee)
> (In the meane time, let 'hem imprison mee)
> But I will speake (and know I shall be heard)
> Touching this cause, where they will be affeard
> To answere me. And sure, it was th'intent
> Of the grave fart, late let in parliament,
> Had it beene seconded, and not in fume
> Vanish'd away: as you must all presume
> Their MERCURY did now.   (lines 93–111)

The passage frustrates attempts at visualisation. In one sense, it relies on the epic mode, which legitimises the manifestation of deities; simultaneously, in accordance with the mock-epic, it invites the reader to imagine gobbets of the metal mercury buried in a falling turd. The resultantly beshitten state of the classical god underlines a familiar Jonsonian lament about corruption and commercialisation, particularly in the author's own realm of 'eloquence'. This satiric point collapses neatly into another familiar attack on medical practices, specifically those employed by the followers of Paracelsus, who argued the physiological benefits of maintaining a balance of mercury, sulphur and salt in the human body. Paracelsus favoured purges – the common use of which threatens the voyagers with befoulment – and he may also have introduced the use of mercury in the treatment of venereal disease.[67] Jonson thus clinches his point about moral corruption and its physical manifestations through a further allusion to the disfiguring illness which haunts contemporary representations of urban sexuality. Interestingly,

Holborn was known not only for its small number of brothels, but also as the metropolitan centre for mercurial sweat baths.[68]

Mercury's threat to take his case 'where they will be affeard / To answere me' carries a possible allusion to Jonson's masque *Mercury Vindicated*, performed in 1615 and perhaps already in the author's mind when he wrote the 'Famous Voyage'.[69] Immediately following this declaration, however, Jonson modifies his tone. The comment about 'the grave fart, late let in parliament', which may be intended as the continued speech of Mercury, refers to an eruption immortalised in one of the most popular poems in manuscript distribution in the early decades of the seventeenth century. 'The Parliament Fart' is an amalgam of scatological comedy and witty character sketches, its jocular tone only mildly disturbed by the insubstantiality of an interjection which resists all attempts to record, arrest or measure it.[70] Jonson's allusion therefore moderates the preceding satire.[71] A turd might widely be accepted as offensive, but a fart was rather a source of humour; its literary allegiance was with the jest-book rather than formal satire.[72] Hence the teasing intonation of a subsequent passage, in which the myriad forms of the 'ghosts ... of farts' are employed to debunk the atom theory initiated by Democritus, pursued by Nicholas Hill, and distrusted by Jonson (lines 124–9). The humour of the lines dissipates the threat of atom theory, without the savage assault characteristic of much contemporary verse satire.

The fart thus establishes a carnivalesque momentum in the poem. This initiative is typified in the speculation on the passing barge, 'the Lord *Maiors* foist', in which Jonson undercuts discourses of civic dignity while concurrently gesturing towards the more common stench and practices of 'Beares colledge, *Paris-garden*' (l. 117). The momentum is sustained as the poem moves towards images of food and consumption. The voyagers reach the 'bankes', upon which,

> Your *Fleet*-lane *Furies*; and hot cookes doe dwell,
> That, with still-scalding steemes, make the place *hell*.
> The sinkes ran grease, and haire of meazled hogs,
> The heads, houghs, entrailes, and the hides of dogs:
> For, to say truth, what scullion is so nastie,
> To put the skins, and offall in a pastie?
> Cats there lay divers had beene flead, and rosted,
> And, after mouldie growne, againe were tosted,
> Then, selling not, a dish was tane to mince 'hem,
> But still, it seem'd, the ranknesse did convince 'hem.
> For, here they were throwne in wi'the melted pewter,
> Yet drown'd they not. They had five lives in future. (lines 143–54)

The catalogue reads as a parody of Jonson's eminently civilised menu in 'Inviting a Friend to Supper' (*Epigrammes* 101). Yet couched between images of the spoiled flesh of dogs and cats is the apparently discordant couplet, 'For, to say truth, what scullion is so nastie, / To put the skins, and offall in a pastie?' The subdued note of relish that informs this aside accords with images elsewhere in Jonson's poems, of the author as a man of 'mountaine belly' and monstrous appetite.[73] The passage thus acknowledges signs of revitalising consumption amidst the welter of refuse, in a manner consistent with the 'material bodily principle' Bakhtin identifies in his study of Rabelais. Like the Frenchman, Jonson works through images of the lower bodily stratum, its orifices and its excrement, to glimpse a 'triumphant, festive principle'.[74] The 'confusion' of London in the 'Famous Voyage' looks towards filth and corruption but evokes simultaneously a strangely subversive vitality.

The final substantial section, centring on Banks and his horse transmigrated into the corpse of a cat, clarifies this development. In this image, Jonson audaciously juxtaposes putrefaction and sustenance, death and sexuality, in a manner which typifies his purpose in the poem. He focuses on this one cat after surveying the 'divers' other corpses, the existence of which mocks taboos against eating domestic animals and cooking corrupt flesh. As acknowledged in Jonson's aside that the corrupted bodies still have 'five lives in future' (l. 154), however, the cat is also an animal known proverbially for its ability to flout death. Further, the cat was associated with lechery and nocturnal straying for sexual purposes; more specifically, 'cat' was in use as a euphemism for a whore, a bawd, the penis and the vulva.[75] (These associations inform the punning humour of the voyagers' response to the mysterious beast, when 'They cry'd out PUSSE' (l. 183), and Bankes identifies himself.) Even this beast's 'great gray eyes' may play on another popular sign of wantonness (l. 161).[76]

Within this context, Jonson's identification of Banks and his horse is particularly apt. Banks taught his horse various tricks, including counting and singling out individuals in a crowd, and exhibited the beast at taverns for over a decade from the late 1580s.[77] Although his actions were trailed by suggestions of infernal trickery, the act remained rooted in the realm of popular entertainment. One anecdote records Dick Tarlton and Banks trading jests, the horse first identifying the former as 'the veriest foole in the company', then selecting his master as 'the veriest whore-master'.[78] Their status within London street culture is reinforced by a 1595 pamphlet, in which 'Bankes Bay Horse in a Trance' performs a comparable function to 'the oxe in LIVIE' (l. 74), attacking

contemporary abuses in London, focusing especially on the exploitation of those of lower degree.[79] The role of landlords in promoting
prostitution and abusing prostitutes is a recurrent theme; of one lecherous individual, the horse says, 'Let him passe for a farting churle, and
weare his mistres favours, viz. rubies and precious stones on his nose'.[80]
Jonson's reference to Banks and the horse being 'burned for one witch'
in France need not be taken too seriously (l. 158), since in 1608 Banks
was safely returned from his continental tour and employed by Prince
Henry.[81] Rather, the line appeals to the knowledge of Jonson's community of readers, who might be expected to set the rumour against their
awareness of the living jester, and thus appreciate the essential humour
of the passage.

When Banks as cat cadaver identifies himself, the voyagers 'laugh't, at
his laugh-worthy fate' (l. 185). Given Banks's preceding speech, mocking
the voyagers and reminding them of his 'merry prankes' (l. 184), this can
hardly be read as a derisive reaction. Rather, the professional jester and
the men whose likely quest for the services of 'MADAME CAESAR' (l. 180)
and her whores has amounted to nothing, are united in laughter of
common buffoonery.[82] For the reader, though, the laughter is ambiguous. On the one hand, it involves the detached ridicule of a coarse form
of satire, in which Banks and the voyagers alike are constructed as
embodiments, in various forms, of moral dissolution. On the other
hand, reader and characters share in the laughter of the jest, which
carries in its licentiousness and unofficial character a 'positive, regen-
erating, creative meaning'. In Bakhtin's conception, 'laughter in its most
radical, universal, and at the same time gay form emerged from the
depths of folk culture', and in the Renaissance played 'an essential role'
in the work of many prominent writers.[83] An apt physical context for this
laughter, in accordance with the popular culture of Bakhtin's 'market-
place', is evoked in the poem's final domesticating images, of the
'sope-boyler', alehouse-keeper and 'ancient pur-blinde fletcher' (lines
188–90). The fletcher, offered as a mock-epic version of the lecherous
Cretan king Minos, recalls also Cupid in his occupation, and sexual
over-indulgence in his lack of sight and phallic 'high nose' (l. 190).[84]

III

'In memorie' of the voyagers' 'most liquid deed', Jonson declares at the
close of the poem, '[t]he citie since hath rais'd a Pyramide' (lines 193–4).
These lines have an air of topicality, and may refer to a construction
associated with the New River scheme.[85] Their principal effect, how-

ever, is derived from the paradoxical conjunction of dissolute action and solid monument. The 'liquidity' of the deed is multivalent, acknowledging the alcohol which the men consumed, and the confused mix of water and bodily fluids in which they journeyed. The very fluidity of their experience of the city marks the reference to that most ancient of monumental forms as especially ironic. Indeed the poem threatens to dissolve the carefully contrived order of monumental space, encoded as it is with values of physical and ideological durability.[86] Jonson furthers this play of irony in the final couplet: 'And I could wish for their eterniz'd sakes, / My *Muse* had plough'd with his, that sung A-JAX' (lines 195–6). Juxtaposing the inconsequential action with the eternising conceit, Jonson punningly invokes both the ancient epic poetry of Homer and the infamous work of Harington: the poetry of classical mythology and the prose of contemporary toiletry practice.

Jonson's mock-heroic practice in the 'Famous Voyage', as this pun suggests, principally operates by exposing the unmentionable. Whereas prevailing discourses of civic description tended to occlude London's sewage and its underworld of alehouses and commercial sexuality, Jonson's exploration of the Fleet Ditch and its precincts delineates a radically divergent spatiality, characterised by confusion and instability. And while confusion involves the 'filth, stench, noyse' of disorder and decay (l. 9), it also fosters a distinctive creativity, evident as much in the tumultuous character of Jonson's distended epigram, as it is in the grotesque environment of the London underworld. The Fleet Ditch is thus figured as a kind of heterotopia. For Michel Foucault, heterotopic spaces 'are something like counter-sites . . . in which the real sites, all the other sites that can be found within the culture, are simultaneously represented, contested, and inverted. Places of this kind are outside of all places, even though it may be possible to indicate their location in reality.'[87] The environment of Jonson's poem accordingly invites and evades identification, suggesting at once a concrete place of human activity and an alternative spatial principle informing the whole city. His heterotopia is subversive and unsettled, fusing satire and saturnalia, disgust for petty commercialisation and delight in the popular.

The most important analogy in Jonson's works is the transient carnivalesque world grafted onto the city in *Bartholomew Fair*.[88] Like the 'Famous Voyage', this play betrays a familiar Jonsonian ambivalence towards the realm of popular culture. It also contains Littlewit's translation of *Hero and Leander* into a puppet-play of London low-life, a text which marvellously parallels the epigram. The environment of the fair, with its central enclosed sites of makeshift puppet theatre and pig-

woman's booth, is vibrantly grotesque, and pregnant with significance
for the city as a whole. 'Acting as a tavern, a brothel, a public lavatory
and a bank for stolen goods', Neil Rhodes notes, 'the pig-booth is also
the seedy metropolis in microcosm.'[89] The embodiment of that booth is
Ursula, whose vast body is 'all fire, and fat', continually replenished with
pig and ale, though she claims to be in perpetual danger of 'melt[ing]
away to the first woman, a ribbe again' (2.2.50–1). In the 'Famous
Voyage', an analogous female body is mapped onto the city, through
the spatial conceit of a journey up its 'dire passage'. This poem, too,
equivocally endorses the radical materialism and festive populism of the
material bodily principle. The 'Famous Voyage', with its singular blend
of learning and buffoonery, urbanity and jest, constructs a spatiality of
intermeshed dissolution and creativity in the very guts of early modern
London.[90]

NOTES

1. See especially Thomas M. Greene's seminal essay, 'Ben Jonson and the
Centered Self', *Studies in English Literature* 10 (1970), 325–48; and Don E.
Wayne, *Penshurst: The Semiotics of Place and the Poetics of History* (Madison:
University of Wisconsin Press, 1984).
2. Peter E. Medine, 'Object and Intent in Jonson's "Famous Voyage"', *Studies
in English Literature* 15 (1975), 97–110. (And see also Bruce Thomas Boehrer,
'The Ordure of Things: Ben Jonson, Sir John Harington, and the Culture
of Excrement in Early Modern England', James Hirsh (ed.), *New Perspectives
on Ben Jonson* (London: Associated University Presses, 1997), pp. 174–96.)
References to Jonson's poems are from *Ben Jonson: Works*, ed. C. H.
Herford, Percy and Evelyn Simpson, 11 vols. (Oxford University Press,
1954–70), vol. VIII.
3. Lawrence Manley, *Literature and Culture in Early Modern London* (Cambridge
University Press, 1995), pp. 87, 422, 515; Steven Mullaney, *The Place of the
Stage: License, Play, and Power in Renaissance England* (London: University of
Chicago Press, 1988).
4. Algernon Charles Swinburne, *A Study of Ben Jonson* [1889], ed. Howard B.
Norland (Lincoln: University of Nebraska Press, 1969), p. 95.
5. 'Ben Jonson', *The Cambridge Companion to English Poetry: Donne to Marvell*, ed.
Thomas N. Corns (Cambridge University Press, 1993), p. 152.
6. Sara J. van den Berg, *The Action of Ben Jonson's Poetry* (Newark: University of
Delaware Press, 1987), p. 104.
7. Medine, 'Object and Intent', 98. Helgerson is broadly in agreement with
this interpretation ('Ben Jonson', p. 152).
8. George Burke Johnston, *Ben Jonson: Poet* (New York: Columbia University
Press, 1945), p. 24.
9. J. G. Nichols, *The Poetry of Ben Jonson* (London: Routledge and Kegan Paul,

1969), p. 108. The distinction between mock-heroic and burlesque is adopted from Gilbert Highet, *The Anatomy of Satire* (Princeton University Press, 1967).

10. The seminal work in this field is Henri Lefebvre, *The Production of Space*, trans. Donald Nicholson-Smith (Oxford: Blackwell, 1991); see especially pp. 34, 36–7.

11. Edward Soja notes that '[t]he presentation of concrete spatiality is always wrapped in the complex and diverse re-presentations of human perception and cognition, without any necessity of direct and determined correspondence between the two. These representations . . . play a powerful role in shaping the spatiality of social life.' (*Postmodern Geographies: The Reassertion of Space in Critical Social Theory* (London: Verso, 1989), p. 121.)

12. I am adapting here the conception of the grotesque developed in Neil Rhodes, *Elizabethan Grotesque* (London: Routledge and Kegan Paul, 1980), especially p. 7.

13. See Edmund Wilson, 'Morose Ben Jonson', *The Triple Thinkers: Twelve Essays on Literary Subjects* (New York: Oxford University Press, 1947), pp. 213–22.

14. See Lawrence Manley, who adopts the notion of 'mentalities of settlement' as the foundation of his study of *Literature and Culture* (p. 16).

15. John Stow, *A Survey of London* [1603], 2 vols., ed. Charles Lethbridge Kingsford (Oxford: Clarendon Press, 1908), vol. I, especially pp. 139, 165.

16. Manley, *Literature and Culture*, pp. 159–60, 240.

17. Michel de Certeau, *The Practice of Everyday Life*, trans. Steven Rendall (Berkeley: University of California Press, 1984), p. xiv, and chapter 7, 'Walking in the City'.

18. *Ibid.*, p. 103.

19. See Paul Griffiths, *Youth and Authority: Formative Experiences in England 1560–1640* (Oxford: Clarendon Press, 1996), p. 209. (Dr Griffiths has written two articles, as yet unpublished, which deal with this matter in greater detail.)

20. [George Peele?], *The Merrie Conceited Jests of George Peele* [1607] (London: G.P. for F. Faulkner, 1627).

21. *Shameless Joan: Or, The Old Woman of Finsbury*, in *The Pepys Ballads*, ed. W. G. Day, 5 vols. (Cambridge: Brewer, 1987), vol. IV, p. 423. The ballad is not dated, nor is it listed in the short-title catalogues for the seventeenth and eighteenth centuries; however its survival in the Pepys collection suggests likely publication in the latter half of the seventeenth century.

22. *The most dangerous and memorable adventure of Richard Ferris* [1590] and *Kemps nine days wonder* [1600] are reprinted in *An English Garner: Social England Illustrated, A Collection of XVIIth Century Tracts*, ed. Andrew Lang (London: A. Constable and Co., 1903), pp. 101–14, 139–62. On Taylor, see *The Pennyles Pilgrimage* and *The Praise of Hemp-Seed. with the Vovage of Mr. Roger Bird and the Writer hereof in a Boat of browne-paper, from London to Quinborough in Kent*, both reprinted in his *All the Workes* (1630).

23. Max W. Thomas, '*Kemps Nine Daies*: Wonder Dancing Carnival into Market', *PMLA* 107 (1992), 511–23.

24. Greene, 'Ben Jonson and the Centered Self', 329, 326–7.

25. Richard S. Peterson, *Imitation and Praise in the Poems of Ben Jonson* (New Haven and London: Yale University Press, 1981), p. 42.

26. 'Inviting a Friend to Supper' (*Epigrammes* 101), lines 28–30.

27. Michael Strachan, *The Life and Adventures of Thomas Coryate* (London: Oxford University Press, 1962), pp. 124–5.

28. Thomas Coryate, *Coryats Crudities*, facsimile edn (London: Scolar Press, 1978), sig. A1v.

29. In his subsequent publication, Coryate sends his 'dutifull respect' to Jonson, who is listed among 'lovers of vertue, and literature'. (*Greeting from the Court of the Great Mogul* [1616], facsimile edn (Amsterdam: Da Capo Press, 1968), pp. 43, 45.)

30. Medine, 'Object and Intent', 100–1, 103.

31. Jonson's attitudes towards astrology are well known. Medine documents his similarly low opinion of *Don Quixote*, which was widely perceived in early seventeenth-century England as merely a popular romance ('Object and Intent', 101–3).

32. *Ibid.*, 100.

33. *Ibid.*, 101.

34. Medine himself demonstrates the search for prostitutes as a possible motivation for the voyage ('Object and Intent', 104–5).

35. In *The Alchemist*, Sir Epicure Mammon dreams of an elixir that will give him 'a back / . . . that shall be as tough / As HERCULES, to encounter fiftie a night' (2.2.37–9). See further Gordon Williams, *A Dictionary of Sexual Language and Imagery in Shakespearean and Stuart Literature*, 3 vols. (London and Atlantic Highlands: Athlone Press, 1994), vol. II, p. 662.

36. *Ibid.*, p. 660.

37. John Strype, *A Survey Of the Cities of London and Westminster*, 2 vols. (London: n.p., 1720), vol. I, book 1, p. 191. Stow himself is less expansive, speaking of Bridewell as a place 'wherein a great number of vagrant persons be now set a worke, and relieved at the charges of the cittizens' (*Survey of London*, vol. II, p. 145).

38. Thomas Middleton, *A Fair Quarrel* (*Works*, ed. A. H. Bullen, 8 vols. (London: John C. Nimmo, 1885), vol. IV), 4.1.39. See further Edward H. Sugden, *A Topographical Dictionary to the Works of Shakespeare and His Fellow Dramatists* (Publications of the University of Manchester (no. 168), 1925), pp. 252–3.

39. Stow, *Survey of London*, vol. I, pp. 11–19.

40. *Ibid.*, p. 266.

41. Manley, *Literature and Culture*, p. 225.

42. 'This Is Not a Pipe: Water Supply, Incontinent Sources, and the Leaky Body Politic', Richard Burt and John Michael Archer (eds.), *Enclosure Acts: Sexuality, Property, and Culture in Early Modern England* (Ithaca and London: Cornell University Press, 1994), p. 215.

43. Even Stow's enthusiasm is surpassed by *An Apologie of the Cittie of London*, appended to his text, which declares that 'none other place is so plentifully watered with springs, as London is' (*Survey of London*, vol. II, p. 220).

44. *Ibid.*, vol. I, p. 128.
45. *Ibid.*, p. 13.
46. On pissing alleys, see Sugden, *Topographical Dictionary*, p. 414; and Gail Kern Paster, *The Body Embarrassed: Drama and the Disciplines of Shame in Early Modern England* (Ithaca: Cornell University Press, 1993), p. 35n.
47. Anthony Munday's continuation of the *Survey* amply redresses this matter.
48. J. W. Gough, *Sir Hugh Myddleton: Entrepreneur and Engineer* (Oxford: Clarendon Press, 1964), pp. 24–58; he documents the aim to cleanse the city ditches at p. 28.
49. Manley, *Literature and Culture*, pp. 271, 285.
50. The phrase 'foysting Arse' is used in a contemporary poem to which Jonson alludes at lines 107–10, 'The Parliament Fart' (*Musarum Deliciae: Or, The Muses Recreation* [1655], ed. John Mennes and James Smith, facsimile edn (Delmar, New York: Scholars' Facsimiles and Reprints, 1985), p. 65).
51. Paster, *The Body Embarrassed*, p. 11.
52. Williams, *Dictionary of Sexual Language*, vol. I, p. 399. The word is used to denote an arse in 'The Parliament Fart' (*Musarum Deliciae*, p. 65).
53. See Paster, *The Body Embarrassed*, chap. 1.
54. *The Description of England*, ed. Georges Edelen (Ithaca: Cornell University Press, 1968), p. 189; quoted in E. J. Burford, *Bawds and Lodgings: A History of the London Bankside Brothels* (London: Owen, 1976), p. 138.
55. Williams, *Dictionary of Sexual Language*, vol. III, p. 1251. In *The Faerie Queene*, Error 'poured forth out of her hellish sinke / Her fruitfull cursed spawne of serpents small' (1.i.22).
56. Margaret Pelling, 'Appearance and Reality: Barber-Surgeons, the Body and Disease', A. L. Beier and Roger Finlay (eds.), *London 1500–1700: The Making of the Metropolis* (London and New York: Longman, 1986), p. 99.
57. Williams, *Dictionary of Sexual Language*, vol. III, pp. 1170–2.
58. 'Bone-ache' is a euphemism for syphilis in *The Alchemist*, 3.2.37 (Williams, *Dictionary of Sexual Language*, vol. I, pp. 129–30).
59. Rhodes, *Elizabethan Grotesque*, p. 4.
60. Mikhail Bakhtin, *Rabelais and His World*, trans. Hélène Iswolsky (Cambridge, Mass.: MIT, 1968), pp. 26–7.
61. The Bakhtinian theorising of Peter Stallybrass and Allon White clarifies the significance of the bodily orifices in the grotesque: 'It is an image of impure corporeal bulk with its orifices (mouth, flared nostrils, anus) yawning wide and its lower regions (belly, legs, feet, buttocks and genitals) given priority over its upper regions (head, 'spirit', reason)'. (*The Politics and Poetics of Transgression* (Ithaca: Cornell University Press, 1986), p. 9.)
62. 'vestibulum ante ipsum primisque in faucibus Orci / Luctus et ultrices posuere culilia Curae, / pallentesque habitant Morbi tristisque Senectus / et Metus et malesuada Fames ac turpis Egestas, / terribiles visu formae, Letumque Labosque; / tum consanguineus Leti Sopor et mala mentis / Gaudia, mortiferumque adverso in limine Bellum / ferreique Eumenidum thalami et Discordia demens, / vipereum crinem vittis innexa cruentis.'

Aeneid, VI, lines 273–81; translations from the Loeb edition, trans. H. Rushton Fairclough (Cambridge, Mass.: Harvard University Press, 1935.)

63. *Purity and Danger: An Analysis of Concepts of Pollution and Taboo* (London: Routledge, 1966), p. 5.

64. See Wilson, 'Morose Ben Jonson'.

65. See the important discussion of Norbert Elias, in *The Civilizing Process: 'The History of Manners' and 'State Formation and Civilization'*, trans. Edmund Jephcott (Oxford: Blackwell, 1994), chapter 3.

66. For contemporary associations of (Jewish) usurers with faeces, see Peter J. Smith, *Social Shakespeare: Aspects of Renaissance Dramaturgy and Contemporary Society* (London: Macmillan, 1995), pp. 166–8.

67. Miles Weatherall, 'Drug Treatment and the Rise in Pharmacology', Roy Porter (ed.), *The Cambridge Illustrated History of Medicine* (Cambridge University Press, 1996), pp. 250–2.

68. Burford, *Bawds and Lodgings*, p. 173.

69. Herford and Simpson tentatively date the poem 'about 1610' (*Ben Jonson: Works*, vol. XI, p. 29); however their evidence is merely conjectural, and Jonson may have written or revised the piece at any time up to its publication in the Folio of 1616.

70. Commonly titled 'The Parliament Fart' in manuscript sources, the poem is printed as 'The Fart censured in the Parliament House' in *Musarum Deliciae*, pp. 65–71.

71. Compare Medine, who interprets the allusion as an earnest criticism of the standard of parliamentary debate ('Object and Intent', 108).

72. On the semiotics of the fart, see further Peter J. Smith, 'Ajax by Any Other Name Would Smell as Sweet: Shakespeare, Harington and Onomastic Scatology', André Lascombes (ed.), *Tudor Theatre: Emotion in the Theatre* (Bern: Peter Lang, 1996), pp. 125–58 (especially pp. 133–4).

73. 'My Picture left in Scotland', line 17; in *Works*, vol. VIII, pp. 149–50. On his 'gluttony', see, for example, 'To Penshurst', line 68; in *Works*, vol. VIII, pp. 93–6.

74. Bakhtin, *Rabelais and His World*, p. 19.

75. Williams, *Dictionary of Sexual Language*, vol. I, pp. 214–6.

76. *Ibid.*, p. 455.

77. *The Dictionary of National Biography*, ed. Sir Leslie Stephen and Sir Sidney Lee, 22 vols. (London: Oxford University Press, 1917), *s.v.* Banks.

78. *Tarltons Jests* [1613]; facsimile edn, *Kemp's nine days wonder [and] Tarlton's jests*, intr. J. P. Feather (New York and London: Johnson Reprint Corp., 1972), sig. C2v.

79. The ox in Livy is accorded a weightier statement, portentous of military and political calamity, 'saying, "Rome, for thyself beware" ('Roma, cave tibi')'. (*Livy*, Loeb Classical Library, trans. Evan T. Sage, 14 vols. (Cambridge, Mass.: Harvard University Press, 1958), vol. X, XXV, xxi, pp. 60–1.)

80. *Maroccus Extaticus: or, Bankes Bay Horse in a Trance* [1595], ed. Edward F.

Rimbault, *Early English Poetry, Ballads, and Popular Literature of the Middle Ages*, 30 vols. (London: Percy Society, 1844), vol. IX, p. 15.

81. The *DNB* records that Banks 'continued to give entertainment in London' after his return from the continent. Its earliest reference to the supposed rumour of Banks' execution is from this poem.

82. Madame Caesar also appears as a brothel-keeper in *The Alchemist*, 5.4.142.

83. Bakhtin, *Rabelais and His World*, pp. 71–2.

84. On the association of excessive sexual activity and blindness, see Williams, *Dictionary of Sexual Language*, vol. I, pp. 455–6.

85. Ian Donaldson's edition suggests a possible reference to the New River scheme (Jonson, *Poems* (Oxford University Press, 1975), p. 84).

86. See Lefebvre, *The Production of Space*, pp. 220–3.

87. 'Of Other Spaces', trans. Jay Miskowiec *Diacritics* 16 (1986), 24. See also Edward W. Soja's commentary on Foucault, in *Thirdspace: Journeys to Los Angeles and Other Real-and-Imagined Places* (Oxford and Cambridge, Mass.: Blackwell, 1996), pp. 154–63.

88. Compare Foucault on fairgrounds as heterotopias ('Of Other Spaces', 26).

89. Rhodes, *Elizabethan Grotesque*, p. 142.

90. A version of this chapter was published in *Early Modern Literary Studies*, Special Issue 3 (1998). I am grateful for the comments of Joanne Woolway Grenfell, Kristin Hammett, Richard Helgerson, Bill Maidment, Anthony Miller, Peter J. Smith and the editors of this volume.

CHAPTER 10

Imaginary journeys: Spenser, Drayton, and the poetics of national space

Bernhard Klein

Writing about the cultural transmission of the national idea, Homi Bhabha notes that '[n]ations, like narratives, lose their origins in the myths of time and only fully realize their horizon in the mind's eye.'[1] What concerns me here is less Bhabha's notion of the temporal disruptions and displacements specific to the modern myth of nationhood than the spatial metaphor of the mental *horizon* which silently frames the national image in a language borrowed from geography. In early modern Britain, the 'nation' lent itself equally smoothly to its articulation in spatial terms,[2] acting as both the implicit referent and the authorising instance of much geographical discourse. Yet to imagine the nation as a spatial entity was never a socially neutral exercise, and each textual version of the national territory had to negotiate not only its adequate external shape but also, and importantly, its internal social configuration. In this essay, my aim is to show how the space of the nation was mapped out in two massive poetic narratives written within a few decades of each other, Edmund Spenser's *Faerie Queene* (1590/96) and Michael Drayton's *Poly-Olbion* (1612/22). The link between Spenser and Drayton is most often described as that between master and student: if Spenser was the Elizabethan prince of poets, Drayton was his most industrious disciple in the Jacobean age, the foremost 'Spenserian' poet of his time.[3] Yet other than the nostalgic longing for a lost Elizabethan sensibility governing *Poly-Olbion*'s productive context, these two monumental works show few signs of internal contact; and the essay that follows looks to explore not their similarities but the opposition between them in terms of their contrasting conceptions of space. To prepare the ground for this discussion I will first briefly consider two contemporary works of national chorography that equally constructed different spatial images of the emerging nation, William Harrison's *Historicall Description of the Islande of Britayne* (1577) and William Camden's *Britannia* (1586).

I

What, from a contemporary perspective, was the use value of a map? One of the most extensive answers to this question was offered by Cyprian Lucar whose manual on surveying, published in 1590, is ample evidence that the analysis of maps should not be restricted to a discussion of their topographical data. For Lucar a map needed first to inform about the local practice of agriculture, the situation of the ground, vegetation, forests and parks; then about harbours, ports and other landing-places, the size of the king's navy kept there, the tidal rhythm 'and whatsoeuer else that said described land hath strange, new, notable, and commodious.' Maps should also include information about houses and buildings, settlements and fortifications, climatic conditions, rivers, bridges and roads, the legal status of towns, 'whether the people there are wittie and of quick conceite', their moral virtues, the number of inhabitants and soldiers, the extent and storage of their weaponry. Lucar ends by urging the cartographer to mention 'whether the said described place is by nature, or art so scituated, as that it cannot be scaled with ladders, beaten downe with great ordinance, or vndermined to be blowne vp with gunpouder'.[4] Evidently, maps also helped destroy what had taken such effort to describe in detail. The excessive demands made on the map-maker's skills in this passage illustrate that the process of transferring world into map required more than proficiency in technical surveying. Lucar does not conceive of maps as geometrical accounts of superficial topographies but as strategic instruments of knowledge whose function was to add vital topographical information to their economic, political and ethnographic scripts. Yet his comments clearly exceed the concept of a map as a visual image and their relevance is more readily grasped when applied to textual rather than cartographic descriptions: written chorographies, a genre that began to flourish in late Tudor Britain, contain much of the type of information Lucar claimed to belong to the domain of the map.

As a genre, written chorographies provided topographically organised accounts of individual regions, not narratives of political events; the chorographer's method was antiquarian, not historical. William Lambarde, in his *Perambulation of Kent*, stated that it was his 'purpose speciallye ... to write a *Topographie*, or description of places, and no

Chronographie, or storie of times'.[5] Concerned with space rather than time, with place rather than person, late Tudor and early Stuart antiquarianism looked back to the pioneering work of John Leland, royal librarian under Henry VIII, who had assembled, on a nationwide itinerary lasting several years, a vast collection of notes intended to form the basis of a multi-volume chorographical description of Britain. In a promotional tract presented to the king (and later edited by John Bale) he described himself as 'totallye enflamed wyth a loue, to se throughlye all those partes of thys your opulent and ample realme'. His subsequent travels were so exhaustive, he wrote, that 'there is almost neyther cape nor baye, hauen, creke or pere, ryuer or confluence of ryuers, breches, washes, lakes, meres, fenny waters, mountaynes, valleys, mores, hethes, forestes, woodes, cyties, burges, castels, pryncypall manor places, monasteryes, and colleges, but I haue seane them, and noted in so doynge a whole worlde of thynges verye memorable.'[6] Leland's project, unprecedented in scope and intent, clearly centred on the land itself as the source for a description capable of capturing the essence of Britain. But confronted with an undigested mass of data Leland was unable to give his discoveries a coherent textual structure. His fate, contemporaries reported, was to go insane over the vast material he had collected.[7] Despite his failure Leland inspired much subsequent chorographical writing and was acknowledged as a central source in both Harrison's *Description* (1577) and Camden's *Britannia* (1586), the two most substantial national chorographies to be written in the latter half of the sixteenth century. Leland's description was intended to embrace a comprehensive 'British' view of its subject matter, a model adopted (and even expanded to include Ireland) both in the *Britannia* and in *Holinshed's Chronicles* (which opened with Harrison's *Description*). Yet although Harrison and Camden shared Leland's emotional response to his native soil and continued, in a sense, his search for an appropriate textual format, their respective constructions of the social space of the nation operate within opposing conceptual frameworks.

Following the medieval model of prefacing historical narratives with topographical introductions, Harrison's *Description* offers 'a broadly imagined, geographical, social, and institutional account of a country, whose function is to lay down the base for the history to follow.'[8] The text provides a spatial setting for the ensuing chronicle but moves beyond a mere illustration of England's topography[9] by addressing a variety of social, economic and political themes, ranging from topics of national interest, such as the structure of society, the legal system, the distribution of fairs and markets, etc., to regional peculiarities, like the 'infinite number of swannes'[10] near London Bridge or the Halifax public execution ritual which requires the active participation of the local populace. Though dominated by a patriotic stance the text is frequently interspersed with complaints about the country's inner decay and the moral corruption brought about by cultural and economic change. The material, Harrison explained in the preface, was gathered from a variety of sources. He had consulted all available reference works, among them Leland's notes, 'bookes vtterly mangled, defaced with wet, and weather',[11] corresponded with residents throughout the country and discussed his findings with his fellow antiquaries. The result of this scholarly exercise is a topographical description that attempts to marshal its material through a loose sequence of thematic sections: 'of cities and towns', 'of palaces belonging to the prince', 'of the building and furniture of our houses', 'of prouision made for the poore' are typical chapter headings. In moving across a multi-faceted spatial reality, the *Description* looks at topics as diverse as England's architecture, its inns and fairs, forests and parks, law courts and universities; it describes local customs and the dietary habits of its population; it includes passing observations on daily life and bitter complaints about the vagaries of contemporary fashion; it sketches out the history of England's political landscape, its ancient road system and current clerical and administrative divisions.

Topographically, the text is organised around an account of England's rivers, a dominant descriptive convention in the chorographical tradition. Rivers are the dynamic element of landscape, they produce the movement and fluidity chorography requires in order to overcome the impression of representational stasis. When Harrison, an armchair geographer who never ventured far beyond his local parish, describes his own work as an imaginary journey – 'I sayled about my country within the compasse of my study'[12] –, the travelling metaphor is not mere poetic flourish but a constitutive principle of the dynamic space constructed in the text of the *Description*. Bringing the first stage of his textual river journey to an end, Harrison looks back over the terrain his writing has covered: '[F]rom the hauen of Southampton, by south vnto the Twede, that parteth England and Scotland, by north (if you go backward contrary to the course of my description) you shall finde it so exacte, as beside a fewe bye ryuers to be touched hereafter, you shall not neede to vse any further aduise for the finding and falles of the aforesayd streames.'[13] Sending his readers backwards through the linear sequence of his chapters, Harrison gestures at the multiplicity of possible journeys across the map of the nation, through its physical, cultural and political space. But although the second edition of *Holinshed's Chronicles* includes a direct reference to Saxton's atlas at this point, Harrison's textual cartography cannot be fully reduced to the figure of the map. In tracing England's rivers across the national territory it is interlaced with another mode of representing space, the itinerary. The description of place, according to Michel de Certeau, 'oscillates between the terms of an alternative: either *seeing* (the knowledge of an order of places) or *going* (spatializing actions).'[14] The former is the privilege of the map, projecting on to a plane, and presenting to full view, a totality of spatial relations; the latter belongs to the order of the itinerary or tour, exploring space through movement and operative action. Harrison's *Description* fluctuates between these two moments, between a space planned and centrally regulated, and a space of lived experience, shaped and used by its inhabitants, defined principally through its social dimension.

Against this background of a structural network of routes and trajectories across England's topography, Harrison's 'poeticall voiage'[15] takes the reader through a seemingly incoherent series of thematic chapters, foregrounding a degree of diversity and fluidity that challenges any monolithic view of the nation's cultural and social configuration. The text provides the elements for alternative narratives, other discursive voyages, that might convey spatial experiences of a complex social realm at odds with the dominant royal perspective inscribed in the massive chronicle history that follows. In offering cultural diversity as a structural principle of its textual progress, the *Description* is perhaps better considered a conceptual alternative to, rather than merely the imperfect precursor of, William Camden's hugely successful *Britannia*, whose first publication in 1586 coincided to a year with the second (and last) contemporary edition of *Holinshed's Chronicles*. The *Britannia* grew vastly in bulk over the years and the substantially revised Latin edition of 1607, translated three years later by Philemon Holland, 'stands as the central achievement of the English chorographical tradition.'[16] Camden's conception of national space corresponds to the synthesis of a unifying cartographic order. Like the maps in Saxton's atlas (1579), the *Britannia* seizes on the county as the central unit of chorographical description, devoting a full chapter to each: the partial view of the individual shire validates the overarching national frame of reference. The horizontal division of a political landscape, essentially an administrative pattern, thus precedes all further detail on British topography.

Masking its textual linearity, its successive unfolding in time, the *Britannia* treats space from the outset as the object of an immediate knowledge, imitating the totalising approach of the map: as if at every stage of the narrative the space of the nation is 'always already visually present, fully offered to full view and potential speech.'[17]

In opening the voluminous tome with a historical section that introduces the much longer perambulation of the individual counties, Camden turns on its head the medieval model *Holinshed's Chronicles* had adopted: in the *Britannia*, history sets the stage for geography. It may indeed be 'difficult to give an adequate indication of the contents of the *Britannia*',[18] yet the topographical descriptions of the counties follow a more or less coherent format. Outlining his agenda, Camden notes that '[i]n the several discourses of every of [the Provinces or Shires of Britaine], I wil declare as plainly and as briefly as I can, who were their ancient Inhabitants; what is the reason of their names; how they are bounded; what is the nature of the soile; what places of antiquity and good account are therein; what Dukes likewise or Earles have beene in ech one since the Norman Conquest.'[19] Preoccupied with names and boundaries, with genealogies and the continuity of human settlement, the *Britannia* streamlines its topographical and antiquarian information into the celebration of a landscape shaped by successive generations of the leading families of the gentry. Even when the description follows a county's rivers, these are shown to be flowing exclusively around stately mansions, ancient castles and private parks. The equation of national space with the realm of a social elite, of which a historicized landscape bears witness, guarantees the stability of a political order and allows its translation into the static coexistence of individual plots on the imaginary plane surface of cartographic projection. In contrast to the mobile landscape of Harrison's *Description*, space in the *Britannia* is less the product of social interaction, defined across a wide spectrum of possible readings, than a political narrative claiming the nation as the exclusive domain of its landowning 'Dukes' and 'Earles'. In employing the land itself as the central element of historical stability, Camden's gentry-oriented representations fashion Britain as a static spatial (and hence social) order, markedly at odds with Harrison's vibrant cultural landscapes. Geographical discourse is enlisted to construct a national topography as the correlate of a social space compatible with the political interests not of a broadly defined national community, but of a narrow 'brotherhood' of landowners.

II

In terms of the various spatial constructs implicit in the national project, the distinction between *The Faerie Queene* and *Poly-Olbion* is partly analogous to the shift from itinerary to map which characterises the reworking of Harrison's fluid national topography into Camden's rigid atlas structure. Yet by giving rise to a vision that processes national space through specific literary and mythological frameworks, the poetic attention geographic material attracts in the work of Spenser and Drayton pushes this duality to a higher level. Put briefly, I will argue that *The Faerie Queene* persistently invites its readers to engage actively in the dynamic performance of space, while *Poly-Olbion* unfolds its national scenario against the secure background of a fixed and intransigent geographical order. In light of the generic affiliation between Drayton's *opus magnum* and the chorographic tradition considered above, I will disregard chronological sequence and begin my discussion with *Poly-Olbion*.

The awkwardness and forced conceit of 'Drayton's painful *Poly-Olbion*'[20] have baffled many readers, and some critics have even suggested that its overpowering length – fifteen thousand mighty alexandrines – should not be mistaken for an indication of its representative status in the Drayton canon. Jean Brink, in the most recent monograph on the poet's work, thinks that 'we have paid too much attention to [Drayton's] chorographical poem and too little to his satire. *Poly-Olbion* ... has always appealed only to the "curious antiquaries"'.[21] Whatever the reasons for its failure to attract a wider readership, it will be argued here that *Poly-Olbion* should not be dismissed so easily as the inexplicable slip of an otherwise decent enough poet. Its textual conception of national space is hardly as belated or backward-looking as the poem's popularity among 'curious antiquaries' seems to imply; and in its attempted fusion (yet actual separation) of various discourses focused on an emergent sense of national identity – poetic, historiographical, cartographic – it creates in the figure of the invisible 'Muse' a fitting emblem for the disembodied nature of modern functional space.

In writing *Poly-Olbion*, Drayton's object was at least partially a versification of Camden's *Britannia*, or rather, its 'digestion in a poem' – a project fully summarised on the title-page: *Poly-Olbion. or A Chorographicall Description of Tracts, Riuers, Mountaines, Forests, and other Parts of this renowned Isle of Great Britaine, With intermixture of the Most Remarquable Stories, Antiquities, Wonders, Rarityes, Pleasures, and Commodities of the same: Digested in a Poem.*[22] The implicit equation in the word 'digested' between a bodily function and the mental accommodation of disparate data into a single text is hardly accidental. The governing trope of the poem, as various critics have noted, is the familiar Renaissance conception of *discordia concors* – the yoking together of opposites to produce structural harmony – which Drayton achieves through his reliance on somatic metaphors: in *Poly-Olbion*, the 'organizing form or conceptual myth' which 'define[s] the relationship of disparate parts to the whole even as they suggest its multivalent meanings' is the image of the 'human body, a peculiarly apt metaphor for the kind of organic unity Drayton wishes to predicate of England.'[23] Casting the land as a human body, *chorography* is subtly *choreographed*[24] to figure as an animated and deeply historicised landscape, producing a composite image where isolated natural features are woven at every turn into the broad canvas of a unified whole.[25] As the Muse proceeds on her journey through England and Wales, place consistently activates historical memory: the nation turns into poem through an evocation of its geographical territory which in turn can be achieved only by firmly imposing on the land the chronology of British history. This parallel exploration of temporal and spatial trajectories through the 'renowned Isle of Great Britaine' converges in a ceaseless celebration of the rich and varied countryside of England and Wales. Diverse landscape features – hills and valleys; rivers and forests; bays, pastures and plains – all get the chance to sing their own praises, to engage in amorous contests or bitter rivalries, and to advertise the advantages of their specific natural attributes.

A national space exclusively animated by the spirits of the natural landscape, with little or no reference to the resident gentry and 'their proprietary attachment to the land',[26] relies heavily on the triumph of the cartographic paradigm. Indeed, the representational work of *Poly-Olbion*, filtering images of landscape through the visual powers of the invisible Muse, is unthinkable without the conceptual precedent of the map: the gaze that guides our own view as readers, that acts as an intermediary agent between land and text, is identical with the view of the modern cartographer. Early on in the poem, 'smooth-brow'd' (3, 122) Salisbury Plain defends its wide open space against 'barb'rous woods' (111) in whose 'darke and sleepie shades' hang 'mists and rotten fogs / ... in the gloomie thicks, and make unstedfast bogs, / By dropping from the boughs, the o're-growen trees among, / With Caterpillars kells, and duskie cobwebs hong.' (117–20) Dark and impenetrable woods block the unrestricted view a map provides but 'upon the goodlie *Plaines*' the light of the sun spreads into every corner of the terrain,

illuminating 'this upper world' (128) with the glaring lucidity of its
'farre-shooting sight' (130). Such passages emphasise the indebtedness of
Drayton's poetic construction of national space to the penetrating
clarity of the cartographer's view. Indeed, the poem frequently draws on
the technical vocabulary of the land surveyor to describe the activity of
the peripatetic Muse: she 'measures out this Plaine; and then survayes
those groves' (3, 348), she 'take[s] a perfect view / Of all the wandring
Streames' (5, 90–1), she 'look[s] from aloft' to '[survey] coy *Severns*
course' (7, 3–4), and she 'survayeth' the land alternatively with an
'amorous' (8, 3) or an 'ambitious' (9, 2) eye. Like Camden, Drayton's
Muse views the land from the lofty position enabled by cartographic
representation, she inspects national space not as the 'raw material' of
landscape but as an image already filtered, already subjected to the
scrutiny of the surveying eye: the space thus inspected is fully exposed in
the act of representation; the surface of the land yields completely to her
observant eye; and her travelling vocabulary owes its idiom of movement and action entirely to the finger moving across the map. It is
important in this context that the Muse never enters the realm of the
visible herself; like a 'point' in Euclid she remains elusive and insubstantial throughout the poem. In the same sense that the implied
chorographer of the *Britannia*, equipped with preconceived principles of
classification, resembles not so much a genuine traveller but a surveyor
viewing landscape through a textual theodolite, the Muse appears as the
prosopopeia of the cartographic gaze, as the poetic abstraction of the
visual synthesis offered by the geometric scale-map.

If the central function of the Muse could be described as the attempt
to impose structural unity on what is experienced as a fragmented
world, to re-discover an essential coherence in a geographical space
defined by quarrelling rivers and warring mountains, this textual attempt at harmonisation finds its most prominent complementary visual
feature in the inclusion of thirty maps that preface the individual songs
of the poem. These are curious maps, to say the least, but although
many critics have noted their indebtedness to Saxton's atlas few have
bothered to inquire into the nature of this derivative transfer.[27] In each
case the terrain depicted corresponds roughly to the poetic description
which follows, but the topographical information on offer is radically
reduced: disregarding signs of human settlement such as towns or
villages they focus almost exclusively on rivers, each graphically animated by its personal nymph; and the selection of toponyms spread over
the cartographic surface follows no recognisable principle of order

(other than the need to cross-reference the place-names mentioned in the poem). Compared to the maps of Saxton or Speed, from which Drayton's maps derive, the most obvious difference is their complete unwillingness to present landscape as a product of human civilisation, as a cultural space shaped by the continuous presence of human society: these maps utterly ignore traces of the land's inhabitants; people are merely the accidental product of an environment that precedes all human interference with landscape.[28] Drayton's Britain – in marked contrast to Camden's – is exclusively inhabited by mythical creatures growing out of rivers or occupying the solitary hilltops of an ancient immutable landscape.

Lacking all further ornamental framework, these maps hover awkwardly between their referential attachment to a real landscape and the Edenic idealisation of cornucopian abundance. What appears as the most striking aspect of the maps in *Poly-Olbion* is their mythic quality: the landscapes they chart seem utterly removed from the political territory registered in earlier cartographic work. One immediate indication of this discontinuity is the missing division into counties. Drayton's maps (though produced by the same engraver as Camden's[29]) circumscribe vaguely defined geographical regions, not administrative units. In fact, the maps in *Poly-Olbion* are hardly recognisable *as* maps, let alone as maps of Britain: the featureless terrain resists even the most common cartographic impulse to focus on borders, and their geographic information hardly offers more than a bare 'summary' of the most prominent landscape elements, rivers and mountains. Their central function, I suggest, is to imagine the link with the subsequent poetic excursions across their surface as the implicit narrative of national purity which constructs the smoothness of the land's temporal transit from mythic prehistory (map) through the events leading up to the present (poem). The undisturbed constancy of this parallel move through space and time is further implied by the iconography of the maps' river network which features curving streams meandering wave-like across the terrain, like the pulsating veins of the national body, or the fertile roots implanted in the imperial garden.

But while the conscious symbolism of these maps may sustain Drayton's dream of an original historical purity of landscape recognisable in the very lie of the land, they fail to hide the tension implicit in *Poly-Olbion*'s multi-layered representational work; a tension that threatens to obliterate his project of national synthesis based on cartographic homogenisation. If the maps are attempts to capture in mythological imagery an eternal and original truth about land, parading before the viewer a pictorial version of Britain's divinely ordained geography, they also admit their uselessness as a means of social and political orientation in the present. For the Britain of Drayton's thirty songs, as opposed to the Britain of his maps, is unable to continue the timeless mythology of its cartographic 'prefaces'. Instead, it engages in a narrative of constant historical change. At the same time as this symbolic cartography offers to depoliticise Britain, an attempt that is itself already reliant on a cartographic discourse firmly locked in a contest over the accurate representation of the social space of the nation, the text of the poem affirms the historical reality of continuous political factionalism. In reducing to a mere sporting contest the bitter rivalries between the constituent parts of its personified landscape, the nation *Poly-Olbion* imagines poetically may repeat the cartographic dream of an original spatial harmony, capable of transcending all social difference, but hardly serves as a model for a nation shaped by invasions and internal political conflicts, or as the image of a society in transition.

The function of John Selden's historical commentary on the first eighteen songs of *Poly-Olbion* could be seen in similar terms. The relation of these notes to the poetic text reproduces the relationship between history and geography in the poem itself, where the temporal is equally treated as little more than a loose collection of footnotes to the spatial. The overt separation between *story* and *history* on the pages of *Poly-Olbion*, even if the categorial distinction between truth and fiction was still a fragile construction when the poem was being written,[30] serves to further disrupt any overall sense of spatial coherence, adding to the conflict between the visual and the verbal, between the poetic and cartographic trajectories of the book. For in its triadic structure of map, poem and history, *Poly-Olbion* seems less to unite disparate areas of knowledge in a comprehensive account than to underline their dissimilar nature, presenting to contemporary readers an image not of eternal union but of internal fragmentation, affecting nation and knowledge alike. What the introductory maps attempt to cover up, the existence of discord and dissent, is re-imported into the poem through the explicit segregation, and mutual incompatibility, of the discursive communities assembled on its pages.

III

The difference between the respective spatial models organising the poetic worlds of *Poly-Olbion* and *The Faerie Queene* is best formulated, I suggest, as the opposition between static and dynamic visions, between still life and performance. Where Drayton's poetry persistently aims to offer a full and final description of its chosen theme, working meticulously (like a map) through a complete and immobile pictorial enclosure, Spenser's verse never displays a similar degree of descriptive fixity. Rather, the spatial imagination of *The Faerie Queene* is shaped by a conceptual design which consistently undermines the impulse to pull out a map and ground the action of the romance plot in geographical space. An obvious instance of this anti-cartographic trace is the voyage of Arthur and Guyon to Acrasia's lustful abode in the closing canto of book II. The complexities of their approach to the Bower of Bliss has troubled criticism. In an incautious moment, one commentator suggests in an introductory textbook on *The Faerie Queene* that students of the poem should draw a map of the eventful journey to facilitate understanding of Spenser's allegorical scheme.[31] This mapping impulse may initially seem a plausible pedagogical device in teaching the section of *The Faerie Queene* which has been identified as 'the most landscaped part of the poem'.[32] But it is hard to imagine practically how a map could be drawn of a perpetually changing landscape that includes such topographically unstable elements as wandering islands which 'seeming now and than, / Are not firme lande, nor any certein wonne, / But straggling plots, which to and fro do ronne, / In the wide waters' (II.xii.11).[33] And it is equally difficult to see how a map could be of aid conceptually to a Spenserian knight (and thus, by hermeneutic implication, to Spenser's readers) who need to move through an incessantly moralised landscape where the right path of virtue will only be discovered after the endurance of extensive moral trials.

Spenser's allegorical landscapes are realms of constant illusion and deceit, posing challenges which the characters first need to successfully confront before they can safely move on. The degree to which Fairie land consistently evades the cartographic paradigm is perhaps best illustrated by Britomart's predicament in the book of chastity, when she embarks on her perilous quest '[w]ithouten compasse, or withouten card' (III.ii.7).[34] Rather than offering the full transparency and safe orientation of a map, the geography of Fairie land is composed of standardised elements which need to be read accurately both by passing knights and learning readers: castles are divided into houses of virtue and anti-virtue; forests are 'always a place of mystery, full of unseen dangers and occasional pleasant surprises';[35] caves may be dens of wild beasts or places of temptation; water – fountains, rivers, lakes – tends to be associated with the spiritual force of baptism but may harbour either chaste or unchaste nymphs. Plains alone appear relatively free of hidden moral perils, acting most frequently as the stage for chivalric combat or chance encounters between travelling knights. But even in unrestrained, open space, identities are more often misread than not. Mastering the complex road network of *The Faerie Queene* is an equally double-edged task. Ten cantos into the legend of holiness, the Red Cross Knight is finally told what he painfully found out for himself, that he should shun the 'broad high way' in favour of 'the narrow path' (I.x.10); but this he cannot, indeed *must* not know prior to his first major adventure – if the poem is to fulfill its didactic purpose.

Thus, his initial challenge in the first canto of book I is duly presented as a lesson in perception.[36] Forced to seek shelter from 'an hideous storme of raine', Red Cross and his companion Una enter into 'a shadie groue' (I.i.8–9). What appears at first sight like a secure network of 'pathes and alleies wide' (9) quickly metamorphoses into a confusing maze: 'wander[ing] too and fro in wayes vnknowne, / Furthest from end then, when they neerest weene, / ... So many pathes, so many turnings seene, / That which of them to take, in diuerse doubt they been.' (10) Their aimless wandering only announces, by way of etymology, a mortal danger hiding in the centre of the forest, the dragon 'Errour'.[37] Since the beast is as much a physical threat as a mental condition, moral and geographical orientation will only set in after the dragon has been slain by the knight; and Red Cross' initial choice of the path 'that beaten *seemd* most bare' (11, my italics) as a potential exit proves, almost by necessity, *erroneous*. Bragging to his anxious companion Una, in true male fashion, that '[v]ertue giues her selfe light, through darknesse for to wade' (12) he ploughs on, only to stumble straight into Errour's den. The promise of full illumination is ironically reduced to a 'litle glooming light, much like a shade' (14) – an accidental reflection from his armour which keeps himself in the dark but wakes the dragon – yet with the support of Una's *unerring* faith, he successfully manages to defeat Errour (and thus to correct his own near fatal error). It is only after this heroic deed that the landscape opens up to his gaze; and the narrow path that before '*seemd* most bare' now turns into the path 'that beaten *was* most plaine' (28, my italics), to lead them safely out of danger – until they encounter the next spatial challenge.

The example shows that the physical space of *The Faerie Queene* has to be mastered first before it can become fully transparent to any knight passing through it; Fairie land is above all a moral testing ground which is not accessible from the privileged position afforded by the topographical map. The attempt to situate the action of Spenser's poem in a historically specific geographical space fails to acknowledge this experimental status of *The Faerie Queene*'s setting.[38] The crucial point is not how much 'real' geography finds its way into the poem (there is a good deal) or according to what schemes the fictional landscape is absorbed into a higher cosmological order; rather, the poem undertakes to question the epistemological significance of space as such, and to describe its power to define the existential state of the fictional characters moving through it. Spenser's landscapes are never closed, purged of dangers, or shut off from the intervention of threatening 'others':[39] Fairie land is as much a romantic setting as it is one endless physical and moral struggle. In this aesthetic universe, where place is always also a moral and political condition, cartography borders on a conceptual impossibility: if knowledge is indeed the ideal end result of a lengthy process of moral education – as suggested in Spenser's letter to Ralegh[40] –, not the point of departure, then maps leap straight into an intellectual condition which the troubled knights of *The Faerie Queene* can only ever hope to achieve at the very end of their own inner journey.

If a map is thus an inconceivable shortcut for a Spenserian knight, which may facilitate spatial displacement but only at the cost of dangerously undermining the overall disciplinary project of the poem, this anti-mapping attitude, I suggest, is not just a quaint poetic device but linked to a contemporary discussion over the relative merits of modern cartography. One of the many uncertainties surrounding new methods of measuring land was the realisation that maps were not entirely faithful to the specific natural conditions of the land they depicted. Cartography was always partial and provisional, and it deliberately needed to 'arrange' the ground for the purposes of visual representation; maps forced the irregularities of landscape both onto a flat piece of paper and into a rigid geometric grid. Edward Worsop, an admirer of John Dee and an ardent defender of the superiority of mathematical insight, explained that land measuring was concerned exclusively with 'the vpper face of any thing' and that surveyors 'desire only to know the content of the outward plaine ... not regarding thicknes, weight, grossenesse, or depth: but only the mesure of ye vpper parts as in groundes: which consist onely of length, and bredth, whether they be flats, or leuels, hils, or valleis.'[41] General acceptance of this labour of abstraction, however, was far less widespread than Worsop admitted. According to his fellow surveyor Ralph Agas the map's effacement of the ground's true surface 'hath perswaded many wise and excellent persons, to doubt whether there be perfection in mapping of landes and tenementes for surueigh', for in light of 'the vneuenes of the groundes, ... their great difference, in hill and dale, from al leuell superficies', surveyors 'are necessarily compelled to put downe [their] practise vpon bookes that are leuel and smooth.'[42] Another contemporary surveyor, Aaron Rathborne, even spotted considerable ignorance concerning the complexities of cartographic projection among his own colleagues. Some 'plaine plaine Tablemen', he fumed, would 'at an instant ... conuert the highest mountains to plaine and leuel grounds, pressing them downe, and inforcing them on a Plaine sheete of paper to lye leuell with the rest.'[43]

I find a striking echo of these anxieties about the (im)possibility of cartographic 'accuracy' in an episode from *The Faerie Queene* which is traditionally read as an allegorical warning about the dangers of popular democracy. In book v, canto ii, the stern justice of the titular hero Artegall is visited upon a plebeian giant who takes up his position at the liminal point of the seacoast and proposes to a cheering populace that, since the world has run so much out of its original proportion, he would now weigh it anew with his huge pair of scales – seemingly an attribute of justice – and thus restore an original state of perfect equality.[44] After a lengthy discussion, which duly ends with the giant being thrown over a cliff by the iron man Talus, Artegall exposes this version of justice as dangerous egalitarianism which threatens to undermine the divinely sanctioned hierarchy of earthly affairs. The relevance of this scene for my purposes is the nature of the giant's reformative vision which focuses not on material goods but on the shape of the land. In order to recover the world's original justice the giant proposes to 'throw down these mountains hie / And make them levell with the lowly plaine: / These towring rocks, which reach vnto the skie, / I will thrust downe into the deepest maine, / And as they were, them equalize againe.' (v.ii.38) Though hardly intended as a conscious allegory for the act of mapping, the levelling giant here suggestively assumes the guise of a transgressive cartographer. In forcing mountains to lie 'levell with the lowly plaine' he verbally closes ranks with Rathborne's dilettantish surveyors who equally flatten out landscape by 'pressing down' the highest mountains 'to lye leuell with the rest.' The political dangers of such acts are only too apparent. In book v the natural irregularities of the ground's surface, which the egalitarian giant wrongfully attempts to correct, are conflated with a divinely authorised political landscape reflecting the principle of social order and the distribution of power: 'The hils doe not the lowly dales disdaine; / The dales doe not the lofty hils enuy. / He maketh Kings to sit in souerainty; / He maketh subiects to their powre obay; / He pulleth downe, he setteth vp on hy; / He giues to this, from that he takes away.' (41)

Ever since their rebellion against Jove, related by Ovid and others, giants are a traditional motif of transgression. In book v, the thrust of their activities is significantly reversed: when the '[g]yants' were first reported to 'coelestial Thrones affect [and] to the skies congested mountaines reare',[45] their upward movement sought to usurp an elevated hierarchical centre. Spenser's mock Atlas figure translates this vertical challenge to authoritarian monarchical claims into a horizontal redistribution of landscape elements, an activity that recalls the suggestion of political equality fostered by the cartographic grid image of the national community. Physical landscape, still invested (by Spenser) with the semiotic potential to stand for the body of the monarch, is a direct mirror of political power; unlawful interference with the spatial configuration of the nation is registered as a rebellious act. Smoothing out an irregular surface, if symbolically in literary allegory or materially on a plane piece of paper, contains the suggestion of similar levelling actions in the political sphere. Since the space of the nation is a fragile figure, produced in a narrative process that consistently includes and acknowledges, albeit with destructive intent, the existence of disruptive others – like giants, dragons, and savages –, it demands its constant reiteration through active performance, rather than its mechanical pictorial reproduction through maps. Unlike *Poly-Olbion*, which offers cartography as a fully sufficient generative matrix for the idea of the nation, the space of *The Faerie Queene* is dependent on its prior articulation through the combined collective effort of a national community constitutive (in however imaginary ways) of all its individual members.

This distinction, I would finally like to suggest, recalls terms used by Homi Bhabha in his influential analysis of modern nationalist discourse that I briefly referred to at the outset. According to Bhabha, 'the contested conceptual territory' of the national idea is evidence of two opposing but mutually enabling strategies. First, a 'nationalist pedagogy, giving the discourse an authority that is based on the pre-given or constituted historical origin *in the past*', and second, 'a process of signification that must erase any prior or originary presence of the nation-people to demonstrate the prodigious, living principles of the people as a contemporaneity: as the sign of the *present* through which national life is redeemed and iterated as a reproductive process.'[46] Within the parameters of the former strategy, people constitute the 'objects' of the national discourse, within those of the latter, its 'subjects'. If the terms of Bhabha's critical project – developed in response to the modern postcolonial experience of exile and geographic dispersal – may be accorded relevance for the early modern period, I suggest that Drayton's narration of national space, continuing the work of Camden's *Britannia*, predominantly embraces 'the continuist, accumulative temporality of the pedagogical' while Spenser's vision of the nation as Fairie land, like Harrison's *Description*, is principally owed to 'the repetitious, recursive strategy of the performative.'[47] When Drayton announced that his cartographically inclined 'industrious Muse great *Britaine* forth shall bring' (1, 65), his poetic map of the nation signals two decisive political changes, first, the decline of an ancient constitutional idea that saw land and ruler, space and power, yoked together in a seamless semantic continuum, and second, the replacement of a concept of national integrity based (albeit hesitantly) on inclusion, by an idea of collective identity reliant on strategies of exclusion. For both developments the success of the cartographic paradigm proved crucial; and between the didactic project of teaching the nation as a preconceived image of structural coherence stretching back through linear time, and its constantly reiterated production in the present by a collective social and moral effort, lies the contested terrain of an early modern poetics of national space.

NOTES

1. Homi K. Bhabha, 'Introduction', Bhabha (ed.), *Nation and Narration* (London: Routledge, 1990), p. 1.
2. See Richard Helgerson's seminal analysis 'The Land Speaks', chapter 3 in *Forms of Nationhood. The Elizabethan Writing of England* (University of Chicago Press, 1992), pp. 105–47.
3. See Joan Grundy, *The Spenserian Poets* (London: Edward Arnold, 1969).
4. Cyprian Lucar, *A Treatise Named Lucarsolace* (London: Iohn Harrison, 1590), pp. 51–2.
5. William Lambarde, *A Perambulation of Kent* (London: Ralphe Newberie, 1576), p. 18.
6. John Leland, *The laboryouse Journey & serche . . . for Englandes Antiquitees*, ed. John Bale (London: n.p., 1549), sigs. D4r-v.
7. D. R. Woolf, *The Idea of History in Early Stuart England* (University of Toronto Press, 1990), p. 19.

8. Annabel Patterson, *Reading Holinshed's Chronicles* (University of Chicago Press, 1994), p. 61.

9. The full title of Harrison's treatise is 'An Historicall Description of the Islande of *Britayne*, with a briefe rehearsall of the nature and qualities of the people of *Englande*, and of all such commodities as are to be found in the same' (my italics). In other words, in a move characteristic of early modern geographical and political thought, the text progresses from historical Britain to contemporary England. See the introduction to this volume for a brief comment on the blurring of boundaries between 'Britain' and 'England'. In my own analysis, I will concentrate principally on what Harrison has to say about the latter, except where the context requires otherwise.

10. William Harrison, 'An Historicall Description of the Islande of Britayne', *Holinshed's Chronicles*, 2 vols. (London: Iohn Harrison, 1577), vol. 1, fol. 20r.

11. *Ibid.*, 'Epistle Dedicatorie'.

12. *Ibid.*, fol. 36r.

13. *Ibid.*, fol. 35v.

14. Michel de Certeau, *The Practice of Everyday Life* [1974], trans. Steven Rendall (Berkeley *et al.*: University of California Press, 1988), p. 119.

15. Harrison, 'Historicall Description', fol. 56r.

16. Andrew McRae, *God Speed the Plough. The Representation of Agrarian England, 1500–1660* (Cambridge University Press, 1996), p. 234.

17. Louis Marin, *Utopics: The Semiological Play of Textual Spaces*, trans. Robert A. Vollrath (Atlantic Highlands, New Jersey: Humanities Press, 1984), p. 202.

18. Stan A. E. Mendyk, *'Speculum Britanniae:' Regional Study, Antiquarianism, and Science in Britain to 1700* (University of Toronto Press, 1989), p. 51.

19. William Camden, *Britain*, trans. Philemon Holland (London: George Bishop and John Norton, 1610), p. 182.

20. John Taylor, *Taylor on Thame Isis* [1632]. Quoted in Joseph A. Berthelot, *Michael Drayton* (New York: Twayne Publishers, 1967), p. 108.

21. Jean Brink, *Michael Drayton Revisited* (Boston: Twayne Publishers, 1990), p. ix.

22. Michael Drayton, *Poly-Olbion* [1612/22], William Hebel *et al.* (eds.), *The Works of Michael Drayton*, 4 vols. (Oxford: Basil, Blackwell and Mott, 1961), vol. IV, facsimile of frontispiece. I rely on this edition throughout. Further references quote song and line number in brackets.

23. Barbara C. Ewell, 'Drayton's *Poly-Olbion*: England's Body Immortalized', *Studies in Philology* 75, no. 3 (1978), 298–9.

24. The pun is Paul Gerhard Buchloh's. Cf. his *Michael Drayton. Barde und Historiker – Politiker und Prophet. Ein Beitrag zur Behandlung und Beurteilung der nationalen Frühgeschichte Großbritanniens in der englischen Dichtung der Spätrenaissance* (Neumünster: Karl Wachholtz, 1964), p. 36.

25. The most remarkable instance of this is the book's frontispiece, suggestively analysed by Helgerson, *Forms of Nationhood*, pp. 108–24. Arguably, Helgerson's emphasis on the cover runs the danger of disregarding the text itself: 'too often in criticism of *Poly-Olbion* we are asked to take the frontispiece as a

synecdoche for the poem's essence . . . rather than to read the poem itself.'
Claire McEachern, *The Poetics of English Nationhood* (Cambridge University
Press, 1996), chapter 4: 'Putting the "poly" back into *Poly-Olbion*', p. 167.

26. McRae, *God Speed the Plough*, p. 257.

27. To my knowledge Wyman H. Herendeen is alone in devoting any critical
energy to a reading of the maps rather than merely noting their existence in
passing. See *From Landscape to Literature. The River and the Myth of Geography*
(Pittsburgh: Duquesne University Press, 1986), esp. p. 294.

28. Cf. *ibid.*, p. 294.

29. William Hole, who also engraved the frontispieces of both the *Britannia* and
Poly-Olbion.

30. See Anne Lake Prescott, 'Marginal Discourse: Drayton's Muse and Selden's Story', *Studies in Philology* 88, no. 3 (1991), 307–28.

31. Gareth Roberts, *The Faerie Queene*, Open Guides to Literature (Buckingham
and Philadelphia: The Open University Press, 1992), p. 77. I should point
out that Roberts' book is excellent both in its approach and its discussion of
the poem.

32. James Nohrnberg, *The Analogy of* The Faerie Queene (Princeton University
Press, 1976), p. 326.

33. I am quoting throughout from A. C. Hamilton's annotated edition: Edmund Spenser, *The Faerie Queene* (London: Longman, 1977).

34. Cf. also Joanne Woolway Grenfell's essay in this volume, chapter 11.

35. John Erskine Hankins, *Source and Meaning in Spenser's Allegory. A Study of 'The
Faerie Queene'* (Oxford: Clarendon Press, 1971), p. 60. My brief typology
largely follows Hankins' argument.

36. See Judith H. Anderson, '"The Hard Begin": Entering the Initial Cantos',
David Lee Miller and Alexander Dunlop (eds.), *Approaches to Teaching Spenser's* Faerie Queene (New York: Modern Language Association, 1994), pp.
41–8. My reading of the Red Cross Knight's adventure in Error's den in this
paragraph is indebted to Anderson's essay which analyses the 'episode in
the Wandering Wood . . . [as] essentially an exercise in perception.' (p. 45).

37. From Latin 'errare': to err and to wander.

38. The most recent effort to describe the geography of *The Faerie Queene* is
Wayne Erickson, *Mapping* The Faerie Queene. *Quest Structure and the World of
the Poem* (New York and London: Garland Publishing, 1996).

39. This point is supported by Chris Fitter who argues that 'Spenser in *The
Faerie Queene* eschews serene and closed landscapes, immune to the incursions of challenging reality, and sets his knights among "open" landscapes
whose want of security is underlined.' *Poetry, Space, Landscape. Toward a New
Theory* (Cambridge University Press, 1995), p. 300.

40. Spenser, 'Letter to Ralegh', *The Faerie Queene*, ed. Hamilton, p. 737.

41. Edward Worsop, *A Discouerie of sundrie errours and faults daily committed by
Landemeaters, ignorante of Arithmetike and Geometrie* (London: G. Seton, 1582), sig.
B4r.

42. Radolph Agas, *A Preparative to Platting of Landes and Tenements for Surueigh*

(London: Thomas Scarlet, 1596), p. 6 (wrongly paginated 10).

43. Aaron Rathborne, *The Surveyor* (London: W. Burre, 1616), p. 168.
44. See Annabel Patterson, 'The Egalitarian Giant: Representations of Justice in History / Literature', *Journal of British Studies* 31 (1992), 97–132.
45. Ovid, *Metamorphosis*, trans. George Sandys (Oxford: J. Lichfield, 1632), I, pp. 152–3.
46. Homi Bhabha, 'Dissemination. Time, Narrative and the Margins of the Modern Nation', *The Location of Culture* (London: Routledge, 1994), p. 145.
47. *Ibid.*

CHAPTER 11

Do real knights need maps? Charting moral, geographical and representational uncertainty in Edmund Spenser's The Faerie Queene

Joanne Woolway Grenfell

Although it is the testing ground for many of the allegorical methods and assumptions of the whole poem, book II of Spenser's *The Faerie Queene* is uncharted and unchartable. Red Cross Knight's lack of 'tables' to help him find his way clearly runs counter to the advice given in William Cuningham's *Cosmographical Glasse*, where the traveller is informed, of the uses of geography, that,

[i]n trauailing by land, her tables poynteth which way to folow, that thy iornay may be spedier, safe, short, & plesant, wher you shall ascend vp to hilles, wher to passe ouer waters, where to walk through woodes, and wher most aptly to remaine at night.[1]

Red Cross Knight, though, like Britomart in book III, voyages '[w]ithouten compasse, or withouten card' away from their native soil in order to seek praise and fame in Faerie land.[2] So should George and Britomart have done their geographical homework? Or is there a reason why the lands of *The Faerie Queene* remain largely uncharted and why Spenser's titular knights must proceed without cartographic aids?

To answer these questions, we need to know what is being tested, and on what ground. As George is the Knight of England and of Holiness, when his integrity is tested in book I by a whole host of allegorical challenges, his steadfastness might be seen as demonstrating the unassailability of the simultaneously coherent religious and national values of the Protestant England for which he stands. There were two main challenges to this sense of identity with which English writers had to contend – a largely Roman Catholic Europe, and a New World to the west – and these challenges figure strongly in writing of the period, whether explicitly, or, in Spenser's case, as a sub-text in his more general exploration of place and culture. Each challenge, I would argue, also brings a reconsideration of representation, and of the different kinds of texts which a traveller or reader needs to have to hand. It is in this context, therefore, that I intend to consider the role, or lack of role, of mapping in Spenser's *The Faerie Queene*, first (and briefly) through a discussion of biblical texts and maps, and, second (and at more length) of the hermeneutic implications of New World geography.

First, religion. Emphasising the straight path which Red Cross Knight learns to take in book 1, Spenser alludes, as A. C. Hamilton has suggested, to a biblical model which is highly relevant to the issues of religion and nationhood which the early books of *The Faerie Queene* raise:

> Then mounted he vpon his Steede again,
> And with the Lady backward sought to wend;
> That path he kept, which beaten was most plaine,
> Ne euer would to any by-way bend,
> But still did follow one vnto the end,
> The which at last out of the wood them brought.
> So forward on his way (with God to frend)
> He passed forth, and new aduenture sought;
> Long way he trauelled, before he heard of ought. (I.i.28)

In order to escape from the wilderness the children of Israel are also, according to the account in Deuteronomy, exhorted to,

Take hede therefore, that ye do as the Lord your God hath commanded you: turne no aside to the right hand nor to the left, But walke in all the wayes which the Lord your God hath commanded you, that ye may liue, and that it may go wel with you: & that ye may prolong your dayes in the land which ye shal possesse.[3]

In Deuteronomy, the author then continues to show the benefits for Israel if this straight and narrow path is adhered to.[4] As the geographical movement is expanded into a moral one, so too the theology of the land is seen to be applied to the law and politics of the nation which is founded when the Israelites emerge out of exile. Theology and nationhood are clearly intertwined here and Spenser's reference usefully draws attention to a parallel which had been used by other commentators to portray England's movement away from the Roman Catholic Church and into a strengthening of both its religious and political sovereignty as similar to that of the Israelites as they travelled from Egypt into a new promised land in which theology, law and politics were designed to coincide.[5]

Commentators in the history of bible printing had explicitly pointed to this historical parallel between the Exodus and the Reformation.[6]

Particularly popular in bibles printed on the continent at the height of
the Reformation and in England later on were maps of the Exodus and
of Canaan. The first appeared in Luther's translation of the New
Testament and another version in the first English edition of the Geneva
Bible showed the Israelites crossing the Red Sea.[7] Spenser picks up on
this significant geographical scene in his description of Moses receiving
the law:

> That done, he leads him to the highest Mount;
> Such one, as that same mighty man of God,
> That bloud-red billowes like a walled front
> On either side disparted with his rod,
> Till that his army dry-foot through then yod,
> Dwelt fortie dayes vpon; where writ in stone
> With bloudy letters by the hand of God,
> The bitter doome of death and baleful mone
> He did receiue, whiles flashing fire about him shone.   (I.x.53)

The invocation of Moses' receiving of the law – a sign of God's covenant
with the Israelites, to be played out on the soil of the Holy Land – at a
moment of self-definition for George deliberately writes England's national course into a biblical model of a favoured nation rewarded by
God after years of persecution.

The use of maps of the Holy Land as visual aids to guide individual
Protestant readers through the unfamiliar lands of Old Testament
narrative had a theological as well as a more national / political
significance. In 1549 the printer Reyner Wolfe noted that,

because the knowledge of cosmographie is very necessary, so that he that
lacketh the same, can neither wel rede the Byble, nor yet prophane Historiogra-
phers, nor the New Testament. For the Evangelists do describe the iourneies of
Christ ... Therefore if a man be not seen in Cosmographie, he shall be
constrained to skippe ouer many notable thinges which otherwise shoulde do
him no lytle pleasures.[8]

Because of the theological, as well as practical importance of the
individual reading scripture for herself, visual aids take on a new role,
helping the reader to root her reading in geographical reality and
ensuring that her attention is sustained even in descriptions of unfamiliar places and customs, whether in the Bible, or in Elizabethan political
and literary texts.

The typology of Israel had also been perceived as useful in displays of
monarchical power: in the pageants which were performed at the
accession of Queen Elizabeth, one scene included,

a seate royal where in was placed *Debora*, a Quene of the Jewes that ruled Israel xl yeres, having about her all her counsailours to talk and consult of the State of the Realme and benefite of the common wealth, this was made to encourage the Quene not to feare though she were a woman: for women by the Spirite and power of Almyghty God have ruled both honourably and pollitiquely and that a great tyme, as did *Debora*, which was there set foorth in Pageaunt.[9]

Not only was this precedent a valuable one in that it could be used to counter apparently biblically-based objections to female rule found in texts such as John Knox's *First Blast of the Trumpet Against the Monstrous Regiment of Women* (1558), but it again reinforced the suggestion that England was a new Israel in both religious and political terms, and that England's recent religious course was as justified and favoured by God as was the Exodus which similarly brought the Israelites into new nationhood. Other texts of the period used the same allusions to draw this parallel: in Thomas Bentley's *Monument of Matrones*, God addresses Elizabeth saying, '[t]hou art my Daughter in deede, this daie haue I begotten thee, and espoused thee to thy king CHRIST, my Sonne; crowned thee with my gifts, and appointed thee QUEENE, to reigne upon my holie mount Zion.'[10]

Given this context, and the use of maps in bibles printed by Protestant printers of the period, we would expect there to be maps in *The Faerie Queene*. Coming out of Eden and finding a way through the wilderness, real or metaphorical, required some kind of geographical or moral handbook to aid the uncertain traveller. But Red Cross Knight has no map, and Britomart, we are explicitly told, travels '[w]ithouten compasse, withouten carde'. Why? First, the knights in *The Faerie Queene* have to learn to do without and learn instead to read the typological signs with which Spenser litters their path in order to gain guidance on and justification for their journeys through the theological / ecclesiological terrain of England. It is their lack of maps which ensures that they make just enough mistakes to teach the reader what not to do. And second, we come back to this question of the New World and the challenge that this seems to have created to writers thinking about national identity.

Whilst it was possible for Old Testament editors and printers to adopt Exodus maps to justify the break away from the Roman Catholic Church, no such typology was available to commentators on the New World. The difficulty of assimilating new geographical territory with Christian morality is seen in this late sixteenth-century interpretation of the chivalric scene by the Dutch engraver in London, Jodocus Hondius (Figure 23). It projects the European discovery of America

Figure 23 Jodocus Hondius, *The Christian Knight Map of the World* (1597)

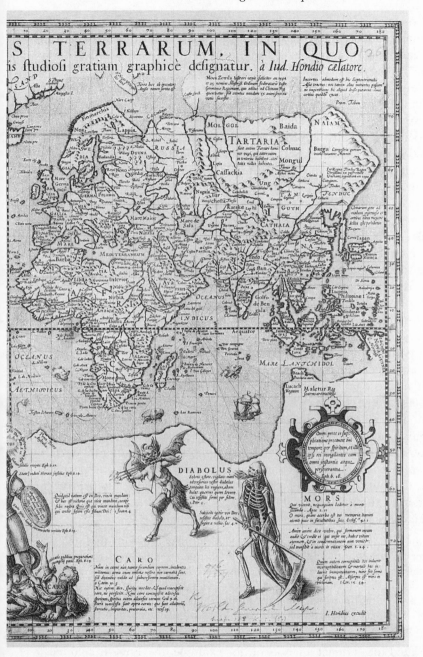

by Christopher Columbus and subsequent voyagers onto a world map. This map contains, in the bottom half of the map frame, the figure of the Christian Knight, armed with the Shield of Faith, the Sword of the Spirit, and the Helmet of Salvation, ready to take on Sin, the Flesh, the Devil and Death. The reference, of course, is to Ephesians 6:13–17.[11] The similarity of the incongruous juxtaposition of the moral and the geographic in the contemporaneously published *The Faerie Queene* is remarkable. The Christian Knight's position on the geometric map grid projection is paralleled by Spenser's knights' journeys across a linguistically mapped out terrain which is equally revealing of concerns and new ideas inspired by a changing understanding of one country's place in relation to a wider – and expanding – world. Through the medium of a romance quest, conducted by virtuous knights traversing uncertain moral territory, the nation is tested and 'proved'. The chivalric journey of *The Faerie Queene* therefore represents a confluence of personal, national and social forces which define the cultural development of England.

But despite the convergence of ideas – particularly the similarly incongruous juxtaposition of moral and geographic ideas in Spenser and Hondius' work – we come back to this problem of the lack of maps in *The Faerie Queene*. I would like to argue that maps are not included – and, by implication, that real knights don't need maps – because the discovery of new territories has ramifications in terms of representation, which means that, as well as finding his way through new places, Spenser was also charting a course through representational boundaries which had suddenly become fluid. It has become almost a commonplace of criticism which deals with geography and literature to assume that colonial writers use the metaphors of mapping to impose cartographic and geometric control and certainty on land – and people – that they wanted to bring under their colonial control. By drawing attention to the theoretical foundation of integrated notions of landscape and seeing, Derek Gregory has observed that,

[t]he classical origins of geography are closely identified with the optical practices of cartography and geometry; its interests have often been assumed to lie in the landscape and the particular 'way of seeing' that this implies; and its decidedly modern interest in theory invokes visualization not only covertly, through the Greek *thea* ('outward appearance') and *horoa* ('to look closely') of 'theory' itself, but also openly, through the display and analysis of spatial structures.[12]

Translated into critical analysis of, for example, the English colonial administration's practices in Ireland, these kind of theoretical insights have been used to propose a model of cartography as a tool of colonial power, its spatial structures ordering and constraining Irish people and culture as well as the Irish land. Whilst there is much to be gained from such an approach, when dealing with Spenser's writing it is not always appropriate and often leads to forced interpretations. For Spenser, I would argue, encounters with geography actually bring about a different response – they make everything uncertain – culture, morality, and, as I will discuss, representation itself.

Tasso's *Discourses* give us some help here about how place can be used to explore literary method. He suggests that in the face of a changing world picture and expanding geographical horizons, there is a great need for artistic selectivity:

[I]mmense too is the diversity of opinions, or rather the contradiction in judgements, the transformation of languages, customs, laws, rites, republics, kingdoms, emperors, and almost of the world itself, which seems to have changed its face and to present itself to us in another form and another guise.[13]

What Tasso here, like Spenser in the proem to book II, suggests is the need for a new poetic representational apparatus – a model which accounts for the role of place and culture in the relations between poetry, language and society. This problem is at the heart of Spenser's discussion of the exploration of the American continent, the consequences of which are that poets must reconsider first what can be seen, and, second, question what the boundaries are between fact and fiction:

> But let that man with better sence aduize,
> That of the world least part to vs is red:
> And dayly how through hardy enterprize,
> Many great Regions are discouered,
> Which to late age were neuer mentioned.
> Who euer heard of th'Indian *Peru?*
> Or who in venturous vessell measured
> The *Amazons* huge riuer now found trew?
> Or fruitfullest *Virginia* who did euer vew? (II.Proem.2)

If the world is a text of which many parts have not previously been 'red' (i.e., made known) then the new texts of discovery propose that there is a whole new world which can be used as metaphorical material for a literary imagination. Moreover, Spenser's understanding that there were worlds beyond what he could see has important consequences for literature. To return to Cuningham's *Cosmographical Glasse*, a dialogue between Philonicus and Spondaeus typifies the way in which geographical writers were stressing that any view of landscape is optically (as well as culturally and historically) dependent upon the position of the viewer.

SPOND: And is this Horizont a fixed Circle or not?

PHILO: It is fixed, and without motion.

SPOND: It should seme contrary. For I beynge at London haue one Horizont, and goyng to Antwerpe, have another, and so at Colein an other, and at Heydelberge another, &c.

PHILO: I confesse no lesse, but that proveth nothinge that the horizont moueth, for loke what errour you shoulde fall: you must graunte (if the horizont moue) that with the turning of the heauens, your Circle must come ouer your verticall point once in 24. houres.

SPOND: Nay, I will not graunt such absurditie in any case: wherefore I see that it is my chaungyg that maketh me to have a new horizont, and not the horizont to move with me.[14]

Likewise, Spenser acknowledges that the eye's horizon is limited and that there are lands beyond his vision. But, consequently, what the individual does see is important: Spondaeus' realisation that changing his position makes him have a new horizon, even though the horizon does not physically move with him, simultaneously confirms human limitation and proclaims individual uniqueness.

Spenser deploys this acknowledgment of human limitation to construct a defence of fiction against the charge of mendacity. As a framework to the evocation of new continents, he appears to propose the collapsing of oppositions which characterise theories of representation – particularly the false dichotomy, as he sees it, between historical writing, the 'matter of iust memory', and the figurative tropes of poetry, seen as the 'aboundance of an idle brain' and 'painted forgery' (II.Proem.1). There is a difference, as he notes in the letter to Sir Walter Raleigh between history which 'discourseth of affayres orderly' and poetry which may play around with time scales and 'maketh a pleasing Analysis of all', but the criticism which could be made of poetry, that it is based on a falsehood because it can create an illusion of reality out of nothingness, is a false one. For what the discovery of the New World suggests is that lack of personal knowledge of a place is not reason enough to dismiss it as a fiction and falsehood; the existence of Peru, the Amazon, or Virginia would not have been credited in the past, yet, 'all these were, when no man did them know; / Yet haue from wisest ages hidden beene.' (II.Proem.3)

Bearing in mind the example of the American continent, the incredulous reader (Queen Elizabeth, and the general reader, who is party to this communication between poet and monarch) is therefore warned of the dangers of assuming that it is her comprehension or viewing of something that makes it real: 'Why then should witlesse man so much

misweene / That nothing is, but that which he hath seene?' (II.Proem.3)
She is then invited to apply this new-found skill to her reading of the rest
of *The Faerie Queene*. Turning back in the next stanza to England, having
learned about the challenges of representation, the reader is then
educated in the conventions of Faerie land allegory which are again
figured through ideas of landscape setting. She is taught '[b]y certaine
signes here set in sundry place' to approach depictions of the country
semiotically, to decipher the clues which allow correspondences to be
made between and through the fictional, physical and social worlds and
see 'thine owne realmes in lond of Faery / And in this antique Image thy
great auncestry.' Charting the development of Albion in book II and
exploring unknown moral territory elsewhere in *The Faerie Queene*, Spenser relies on the reader's understanding of these 'certaine signes' to make
connections between the 'lond of Faery' and England.

It is partly because of the varied cultural connotations of early
modern writing about landscape that it has become a subject particularly suited to working out the representation of nature and nation, culture
and civilisation. And as such, it appears to give us some insight into
cultural history – what Roger Chartier has called the

configurations and motifs – of representation of the social sphere – that give
unconscious expression to the positions and the interests of social agents as they
interact, and that serve to describe society as those social agents thought it was
or wished [it] to be.[15]

At a time when the scope of these configurations and motifs was being
considerably widened, landscape provided a whole field of interpretative possibilities which, for Spenser, inevitably led to new ways of
describing the interrelations of the poet, textual representation and the
nation. Referring to the very real geographical landscape of the marriage of the Thames and Medway, he seems to question the ability of
language and literature adequately to represent the nation; in the
conventional rhetoric of poetic doubt he asks,

> But what do I their names seeke to rehearse,
> Which all the world have with their issue fild?
> How can they all in this so narrow verse
> Contayned be, and in small compasse hild? (IV.xi.17)

Yet *The Faerie Queene* is full of passages that indicate that the truth of
literary representation was far removed from such self-effacement; and
that, indeed, there was in English writing ample opportunity for charting the growth of the nation. Alongside traditional texts about
the culturing of the land – the old husbandry manuals, shepherds'

calendars, and religious-cultural histories – there were also the texts of
the mapping of the New World and new English historical-geographical
writings which attempted to provide comprehensive coverage of English
culture and place. For Spenser, texts such as Camden's *Britannia* seemed
to acquire a monumental status and to provide some reassurances that
what has since been termed the Elizabethan 'project' of charting England's place within the world would not be forgotten in future generations. Recalling the end of Ovid's *Metamorphoses*, he proclaims, in 'The
Ruines of Time',

> *Cambden* the nourice of antiquitie,
> And lanterne vnto late succeeding age,
> To see the light of simple veritie,
> Buried in ruines, through the great outrage
> Of her owne people, led with warlike rage;
> *Cambden*, though time all moniments obscure,
> Yet thy iust labours euer shall endure.[16]

By the completion of *The Faerie Queene*, there were far more depictions of
England – in all kinds of texts – which could both redefine England's
place within a changing world and make available to poets a wider
geographic vocabulary with which to consider their relation to it. But
Spenser's knights cannot yet have the maps which formally acknowledge this possibility . . . there is more learning about signs and place to
be done before such knowledge can be codified.

So, coming back again to the point with which we began: do real
knights need maps? Perhaps the point is that maps cannot be available
to the characters, the readers, or the author, because Spenser seems to
have felt that there were no texts which could adequately represent the
complexity – moral as well as geographical – of England's situation. To
be sure, maps of England and the New World were in circulation, but
these could offer very little help in response to the challenges to accepted
conventions of morality, culture and literature which were posed.
Preparing his readers to encounter this new moral world, Spenser has to
make the landscape of book i unknown in order to create a challenge to
his knight and reader, to allow George, particularly, to misread the signs
around him, and to misinterpret the challenges to his faith so that he
becomes morally as well as physically lost to the point where,

> So many pathes, so many turnings seene,
> That which of them to take, in diuerse doubt they been.   (i.i.10)

This then provides the occasion for a lesson on how to read the signs,
not just of landscape, but also of religion and literary interpretation. The

importance of a semiotic rather than a specifically cartographic interpretation of landscape is established early in book 1 through techniques
of poetic description in the scene where Red Cross Knight stumbles
upon a false hermitage:

> A little lowly Hermitage it was,
>> Downe in a dale, hard by a forests side,
>> Far from resort of people, that did pas
>> In trauell to and froe: a little wyde
>> There was an holy Chappell edifyde,
>> Wherein the Hermite dewly wont to say
>> His holy things each morne and euentyde:
>> Thereby a Christall streame did gently play,
> Which from a sacred fountaine welled forth alway.   (1.i.34)

As Hamilton has noted, 'this false hermitage at which the Knight
abandons his religious role is "[d]owne in a dale" because his descent
into sin begins here', but of course Red Cross Knight has not yet learned
to make such connections. Nor indeed should he have, for his mistake is
essential to the hermeneutic lesson of the canto to the reader, suggesting
that landscape, like people, does not always signify what it seems to
signify. As elsewhere, the failing of the knight allows the reader to learn
by 'ensample', rather than religious didacticism, that something which
appears to be holy need not be. She is made aware that it is possible to
work out the integrity of symbols by paying appropriate attention to the
signs that accompany them – in this case the geographical location of
the hermitage. Furthermore, the hermeneutic lesson allows for the
possibility of symbols in representation being persuasive without being
iconoclastic. Confronting the reader later in the same book with the real
hermitage on the top of the Hill of Contemplation ('Forth to an hill, that
was both steepe and hy; / On top whereof a sacred chapell was' [1.x.46])
and with the knight's re-dedication of himself to his quest there, Spenser
offers a revision of the signs of landscape which reinforces the interpretative lesson of the first, false, scene. Apart from the significance in
spatial terms of one hermitage being '[d]owne in a dale' whilst the other
is on a steep and high hill, the versification of the passages also gives
clues to their meaning and to the representative methods of the poem as
a whole. Unusually, both begin with an inverted metrical foot, a tro-
chee, which immediately draws attention to the change in pace as the
knight approaches the significant setting. But whereas at the scene of the
true hermitage, the verse then reverts immediately to the usual iambic
pattern – 'that was both steepe and hy' – and continues in that manner

as the view is unfolded, the description of the false hermitage continues the inverted and rather awkward metre for rather longer: this hermitage is 'hard by a forests side; / Far from resort of people, that did pas', the trochaic feet and stressed endings of the next line adding to the effect of unease before the stanza turns again to the more comfortable (though clearly deceptively comfortable) iambic pentameter of all lines but the last (a hexameter with caesura). The reader thus learns to decode meaning from a combination of the signs of medium, context and allegory. This, it seems the author hopes, ensures that error and misunderstanding of the nature and function of signs do not lead to misinterpretation. (See 1.i.18: 'God helpe the man so wrapt in *Errours* endlesse traine'.) The scene therefore sets up an interpretative guide – the key, if you like, to the non-existent map – to which both knights and readers can refer throughout the poem.

So it is not that real knights don't use maps, rather that a map cannot be created until the territory becomes known and familiar. The unchartedness of Faerie land's literary, moral and geographical territory emphasises the testing of the knight and reader, so that Red Cross Knight has to use the 'little glooming light' (1.i.14) from his armour to light his and our way. In this sense his quest stands both for the testing of his temperament and associated Christian values, and of the country which he emblematically represents. Furthermore, it establishes a typology of journeying for England which offers guidance to future travellers in the same way that the model of the Exodus provided a way of understanding religious and national conflict in history. It also reminds the reader from the outset of the uncertain literary terrain which Spenser is beginning to traverse as he moves from pastoral to a combination of romance and epic with the aim of producing a poem which could allow England to compete with the best that Europe could offer and which could adapt to the collapsing of oppositions between fact and fiction which increasing knowledge of old and new worlds made necessary.

NOTES

1. William Cuningham, *The Cosmographical Glasse* (London: John Day, 1559), sig. A5r. See also Machiavelli's assertion that '[a prince] must also learn the nature of the terrain, and know how mountains slope, how valleys open, how plains lie, and understand the nature of rivers and swamps; and he should devote much attention to such activities. Such knowledge is useful in two ways: first, one learns to know one's own country and can better understand how to defend it; second, with the knowledge and experience of

the terrain, one can easily comprehend the characteristics of any other terrain that it is necessary to explore for the first time'. *The Prince*, trans. Peter Bondanella and Mark Musa (Oxford University Press, 1979), p. 50. What was more important, though, when colonisers had become established in a country such as Ireland, was that they could use their knowledge of the country in order to hold onto the land they had gained, to identify and protect land which was suitable for cultivation, and to plan how and where trade could develop. The renown in which Sir Henry Sidney was held for his knowledge of Ireland – its 'Havens, Ports, Promontories . . . or whatsoever else could be known . . . not any Man having seen, or observed as much of that Kingdom' – provides some indication of this understanding. Quoted in David J. Baker's essay, 'Off the Map: Charting Uncertainty in Renaissance Ireland', Brendan Bradshaw *et al.* (eds.), *Representing Ireland: Literature and the Origins of Conflict, 1534–1660* (Cambridge University Press, 1993), p. 77.

2. Edmund Spenser, *The Faerie Queene*, ed. A. C. Hamilton (London: Longman, 1977), III.ii.7. All quotations from *The Faerie Queene* refer to this edition.

3. *Deuteronomy* 18: 9–11. All quotations are from *The Bible and Holy Scriptures* (Geneva: R. Hall, 1560) [The Geneva Bible].

4. *Deuteronomy* 5: 32–3. 'And thou shalt come vnto the Priests of the Leuites, & vnto the iudge that shalbe in those dayes, and aske, and thei shal shewe thee the sentence of iudgement . . . According to the lawe, which they shal teach thee, and according to the iudjement . . . which they shal tel thee, shalt thou do: thou shalt not decline from the thing which they shal shewe thee, *nether* to the right hand, nor to the left.'

5. The competition was, of course, cultural as well as religious and political. Lodowick Bryskett summed up this point in his comment that 'the healthfull and delicious fruites which she hath brought with her to furnish this our English soile & clime withal. Whereby we may with the lesse labour and cost henceforth haue them to delight and nourish our minds, since we shall not be constrained to fetch them from *Athens* or from *Rome*, but may find them growing at home with ourselves, if our owne negligence and sloth cause us not to foreslow the cultivation and manuring of the same.' For a full discussion of these ideas, see Richard Helgerson, *Forms of Nationhood: The Elizabethan Writing of England* (University of Chicago Press, 1992).

6. See Catherine Delano Smith and E. Morley Ingram, *Maps in Bibles, 1500–1600: An Illustrated Catalogue* (Geneva: Librairie Droz, 1991), p. xxiii: 'It is not difficult to see why a map of the Exodus would attract Protestant Bible printers. The narrative, with its movement from bondage to salvation, from ignorance to knowledge of God, from promise to fulfilment held a central place in both Hebrew and Christian thought.' Important bible publications in England include the Bishops Bible of 1568 which contains battle illustrations and a plan of the temple as well as maps of Egypt and Arabia. Map illustrations started to be used in other religious works around this time. See e.g. Hugh Broughton, *A Concent of Scripture* (London: Gabriell Simson and

William White, 1590); and John Bale, *The Image of Both Churches after the Revelacion of Sainct John* (London: J. Daye and W. Seres, 1550).

7. The explanation accompanying the illustration further suggests the relevance of the Israelites' suffering and persecution to a sixteenth-century audience: 'In this figure four chiefe points are to be considered. first that the Church of God is euer subiect in this worlde to the Crosse & to be afflicted after one sort or another. The second, that the ministers of God following their vocation shalbe euil spoken of, and murmured against, euen of them that pretend the same cause and religion that thei do. The third, that God deliuereth not his church incontinently out of dangers but to exercise their faith and pacience continueth their troubles, yea and often tymes augmenteth them as the Israelites were now in lesse hope of their lives then when thei were in Egypt. The fourth point is, that when the dangers are most great, then Gods helpe is moste ready to succour: for the Israelites had on either side them, huge rockes & mountaines, before them the Sea, behinde them moste cruel enemies, so that there was no way left to escape mans iudgement.'

8. Quoted in Smith and Ingram, *Maps in Bibles*, p. xxiv.

9. Quoted in J. A. Kingdon, *Richard Grafton, Citizen and Grocer of London* (London: Rixon and Arnold, 1901), p. 105. For a discussion of these ceremonies, see Richard L. DeMolen, 'Richard Mulcaster and Elizabethan Pageantry', *Studies in English Literature 1500–1900* 14 (1974), 209–21.

10. Thomas Bentley, *The Monument of Matrones: conteining seven severall lamps of Virginitie, or distinct treatises* (London: Denham, 1582), p. 307.

11. See A. M. Hind, *Engraving in England in the Sixteenth and Seventeenth Centuries*, 3 vols. (Cambridge University Press, 1952), vol. I, p. 176.

12. Derek Gregory, *Geographical Imaginations* (Oxford: Blackwell, 1994), p. 16.

13. Torquato Tasso, *Discourses on the Heroic Poem*, trans. Mariella Cavalchini and Irene Samuel (Oxford: Clarendon Press, 1973), p. 22.

14. Cuningham, *Cosmographical Glasse*, fol. 18r. For a more sophisticated view of perspective, though, see 'A Short Treatise of Perspective' which notes that landscape (painting) 'expresseth places of larger prospects, as whole contries where the eye seemeth not to be hindered by any objects . . . ether of nature or arte, but to passe as farre as the force thereof can pierce . . . And therfor all thinges seme by littell and little to diminishe and vanishe awaye both in color and shape.' British Library Sloane MS 536. Quoted in Norinan K. Farmer, *Poets and the Visual Arts in Renaissance England* (Austin: University of Texas Press, 1984), p. 5.

15. Roger Chartier, *Cultural History: Between Practices and Representations*, trans. Lydia G. Cochrane (Cambridge: Polity Press, 1988), p. 6.

16. Edmund Spenser, *Works*, 9 vols. (Baltimore: Johns Hopkins Press, 1933–58), vol. VIII, p. 41, lines 169–75.

Epilogue

CHAPTER 12

The folly of maps and modernity

Richard Helgerson

As other essays in this volume amply testify, maps were deeply engaged in the work of early modernity. Maps enabled and inspired Europe's vast overseas expansion, and maps spread the new knowledge that resulted from that expansion. Maps provided rulers with new instruments of control and subjects with a new sense of identity, thus promoting both the political and the affective consolidation of national states. Maps heightened civic pride and regional loyalty. By teaching landowners the precise extent and nature of their holdings, maps pushed Europe's agrarian economy away from the feudal manor and toward the capitalist market. Maps illustrated the ancient and biblical past, reinforcing the historicist inclinations of humanist and Reformation scholarship. And maps made the new geography the model for a scientific revolution that replaced ancient authority with experience and mathematical description. In these and many other ways, maps excited, moved, informed and remade everyone who had contact with them, and through the social, political, economic and intellectual remakings they prompted, they changed the lives even of those who didn't. No wonder then that painters copied maps, that poets made metaphors of them, or that playwrights brought them on stage. Maps were the undeniable makers and markers of modernity, the signs, as well as the tools, of a distinctly new age.

To get just one measure of the unprecedented burst of cartographic production that underlies these effects, consider the history of the atlas. Though for decades mapsellers had been binding miscellaneous sheet maps in single-volume collections, the first true atlas – that is, the first book whose maps were prepared in a common format with the intention of making a book – was the *Theatrum Orbis Terrarum* of Abraham Ortelius, first published in 1570. In the next thirty years more than forty

editions in seven languages of Ortelius' *Theatrum* appeared, and it was
soon joined by Gerard Mercator's *Atlas* – the book that gave the genre
its name – which, under the imprint of Mercator and his successors, the
Hondiuses, went through another forty editions. And soon added to
these were the atlases of the Visschers, the de Wits, the Allardts, the
Blaeus, and many others, enough to have moved Leo Bagrow in his
pioneering *History of Cartography* to have dubbed this 'the century of
atlases'.[1]

The growing size of these books tells the story of commercial expansion in another way. In 1570 Ortelius' single-volume *Theatrum* contained
seventy maps. By the 1660s, the famous Blaeu *Grand Atlas* had grown up
to twelve volumes, containing some six hundred maps. And while these
standard world atlases were increasing in number and size, pocket-size
spin-offs were appearing in dozens of editions from these same publishers, and still other entrepreneurs were adopting the Ortelian model
for urban atlases, beginning with Georg Braun and Frans Hogenberg's
Civitates Orbis Terrarum (1572), and for numerous national and regional
atlases, of which the ones best known to English-speaking readers are
Christopher Saxton's atlas of England and Wales (1579) and John
Speed's *Theatre of the Empire of Great Britain* (1611). And, of course, this
exponentially growing production of atlases of all sorts and sizes went
hand in hand with the booming production of sheet maps, wall maps,
globes and estate surveys. In these years, mapmaking became a very big
business.

But, like other big businesses, this one prompted not only emulation
and further expansion but also negative reaction and resistance. Large-
scale commodification made maps available for purposes quite different
from – sometimes even at odds with – the purposes they were most
obviously meant to serve. If maps were the pre-eminent sign of modernity, they could also be made to speak out against the modern. Indeed,
their very prominence made them especially available for contrarian
appropriation. Maps were regularly inserted into interpretive contexts
that radically altered their meaning, contexts that turned their worldly
uses against themselves, revealing the folly of both maps and the modernity to which they were so actively contributing. But this second-
order system of differences itself proved unstable and tipped – not
intentionally perhaps but no less decisively – from anti-modernity into
still another configuration of the modern, one that found a new way of
anchoring anti-worldly difference.

Tracing these transmutations is the business of this essay. What happened, I'll be asking, when, instead of doing the work of modernity, maps were made to mock that very project and all those who had devoted themselves to it?

THE WORLD IN MOTLEY

To begin, let's go back to Ortelius and the map that initiated his great enterprise, the general map of the world from the first edition of the *Theatrum Orbis Terrarum*, his celebrated *Typus Orbis Terrarum* (Figure 24) – in the words of John Gillies, 'the single most famous manifestation of the new geography in the sixteenth century.'[2] Based on a pioneering wall-map Mercator had brought out a year earlier, Ortelius' *Typus Orbis Terrarum* was as comprehensive, accurate and accessible a world map as could then be found, and it remained the most familiar image of the world for the next forty years. But that very familiarity invited an unexpected retort, when shortly after its first publication the Parisian engraver Jean de Gourmont dressed Ortelius' famous world map in motley (Figure 25).

In his fascinating little book *Maps Are Territories / Science Is an Atlas*, David Turnbull seizes on de Gourmont's woodcut as a handy illustration of how we all have maps in our heads. The brain is a map. Elsewhere, Turnbull has used the same image to make a slightly different point: the figure with the map in his head is a jester, a trickster, 'the spirit of disorder', as Turnbull puts it, 'the enemy of boundaries'.[3] Both points are suggestive and both make intriguing use of the woodcut. But early modern viewers would have seen something quite different. In fact, we have just such a viewer waiting to be called up as a witness. In *The Anatomy of Melancholy*, Robert Burton writes, 'Thou shalt soon perceive that all the world is mad, that it is melancholy, dotes, that it is, [as was] expressed not many years since in a map made like a fool's head with that motto "*caput helleboro dignum*" ['O head worthy of purgation' or, in the French of de Gourmont, '*O teste digne de purgation*'], a crazed head, *cavea stultorum* [a theatre of fools], a fool's paradise . . . and needs to be reformed'.[4] Like Burton, early modern viewers would have seen not so much a map in a trickster's head as the world in the head of a fool. Worldliness is the very essence of folly. The fool is a fool because of his devotion to the things of this world. And 'the number of fools', as Solomon is quoted saying just under the map, 'is infinite'. We all qualify. There is a visual/verbal pun at work here. All the world – *tout le monde* – is a worldly fool. About half the moral mottos strewn over the page have

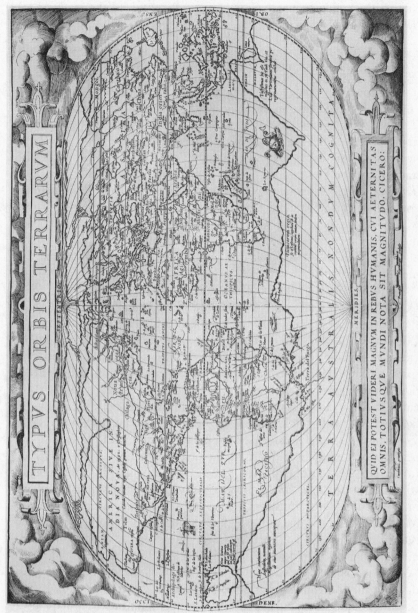

Figure 24 Abraham Ortelius, *Typus Orbis Terrarum* from the *Theatrum Orbis Terrarum* (1570)

Figure 25 Jean de Gourmont, *Fool's Cap Map* (1575)

to do with one side of that pun – that is, with the universality of human folly (for example, 'ass's ears, who's without them?' on the ears of the fool's cap) – and the other half with the other side – with the folly of worldliness (for example, 'vanity of vanities, all is vanity', over the fool's bauble).[5]

But what seems to me most worth remarking on is how Ortelius' world map, one of the most commercially successful cartographic images ever produced, has been appropriated to generate these meanings. The radically new is being energetically reinscribed in terms of the timelessly old. Nor is Ortelius' map just a convenient place filler, a place filler that gives an old moral a tingle of newness. With the new map there, the old moral has a new target. Now it is aiming at modernity itself, at the discovery and conquest of the New World so prominently featured on Ortelius' map, at the technological and commercial developments that have resulted in the map's production and distribution, at the avidity for worldly newness that has led us foolishly to get to know such representations. The Fool's Cap Map, as this image is usually called, uses a map to denounce mapmaking and everything associated with it – though, of course, at the same time, it depends for its own commercial appeal on those very processes. It is thus not surprising that when Ortelius updated his map, the market-canny fool's cap was not far behind, simultaneously denouncing and appropriating this new bit of newness before it had time to get old.[6]

The French National Library in Paris keeps its copy of Jean de Gourmont's Fool's Cap Map with 'facéties et pièces de buffonerie' ['jokes and comic pieces'] and the London Map Collectors' Circle reprinted the updated version in a volume of 'geographical oddities'.[7] As irresistible as they may seem to us, these classifications are no less anachronistic than the idea of the Fool's Cap Map as trickster or illustration of cartographic consciousness. However witty, the juxtaposition of world map and fool's cap made, as Burton testifies, a serious point: 'all the world is mad'. And lest we think that such effects must always be secondary, that no mapmaker could turn his own cartographic labours to such moralistic ends, we should recall Jodocus Hondius' Christian Knight Map, already discussed in this volume by Joanne Woolway Grenfell, a map whose Latin title can be translated as 'The image of the whole world in which is also set forth to please the student devoted to piety the earthly struggle of the Christian knight' (Figure 23 on pp. 228–9). Hondius, the successor of Mercator, was one of the great mapmakers of early modern Europe, and this map, far from being a facetious appropriation of someone else's work, was itself a significant contribution to cartographic learning. In using Mercator's projection as re-articulated by the Cambridge mathematician Edward Wright, Hondius' map innovates in a way that suggests its scientific seriousness, and it confirms that impression by including the latest findings from voyages to Virginia, the Davis Straits and Nova Zembla. As a leading cartographic historian has remarked, this map 'is as up-to-date as geographical knowledge of the time allowed'.[8]

But what then are we to make of the scene that fills the bottom half of the sheet? Here the Christian knight, having put on 'the whole armor of God', as recommended in the verses from St Paul's letter to the Ephesians that surround him, faithfully resists a variety of familiar temptations. Why should this scene be included on a world map? Because the Christian knight's struggle takes place on earth and against worldly foes: Sin and Death, the Flesh, the Devil and the World itself, represented both by the allegorical figure of Mundus in the lower left-hand corner *and* by the map. The world is both the scene of the Christian's struggle and the enemy that must be fought. Thus, as the 'student devoted to piety' poured over this map, delighting in the accomplishments of discovery and scientific representation, he was warned against the very attractions that drew him on, warned to resist the lure of the world that was so temptingly spread out before him. That warning is made explicit in the biblical passages that accompany Mundus. 'What does it profit a man to gain the whole world if he lose his own soul?' asks one of them, and another cries out: 'Unfaithful creatures! Do you not know that friendship with the world is enmity with God?'

Hondius, the ardently Protestant mapmaker, would himself have qualified as the world-besotted *studiosus* at whom these warnings were aimed, and so would a legion of others, including Robert Burton. Burton may have thought the world and worldliness the root of the life-long melancholy from which he was so obsessively working to cure himself, but he liked nothing better than gazing on the world in maps. 'Methinks', he wrote, 'it would well please any man to look upon a geographical map . . . to behold, as it were, all the remote provinces, towns, cities of the world, and never go forth of the limits of his study. . . . What greater pleasure can there now be' – and notice the immediacy of that 'now' – 'than to view those elaborate maps of Ortelius, Mercator, Hondius, etc.? To peruse those books of cities put out by Braunus and Hogenbergius? To read those exquisite descriptions of Maginus, Munster, Herrera . . .?' – and so on through the full repertory of early modern cartographic and chorographic description.[9] Like Hondius, Burton loved the world he thought it folly not to despise, and he loved it even more when he could see it in maps, including those Hondius engraved, maps that were, Burton thought, making him mad with worldly pleasure.

Such denunciations of worldly modernity in the midst of what might just as easily appear its celebration do not stop with these obvious examples. Seen in the light of the Fool's Cap Map, the Christian Knight Map, and *The Anatomy of Melancholy*, even Ortelius' *Typus Orbis Terrarum* can turn against itself. Just under Ortelius' map is a sentence from Cicero: 'Quid ei potest videri magnum in rebus humanis, cui aeternitas omnis, totiusque mundi nota sit magnitudo' ['For what can seem of moment in human occurrences to a man who keeps all eternity before his eyes and knows the vastness of the universe?'].[10] At first glance, these words may appear triumphantly self-congratulatory. With the aid of Ortelius' new world map, we can now see 'the vastness of the universe' as Cicero, for all his wisdom, could never have done. But the intent of the sentence in Cicero's *Tusculan Disputations*, as Ortelius and his human-ist audience would surely have known, is precisely the intent of the Fool's Cap Map: to condemn the folly – a word Cicero uses repeatedly – of all excessive attachment to the world. And the further bits of stoic morality Ortelius added in 1587 to the revised version of his map mark the intersection still more clearly. Included among those additions is, for example, this wry remark from Seneca's *Natural Questions*: 'Hoc est punctum, quod inter tot gentes ferro et igni dividitur. O quam ridiculi sunt mortalium termini!' ['Here is that pinpoint divided by sword and fire among so many nations. O how ridiculous are the boundaries of mortals!'].[11] Just above the map/face of the Fool's Cap Map we find a strikingly similar sentence from Pliny. In de Gourmont's French, it begins 'voici le point du monde' ['Here is the pinpoint of the world'] and then goes on to mock human ambition in much the same terms as Ortelius' Seneca.[12] Like the motto from Cicero, these Senecan and Plinian sentences with their 'hoc est punctum' or 'voici le point' (which became 'hic est . . . punctum' on the Latinized 1590 Fool's Cap Map) take pride in the new visibility of the world afforded by Ortelius' work, but they also condemn both the world Ortelius' maps portray and the folly of all worldly pursuits, including the cartographic pursuits that have made this new world so vividly known.

Whether the source is biblical, as it is on the Christian Knight Map, or classical, as it is with the humanistically educated Ortelius, or a combination of the two, as on the Fool's Cap Map or in Burton, the ancient sentiment takes on a new meaning when attached to maps of a world the ancients ignored. And, as we have seen, that renovated sentiment is as likely to be expressed by early modern Europe's most prominent cartographers, by men like Hondius and Ortelius, as it is by anyone else. The double-consciousness it expresses qualified everything they did.

THE VANITY OF NATIONAL IDENTITY

The art and literature of the sixteenth century repeatedly combine, in much the way mapmakers do, *contemptus mundi* with a delight in the world's modernity. In using a version of the Fool's Cap Map as their dust-jacket illustration, the editors of *The Norton Shakespeare* advertise the connection. Their choice certainly fits their author. The playwright who casually compared the lines on a character's smiling face to the rhumb lines 'in the new map with the augmentation of the Indies' – a map usually identified as Edward Wright's mathematically sophisticated *Hydrographiae Descriptio* (1599) – was obviously no stranger to the new geography. And the playwright who made Hamlet complain 'that this goodly frame, the earth, seems to me a sterile promontory' was at least as familiar with *contemptus mundi*.[13] Like the Fool's Cap Map, Shakespeare's plays work to expose the folly of the world at the same time that they embrace its heady and disruptive modernity.

Nor is Shakespeare unique in this regard. Think, for example, of the moment in *The Lusiads*, when the old man of Restelo rises up to condemn the sinful worldliness of the very voyage of discovery, Vasco da Gama's first trip to India, that Camões' poem is intent on glorifying. 'Do you seek', asks the old man, 'an uncertain and unknown fate so that fame will exalt and flatter you, calling you with extravagant plenty, lord[s] of India, Persia, Arabia, and Ethiopia?'[14] Given that kings of Portugal, including the king to whom Camões' poem was dedicated, had borne precisely these words in their official title since the time of da Gama, the charge is particularly shocking. But it is no more shocking, to cite a still more familiar example, than the anamorphic death's head that cuts across the lower part of Holbein's *The Ambassadors*, radically troubling the painting's elaborate display of its subjects' learned accomplishments. Camões and Holbein are among the greatest sixteenth-century proponents of the new, but the worldliness of what they portray obviously bothered them. So as talismanic insurance against that worldly involvement, they introduce a perspective fundamentally at odds with it.

Shakespeare features maps in crucial scenes of *1 Henry IV* and *King Lear*; Camões tells a story that would be virtually incomprehensible without a map-conditioned sense of geographic space; and Holbein includes among the signifying objects on the shelves between his ambassadors not only a celestial and a terrestrial globe but also a whole host of geometrical instruments. For all three, maps, modern practices of knowledge and power, and a counter-discourse of *contemptus mundi* go together, however much at odds they may seem to us. Elsewhere the bond uniting these disparate perspectives can be still tighter, with the map itself being made a *memento mori*. 'So worldly joys', preached Walter Balcanquahall in 1623, 'are but towns and countries finely painted in the map, which as with a little water anyone may wipe out', and in his 'Hymn to God My God, in My Sickness', John Donne gave the trope still another twist. 'Whilst my physicians', writes Donne,

> by their love are grown
> Cosmographers, and I their map, who lie
> Flat on this bed, that by them may be shown
> That this is my southwest discovery
> *Per fretum febris*, by these straits to die.

But then, in a startling departure from what we may by now expect, Donne goes on to find hope in the map's implicit circularity: 'As west and east / In all flat maps (and I am one) are one, / So death doth touch the resurrection.'[15] For Donne, in the straits of fever, the map figures both death and a life beyond death. Worldliness offers a passage to other-worldliness.

Hope may be less evident, but the association of maps and death is just as apparent in the artistic genre that furnishes the greatest number of examples of *contemptus mundi* in the midst of modernity and its celebration, the 'vanitas' still life. In these paintings, which enjoyed great popularity all over Europe but were especially prized in the Netherlands, maps regularly join other markers of knowledge and power in symbolising the transience of all such worldly accomplishment. A still life, painted in about 1661 by Edwaert Collier, and Jan van der Heyden's *Room Corner with Curiosities* (1712) furnish a relatively conventional and a more wittily inventive version of the kind (Figures 26 and 27). Maps are conspicuous in both. The Collier has two, an open atlas in the right foreground and a celestial globe; and the van der Heyden has four, an atlas, a terrestrial and celestial globe and a large furled wall-

Figure 26 Edwaert Collier, *Vanitas Still Life* (c. 1661–62)

map leaning against the side wall. The musical instruments, the book of music, and the open copy of Plutarch's *Lives of the Illustrious Greeks and Romans* in a recent Dutch translation provide other signs of human achievement in the Collier painting, as do the 'curiosities' collected from distant parts of the world in the van der Heyden: the rare fabrics, the Chinese porcelain, the Japanese pike and *shakujo*, the inlaid cabinet and the hanging armadillo. That armadillo, like the empty shells or dead birds that figure in so many 'vanitas' still lifes, also serves to replace the yet more ubiquitous human skulls as a reminder of death, while in the Collier time's irresistible passage is similarly suggested by the hour glass,

Figure 27 Jan van der Heyden, *Room Corner with Curiosities* (1712)

the watch (which may also recall human ingenuity), and the recently extinguished candle. And lest we miss the point, both paintings clearly announce their genre: the Collier with a note sticking out of the Plutarch that reads 'Vanitas vanitatum et omnia vanitas' (a sentence we have already noticed on the Fool's Cap Map), and the van der Heyden with a Dutch Bible open to the very page in Ecclesiastes where that familiar declaration of the vanity of all things is to be found. But van der Heyden does not stop with the biblical admonition. Instead he couples it with a classical image. Over the mantlepiece at the back of the room, he reproduces a painting of the death of Dido, an episode from Virgil's *Aeneid* that cries out, like Camões' old man of Restelo, against the terrible cost of empire. It is an image that echoes with particular resonance in this room where the spoils of Holland's own far-flung commercial empire are gathered together.

But of all the objects in these two paintings, none is more surprising or more in need of explanation than the open atlas in each, for unlike the map in the fool's cap or the map that looms over the Christian knight or the map that calls forth Ortelius' memories of stoic morality or the map in Donne's meditation on death, these are not world maps. Nor are they the celestial maps that could so easily be made to stand for *mundus* in a visual discourse of *contemptus mundi*. Instead, they are maps of Holland itself, of Collier's and van der Heyden's own national homeland, which was also the homeland of their intended audience.

Some years ago, in a study of the early modern explosion of cartographic and chorographic descriptions of England and its various counties, I found a map-driven shift in the focus of loyalty and identity from the dynastic state to the land itself.[16] In their passionate attention to maps of their own country, the English exposed themselves to the pervasive influence of an image no less compelling and considerably more durable than even that of the monarch, whose royal insignia were necessarily pushed aside on maps to make place for the land and its representation. The very newness of maps lent them an unsettling ideological force. Considered from this perspective, the Delphic motto on the Fool's Cap Map, 'Know thyself', might just as well have found a place on the national and regional maps of England or any other European country. Looking at these maps, early modern Europeans saw a version of themselves they had never seen before, certainly not with such clarity, immediacy, or insistence. Suddenly they saw themselves as belonging to a land-based community whose outline and features could now be seized at a glance. In such moments of unexpected self-recognition, maps helped transform subjects into citizens, dynasts into nationalists.

Nowhere was this impact greater than in the Netherlands. Not only were the Netherlands' chief cities – first Antwerp and then Amsterdam – the European centres of cartographic production, but the Low Countries were also the most intensively mapped region of Europe, and maps were far more broadly distributed there than anywhere else. But more than that, the very conditions that led to the emergence of the Netherlands, or at least its seven northern provinces, as an independent state gave maps a greater symbolic weight. Through eighty years of intermittent war, from the 1560s to 1640s, the Dutch fought to free themselves from their monarchic overlord, the king of Spain. In these circumstances, maps had an extraordinarily potent effect. They stood almost alone for the nation and for whatever national identity the Dutch managed to forge in those years of repeated crisis and seemingly miraculous economic and cultural success. In the Netherlands, maps and the nation were one. Only the heraldic figure of the Dutch lion, Leo Hollandicus or Leo Belgicus, was a close competitor. And even the Dutch lion frequently morphed into a map.[17] More than anywhere else in Europe, in the Netherlands maps – most particularly the survey ordered by the Habsburg emperor Charles V, when in the 1540s he decided to unite the seventeen provinces as a single administrative unit – made the nation. And for well over a century after the emperor's great survey, maps continued to guarantee that the nation, now at war with the emperor's son, grandson, and great-grandson, would retain a vivid sense of itself.[18]

Given this remarkable centrality of maps to Dutch national self-consciousness, what are we to make of the Collier still life or the van der Heyden *Room Corner with Curiosities*, in both of which a map of the Netherlands itself – a map of the province of Holland from Abraham Goos' *New Netherlandish Mapbook* (1616) in the Collier and a regional map of Holland from Willem and Joan Blaeu's *Theatre of the World* (1642) in the van der Heyden – is made to stand, along with many other signs of modernity, for the vanity of all worldly pursuits? How can so positive and even patriotic an image have turned so negative?

Before trying to answer, let me broaden the evidence a bit, for the Collier and van der Heyden still lifes are by no means isolated instances. In the Dutch seventeenth century, there was a strong and extraordinarily flexible tradition of representing worldly vanity in the person of the seductive Lady World.[19] We have already seen her in her most allegorically obvious guise as 'Mundus' in the lower left-hand corner of the Hondius Christian Knight Map, where the orb balanced delicately on her head provides an unmistakable attribute. More naturalistically, Lady World reappears in a 1633 painting by Jan Miense Molenaer, whose title in the last half century has migrated all the way from *The Preparation for a Wedding* to the *The Allegory of Human Vanity* (Figure 28).[20] Having come to this painting by the route we have taken, virtually

Figure 28 Jan Miense Molenaer, *The Allegory of Human Vanity* (1633)

everything in it speaks out for the identification with vanity: the musical instruments (recalling the lute in Holbein's *Ambassadors* and the flute, violin and lute in the Collier still life), the death's head (most ladies in seventeenth-century Holland did not use skulls as footstools), the bubble about to burst, the mirror, the cosmetics, and the monkey (playing a fool's-cap-like role). And though Lady World's orb has flattened into a wall map, a Hondius double-sphere world map that was taken over and several times revised by the Visschers, it continues to function, as world maps had done from Ortelius on, as a sign of vain worldly attachment. Nor is the step from world to nation hard to trace in the Netherlandish metamorphoses of Lady World. Indeed, thirteen years before Molenaer painted Vrouw Wereld, as the Dutch called her, with the Hondius world map, Willem Buytewech had put her into a *Merry Company* with many of the familiar signs of worldly dissipation and folly, but with her orb replaced by a clearly recognisable Jan Saenredam map of Holland (Figure 29). In Buytewech's *Merry Company*, as in the still lifes of Collier and van der Heyden, Holland itself is made to stand for wayward worldliness.

Figure 29 Willem Buytewech, *Merry Company* (c. 1620–22)

Or is it? Drawing on traditions of Dutch national self-representation like those I mentioned earlier, a German art historian, Bärbel Hedinger, has read the map in this painting as a patriotic rebuke to the idle gallants featured in the foreground, and Simon Schama in *The Embarrassment of Riches* reads the similar map in another closely related Buytewech merry company in much the same way.[21] So is the map a positive and patriotic sign or a negative and moralising one? Whatever the artist may have intended, the answer must be 'both'. As we have seen again and again, the same maps that so powerfully represented early modern European accomplishments in government, exploration, commerce, and technology, maps that not only represented those accomplishments but participated actively in them, could also be taken as signs of the vanity of all such pursuits. And if this was true of obviously allegorical images like the Fool's Cap Map, the Christian Knight Map, the Collier and van der Heyden 'vanitas' still lifes, the Molenaer *Allegory of Human Vanity*, and the Buytewech merry companies, it was also true (in whatever attenuated way) of hundreds of less obviously allegorical works, including what is certainly the most famous of them all, Vermeer's *Art of Painting* with its marvellous copy of the 1620s Visscher map of the Seventeen Provinces (Figure 30).

It is hard to imagine a more resonantly beautiful image of national identity and aspiration than this map, a map whose real-life counterparts hung in a great many Dutch burgher households in the seventeenth century. Without the various political and cultural changes that together we label as modernity, such an image is inconceivable. It would simply not have existed. But can we be sure that this bashful Dutch girl, dressed somewhat incongruously as Clio, the muse of history, has nothing of Lady World about her? After all, is the muse of history so different in her implications from Plutarch's *Lives* in the Collier still life? For any early modern viewer, a map like Vermeer's could send both a message of modernity, including the rousingly patriotic modernity of national identity, and a message of anti-modernity, a message warning of the vanity and spiritual hazard of all worldly attachment.

HOME AND THE WORLD

The layering that produced the Fool's Cap Map finds its counterpart in Vermeer's *Art of Painting*. Though critics do not always remark on it, we see here not one but two paintings, the products of two readily distinguishable 'arts of painting'. One is the painting-within-the-painting, the allegorical representation of Fame in the guise of Clio, that the fictional painter has just begun to fill in. The other is, of course, Vermeer's own painting, a genre scene of the artist in his studio. Like the fool's cap encasing Ortelius' map of the world, the second comments ironically on the first. In the terms that have been emerging from our examination of *contemptus mundi* and its vigorous renewal in the midst of early modern, worldly accomplishment, the comment, directed to the painter within the painting, would go something like this: 'The glory you hope to inscribe in the annals of history and that you here invoke with the figure

Figure 30 Johannes Vermeer, *The Art of Painting* (c. 1666–67)

of Clio is mere vanity. The Habsburg Empire, recalled in the chande-
lier's double-headed eagle, is no more; the map's united Seventeen
Provinces are a thing of the past. *Vanitas vanitatum et omnia vanitas.*' But
there is another way to read this contrast. Vermeer mocks the pretension of the allegorical history painter not only in the name of ancient
contemptus mundi but also and more importantly in the name of his own

kind of genre painting. While the painter within the painting celebrates the pretended (but false) transcendence of worldly accomplishment, Vermeer celebrates the everyday beauty of objects and persons, the beauty especially of the magnificently illuminated Dutch map and of the shy Dutch girl who inhabits and perhaps even stands for the land the map represents.

Looking back over the other, more obviously didactic paintings we have seen, particularly the Collier and van der Heyden still lifes, in the light of Vermeer's *Art of Painting*, we can see that they are doing something similar. While they expose the transitoriness of the worldly pursuits represented by maps and books and musical instruments, they lovingly reproduce with an incredible tactile fidelity the ordinary – and sometimes not so ordinary – objects of the world, including those very maps and books and musical instruments. And were we to broaden the field still further to encompass mid-seventeenth-century Dutch genre painting generally, painting that includes a great many maps in familiar domestic settings, we might argue that maps and the worldly modernity with which they are so firmly associated have a new rival – not the unworldly heaven of the traditional religious teaching invoked by the Fool's Cap Map, the Christian Knight Map, and the 'vanitas' still lifes but rather the secular haven of the private middle-class home, 'a haven', as Christopher Lasch called it in the memorable title of his 1977 book, 'in a heartless world'. That homely haven may be variously menaced in these paintings.[22] But whatever the menace, the home emerges in Dutch genre painting as a place of value, a place engaged with maps yet set apart from the world they represent. And that early modern emergence of the domestic as an alternative source of value was itself, I would suggest, the product of the very processes, including the political and affective consolidation of national states, that were coming to define early modernity.

In the shops of Amsterdam, Delft, or The Hague, one could easily buy for about the same price a wall map or a genre painting, a representation of the world or of the home, and the two must often have ended hanging side by side in their purchasers' own homes. Through such representational juxtapositions, the ancient folly of worldliness was being given the new meaning we see emerging in Vermeer's *Art of Painting* and in Dutch genre painting more generally: no longer the world in the head of a fool but now the world within the walls of a burgher house. Thinking only of the Fool's Cap Map and its early modern counterparts, I had planned to end this paper by chiding our inclination to find ourselves in everything we study. We have of course become accustomed in recent years to understanding older maps as more than mere steps in the onward march of positive, scientific knowledge. But even in our newer attention to the political and ideological uses of maps and to their place in a growing market economy, we are still most interested – and understandably so – in what leads up to us. The Fool's Cap Map might have reminded us of what such arguments miss: the ideological resistance and retrogression that continued to exert their claim in the midst of the progress we find it so much easier to see. But now I have found, to my own surprise, a different kind of progress in the midst of that very retrogression, a domestic claim – a claim for the middle-class home – to set against the cartographically inscribed claims of the world. The opposition is of course not the same. Home has taken the place of heaven. But once again we and our modernity are firmly back in the picture.

NOTES

1. Leo Bagrow, *History of Cartography*, revised and enlarged by R.A. Skelton (Cambridge, Mass.: Harvard University Press, 1964), pp. 179–89.
2. John Gillies, *Shakespeare and the Geography of Difference* (Cambridge University Press, 1994), pp. 79 and 202n32.
3. David Turnbull, *Maps Are Territories / Science Is an Atlas* (University of Chicago Press, 1989), p. 1, and '"On With the Motley"': Maps, Map Consciousness and Knowledge Spaces', paper delivered at a conference on 'The Explosion of Cartography in Early Modern Asia and Europe', Center for Japanese Studies, University of California, Berkeley, 1996.
4. Robert Burton, *The Anatomy of Melancholy*, 3 vols, ed. Thomas C. Faulkner, Nicholas K. Kiessling and Rhonda L. Blair (Oxford: Clarendon Press, 1989), vol. I, p. 24. For a discussion of the broader relation between the Fool's Cap Map and *The Anatomy of Melancholy*, see Anne S. Chapple, 'Robert Burton's Geography of Melancholy', *Studies in English Literature* 33 (1993), 99–130.
5. 'Ass's ears, who's without them' comes from Persius 2.1, and 'Vanity of vanities, all is vanity' from the opening verse of Ecclesiastes. Together they suggest the combination of culturally authoritative sources, both pagan and Christian, that stand behind de Gourmont's *contemptus mundi*. Thanks to G.W. Pigman III for spotting the Persius quotation.
6. For an illustration of the updated Fool's Cap Map and a discussion of the cordiform projection used in it, see Giorgio Mangani, 'Abraham Ortelius and the Hermetic Meaning of the Cordiform Projection', *Imago Mundi* 50 (1998), 59–83. Mangani suggests Ortelius' 1564 cordiform world map as the source for the map on this engraving. The geographic details make clear,

however, that the engraver was using the map from the 1587 edition of
Ortelius' *Theatrum*, refitting those details onto a cordiform projection. On
this point, see Rodney W. Shirley, *The Mapping of the World: Early Printed
World Maps, 1472–1700* (London: Holland Press, 1983), p. 189. Thanks to
Catherine Delano Smith for drawing my attention to Mangani's article and
for supplying me with a prepublication copy.

7. R. V. Tooley, *Geographical Oddities, or Curious, Ingenious, and Imaginary Maps and
Miscellaneous Plates Published in Atlases* (London: Map Collectors' Circle,
1963).

8. Shirley, *The Mapping of the World*, p. 219.

9. Burton, *Anatomy of Melancholy*, vol. II, pp. 86–7.

10. Marcus Tullius Cicero, *Tusculan Disputations*, 4.37. The translation is from
the Loeb edition by J. E. King, *Cicero: Tusculan Disputations* (Cambridge,
Mass.: Harvard University Press, 1950), p. 367. For a thorough and insight-
ful discussion of the stoic morality of Ortelius' map, see Gillies, *Shakespeare
and the Geography of Difference*, pp. 79–84.

11. Lucius Annaeus Seneca, *Natural Questions*, 1. I have adapted the translation
from the Loeb edition by T. H. Corcoran, *Seneca in Ten Volumes* (Cambridge,
Mass.: Harvard University Press, 1971), vol. VII, p. 6.

12. For the full quotation, its source in Pliny's *Natural History* and an English
translation, see Chapple, 'Robert Burton's Geography of Melancholy',
115–16.

13. *Twelfth Night*, 3.2.67–8, and *Hamlet*, 2.2.289–90, quoted from *The Norton
Shakespeare*, ed. Stephen Greenblatt *et al.* (New York: Norton, 1997), pp. 1798
and 1697. For a careful discussion of Shakespeare's geographical knowledge, see Gillies, *Shakespeare and the Geography of Difference*, pp. 40–51.

14. Luís de Camões, *The Lusiads*, trans. Leonard Bacon (New York: Hispanic
Society of America, 1950), 4.101.

15. Walter Balcanquhall, *A Sermon Preached at St. Maries Spittle on Munday in Easter
Weeke, the Fourteenth Day of Aprill, Anno Dom. 1623* (London: John Budge, 1623),
p. 50; and John Donne, *The Divine Poems*, ed. Helen Gardner (Oxford:
Clarendon Press, 1952), p. 50. For a discussion of Donne's poem in relation
to Renaissance cartography, see Howard Marchitello, 'Political Maps: The
Production of Cartography and Chorography in Early Modern England',
Margaret J. M. Ezell and Katherine O'Brien O'Keeffe (eds.), *Cultural
Artifacts and the Production of Meaning: The Page, the Image, and the Body* (Ann
Arbor: University of Michigan Press, 1994), pp. 15–21. William E. Engel
discusses maps as *memento mori* in *Mapping Mortality: The Persistence of Memory
and Melancholy in Early Modern England* (Amherst: University of Massachusetts
Press, 1995), pp. 129–94, and Robert Appelbaum provides a telling
example of geographic *contemptus mundi* in 'Anti-geography', *Early Modern
Literary Studies*, Special Issue 3 (1998), which can be found on-line at http://
www.shu.ac.uk/emls/04-2/appeanti.htm. My thanks to Mark Koch for
the Balcanquhall reference and to Garrett Sullivan for drawing my attention to Engel's book.

16. Richard Helgerson, *Forms of Nationhood: The Elizabethan Writing of England* (University of Chicago Press, 1992), pp. 105–47.

17. On these maps of the Netherlands in the form of the Dutch lion, see H. A. M. van der Heijden, *Leo Belgicus: An Illustrated and Annotated Cartobibliography* (Alphen aan den Rijn: Canaletto, 1990).

18. See H. A. M. van der Heijden, *The Oldest Maps of the Netherlands: An Illustrated and Annotated Carto-Bibliography of the 16th Century Maps of the XVII Provinces* (Utrecht: HES, 1987).

19. For the classic account of Lady World and her many disguises, see E. de Jongh, 'Vermommingen van Vrouw Wereld in de 17de eeuw', J. Bruyn *et al.* (eds.), *Album Amicorum J.G. van Gelder* (The Hague: Nijhoff, 1973), pp. 198–206.

20. See *Masters of Seventeenth-Century Dutch Genre Painting*, ed. Peter C. Sutton (Philadelphia Museum of Art, 1984), pp. 262–3. Other examples of Lady World are discussed on pp. 152, 173, 241, 281 and 293.

21. Bärbel Hedinger, 'Karten in Bildern: Zur politischen Ikonographie der Wandkarte bei Willem Buytewech und Jan Vermeer', Henning Bock and Thomas W. Gaehtgens (eds.), *Holländische Genremalerei im 17. Jahrhundert* (Berlin: Gebr. Mann, 1987), pp. 139–68; and Simon Schama, *The Embarrassment of Riches: An Interpretation of Dutch Culture in the Golden Age* (Berkeley: University of California Press, 1988), pp. 216–18.

22. I describe this menace and argue for a political understanding of it in two related articles: 'Soldiers and Enigmatic Girls: The Politics of Dutch Domestic Realism, 1650–1672', *Representations* 58 (1997), 49–87; and 'Genremalerei, Landkarten und nationale Unsicherheit im Holland des 17. Jahrhunderts', Uli Bielefeld and Gisela Engel (eds.), *Bilder der Nation. Kulturelle und politische Konstruktionen des Nationalen am Beginn der europäischen Moderne* (Hamburg: Hamburger Edition, 1998), pp. 123–53. A version of the first of these articles has also appeared in my *Adulterous Alliances: Home, State, and History in Early Modern European Drama and Painting* (University of Chicago Press, 2000), pp. 77–119.

Select bibliography

Agnew, John A., and James S. Duncan (eds.), *The Power of Place: Bringing Together Geographical and Sociological Imaginations* (London: Unwin and Hyman, 1989).

Alpers, Svetlana, *The Art of Describing: Dutch Art in the Seventeenth Century* (University of Chicago Press, 1983).

Andrea, Bernadette (ed.), *Genre* 30, no. 1 (1997), special issue on space, place and signs in Early Modern Studies.

Andrews, J. H., *Shapes of Ireland. Maps and Their Makers, 1564–1839* (Dublin: Geography Publications, 1997).

Avery, Bruce, 'Mapping the Irish Other: Spenser's *A View of the Present State of Ireland*', *ELH* 57 (1990), 263–79.

Bachelard, Gaston, *The Poetics of Space*, trans. Maria Jolas (New York: Orion Press, 1964 [French original 1958]).

Bagrow, Leo, *History of Cartography*, revised and enlarged by R. A. Skelton (Chicago: Precedent Publishing, 2nd edn. 1985).

Baker, David J., 'Off the Map: Charting Uncertainty in Renaissance Ireland', Brendan Bradshaw *et al.* (eds.), *Representing Ireland. Literature and the Origins of Conflict, 1534–1660* (Cambridge University Press, 1993), pp. 76–92.

Barber, Peter, 'England I: Pageantry, Defense, and Government: Maps at Court to 1550' and 'England II: Monarchs, Ministers, and Maps, 1550–1625', Buisseret (ed.), *Monarchs, Ministers and Maps*, pp. 26–98.

Bendall, Sarah, *Maps, Land, and Society: A History, with a Carto-Bibliography of Cambridgeshire Estate Maps, c. 1600–1836* (Cambridge University Press, 1992).

Bennett, J. A., *The Divided Circle: A History of Instruments for Astronomy, Navigation and Surveying* (Oxford: Clarendon Press, 1987).

Beresford, Maurice, *History on the Ground. Six Studies in Maps and Landscape* (London: Lutterworth Press, 1957).

Bhabha, Homi K., *The Location of Culture* (London: Routledge, 1994).

Black, Jeremy, *Maps and Politics* (London: Reaktion, 1997).

Boelhower, William, 'Inventing America: A Model of Cartographic Semiosis', *Word and Image* 4, no. 2 (1988), special issue on cartography, 475–97.

Broc, Numa, *La géographie de la Renaissance, 1420–1620* (Paris: CHTS, 2nd edn. 1986).

Brotton, Jerry, *Trading Territories* (London: Reaktion, 1997).

Buisseret, David (ed.), *Envisioning the City: Six Studies in Urban Cartography* (University of Chicago Press, 1998).

Monarchs, Ministers and Maps: The Emergence of Cartography as a Tool of Government in Early Modern Europe (Chicago University Press, 1992).

Buisseret, David (ed.), *Rural Images: Estate Maps in the Old and New Worlds* (University of Chicago Press, 1996).

Burt, Richard and John Michael Archer (eds.), *Enclosure Acts: Sexuality, Property, and Culture in Early Modern England* (Ithaca and London: Cornell University Press, 1994).

Casey, Edward S., *The Fate of Place: A Philosophical History* (Berkeley: University of California Press, 1997).

Certeau, Michel de, *The Practice of Everyday Life*, trans. Steven Rendall (Berkeley: University of California Press, 1984 [French original 1974]).

Chamberlin, Russell, *The Idea of England* (London: Thames and Hudson, 1986).

Conley, Tom, *The Self-Made Map* (Minneapolis: University of Minnesota Press, 1996).

Cormack, Lesley, *Charting an Empire: Geography at the English Universities, 1580–1620* (University of Chicago Press, 1997).

Cosgrove, Denis and Stephen Daniels (eds.), *The Iconography of Landscape* (Cambridge University Press, 1988).

Cosgrove, Denis (ed.), *Mappings* (London: Reaktion, 1997).

Crone, G. R., *et al.*, 'Landmarks in British Cartography', *Geographical Journal* 128 (1962), 406–30.

Crone, G. R., *Maps and Their Makers. An Introduction to the History of Cartography* (London: Hutchinson's University Library, 1953).

Driver, Felix and David Gilbert (eds.), *Imperial Cities: Landscape, Display and Identity* (Manchester University Press, 1999).

Dunlop, Robert, 'Sixteenth-Century Maps of Ireland', *English Historical Review* 20 (1905), 309–37.

Elliot, James, *The City in Maps. Urban Mapping to 1900* (London: The British Library, 1987).

Erickson, Wayne, *Mapping* The Faerie Queene. *Quest Structure and the World of the Poem* (New York and London: Garland Publishing, 1996).

Evans, Ifor M. and Heather Lawrence, *Christopher Saxton, Elizabethan Map-Maker* (West Yorkshire: Wakefield Historical Publications, 1979).

Fitter, Chris, *Poetry, Space, Landscape. Toward a New Theory* (Cambridge University Press, 1995).

Fletcher, David, *The Emergence of Estate Maps. Christ Church, Oxford, 1600 to 1840* (Oxford: Clarendon Press, 1995).

Fordham, George, *Some Notable Surveyors & Map-Makers of the Sixteenth, Seventeenth, & Eighteenth Centuries and Their Work. A Study in the History of Cartography* (Cambridge University Press, 1929).

Foucault, Michel, 'Of Other Spaces', trans. Jay Miskowiec *Diacritics* 16 (1986 [French original 1969]), 22–7.

'Questions on Geography', *Power / Knowledge. Selected Interviews and Other Writings 1972–1977*, ed. Colin Gordon, trans. Gordon *et al.* (New York: Pantheon Books, 1980), pp. 63–77.

Frenk, Joachim (ed.), *Spatial Change in English Literature* (Trier: Wissenschaftlicher Verlag, 2000).

Gillies, John and Virginia Mason-Vaughan (eds.), *Playing the Globe: Genre and Geography in English Renaissance Drama* (Madison: Fairleigh Dickinson University Press, 1998).

Gillies, John, *Shakespeare and the Geography of Difference* (Cambridge University Press, 1994).

Godlewska, Anne and Neil Smith (eds.), *Geography and Empire* (Oxford: Blackwell, 1994).

Goss, John, *The Mapmaker's Art: A History of Cartography* (London: Studio Editions, 1993).

Gregory, Derek, *Geographical Imaginations* (Oxford: Blackwell, 1994).

Grosz, Elizabeth, *Space, Time, and Perversion: Essays on the Politics of Bodies* (London: Routledge, 1995).

Harley, J. B., 'Cartography, Ethics and Social Theory', *Cartographica* 27, no. 2 (1990), 1–23.

'Deconstructing the Map', *Cartographica* 26, no. 2 (1989), 1–20.

'Maps, Knowledge and Power', Cosgrove and Daniels (eds.), *The Iconography of Landscape*, pp. 277–312.

'Meaning and Ambiguity in Tudor Cartography', Tyacke (ed.), *English Map-Making*, pp. 22–45.

'Silences and Secrecies: the Hidden Agenda of Cartography in Early Modern Europe', *Imago Mundi* 40 (1988), 57–76.

Harley, J. B. and Kees Zandvliet, 'Art, Science, and Power in Sixteenth-Century Dutch Cartography', *Cartographica* 29, no. 2 (1992), 10–19.

Harvey, David, *The Condition of Postmodernity. An Enquiry into the Origins of Cultural Change* (Cambridge, Mass.: Blackwell, 1989).

Harvey, P. D. A., 'Estate Surveyors and the Spread of the Scale-Map in England, 1550–1580', *Landscape History* 15 (1993), 37–49.

Maps in Tudor England (Chicago University Press, 1994).

The History of Topographical Maps: Symbols, Pictures and Surveys (London: Thames & Hudson, 1980).

Hedinger, Bärbel, *Karten in Bildern. Zur Ikonographie der Wandkarte in holländischen Interieurgemälden des 17. Jahrhunderts* (Hildesheim *et al.*: Solms, 1986).

Helgerson, Richard, *Forms of Nationhood: The Elizabethan Writing of England* (University of Chicago Press, 1992).

'Nation or Estate? Ideological Conflict in the Early Modern Mapping of England', *Cartographica* 30, no. 1 (1993), 68–74.

'Genremalerei, Landkarten und nationale Unsicherheit im Holland des 17. Jahrhunderts', Uli Bielefeld und Gisela Engel (eds.), *Bilder der Nation. Kulturelle und politische Konstruktionen des Nationalen am Beginn der europäischen Moderne* (Hamburg: Hamburger Edition, 1998), pp. 123–53.

Helgerson, Richard and Joanne Woolway Grenfell (eds.), 'Literature and Geography', *Early Modern Literary Studies* 4, special issue no. 3 (1998).

Herendeen, Wyman H., *From Landscape to Literature. The River and the Myth of Geography* (Pittsburgh: Duquesne University Press, 1986).

Howgego, James, *Printed Maps of London circa 1553–1850* (Folkestone: Dawson, 1978).

Hulme, Peter and William Sherman (eds.), *'The Tempest' and Its Travels* (London: Reaktion, 2000).

Hyde, Ralph, *Gilded Scenes and Shining Prospects: Panoramic Views of British Towns 1575–1900* (New Haven, Conn.: Yale Center for British Art, 1985).

Jardine, Lisa and Jerry Brotton, *Global Interests: Renaissance Art between East and West* (London: Reaktion, 2000).

Kagan, Richard L., 'Philip II and the Art of the Cityscape', *Journal of Interdisciplinary History* 17, no. 1 (1986), 115–35.

Klein, Bernhard, 'Randfiguren. Othello, Oroonoko und die kartographische Repräsentation Afrikas', Michaela Boenke and Ina Schabert (eds.), *Imaginationen des Anderen im 16. und 17. Jahrhundert* (Wolfenbüttel: Herzog August Bibliothek, forthcoming).

Maps and the Writing of Space in Early Modern England and Ireland (London: Palgrave, 2001).

Koeman, C., *The History of Abraham Ortelius and His Theatrum Orbis Terrarum* (Lausanne: Sequoia S.A., 1964).

Lefebvre, Henri, *The Production of Space*, trans. Donald Nicolson-Smith (Oxford: Blackwell, 1991 [French original 1974]).

Writings on Cities, ed. and trans. Eleonore Kofman and Elizabeth Lebas (Oxford: Blackwell, 1996).

Lestringant, Frank, 'Chorographie et Paysage à la Renaissance', Yves Giraud (ed.), *Le Paysage à la Renaissance* (Fribourg: Editions Universitaires, 1988), pp. 9–26.

Mapping the Renaissance World. The Geographical Imagination in the Age of Discovery, trans. David Fausett (Cambridge: Polity Press, 1994 [French original 1991]).

Livingstone, David, *The Geographical Tradition. Episodes in the History of a Contested Enterprise* (Oxford: Blackwell, 1992).

Lupton, Julia Reinhard, 'Mapping Mutability: or, Spenser's Irish Plot', Brendan Bradshaw *et al.* (eds.), *Representing Ireland. Literature and the Origins of Conflict, 1534–1660* (Cambridge University Press, 1993), pp. 93–113.

Lynam, Edward, 'English Maps and Map-Makers of the Sixteenth Century', *The Mapmaker's Art: Essays on the History of Maps* (London: The Batchworth Press, 1953), pp. 50–76.

Manley, Lawrence, *Literature and Culture in Early Modern London* (Cambridge University Press, 1995).

Marchitello, Howard, 'Political Maps: The Production of Cartography and Chorography in Early Modern England', Margaret J. M. Ezell and Katherine O'Brien O'Keeffe (eds.), *Cultural Artifacts and the Production of*

Meaning. The Page, the Image, the Body (Ann Arbour: The University of Michigan Press, 1994), pp. 13–40.

Marin, Louis, *Utopics: The Semiological Play of Textual Spaces*, trans. Robert A. Vollrath (Atlantic Highlands, New Jersey: Humanities Press, 1984).

Massey, Doreen, *Space, Place, and Gender* (Minneapolis: University of Minnesota Press, 1994).

McEachern, Claire, *The Poetics of English Nationhood, 1590–1612* (Cambridge University Press, 1996).

McRae, Andrew, *God Speed the Plough. The Representation of Agrarian England, 1500–1660* (Cambridge University Press, 1996).

Mendyk, Stan A. E., *'Speculum Britanniae.' Regional Study, Antiquarianism, and Science in Britain to 1700* (University of Toronto Press, 1989).

Morgan, Victor, 'The Cartographic Image of "The Country" in Early Modern England', *Transactions of the Royal Historical Society* 5, no. 29 (1979), 129–54.

'Lasting Image of the Elizabethan Era', *Geographical Magazine* 52 (1980), 401–8.

Mukerji, Chandra, *From Graven Images: Patterns of Modern Materialism* (New York: Columbia University Press, 1983).

Mullaney, Steven, *The Place of the Stage: License, Play, and Power in Renaissance England* (University of Chicago Press, 1988).

Nuti, Lucia, 'The Mapped Views by Georg Hoefnagel: the Merchant's Eye, the Humanist's Eye', *Word and Image* 4, no. 2 (1988), special issue on cartography, 545–70.

Rees, Ronald, 'Historical Links Between Cartography and Art', *Geographical Review* 70 (1980), 61–78.

Richeson, A.W., *English Land Measuring to 1800: Instruments and Practices* (Cambridge, Mass.: Society for the History of Technology, 1966).

Rose, Gillian, *Feminism and Geography. The Limits of Geographical Knowledge* (Cambridge: Polity Press, 1993).

Sawday, Jonathan, *The Body Emblazoned: Dissection and the Human Body in Renaissance Culture* (London: Routledge, 1995).

Schwyzer, Philip, 'Purity and Danger on the West Bank of the Severn: The Cultural Geography of A Masque Presented at Ludlow Castle, 1634', *Representations* 60 (1997), 22–48.

Seaton, Ethel, 'Marlowe's Map' [1924], Clifford Leech (ed.), *Marlowe: A Collection of Critical Essays*, Twentieth-Century Views (New Jersey: Prentice Hall, 1964), pp. 36–56.

Sherman, William, *John Dee: The Politics of Reading and Writing in the English Renaissance* (Amherst: University of Massachusetts Press, 1995).

Shirley, Rodney W., *Early Printed Maps of the British Isles, 1477–1650*, completely revised and updated edition (East Grinstead, West Sussex: Antique Atlas Publications, 1991).

Shirley, Rodney, *The Mapping of the World. Early Printed World Maps, 1472–1700* (London: New Holland Publishers, 1993).

Skelton, R. A. and J. Summerson, *A Description of Maps and Architectural Drawings in the Collection Made by William Cecil, First Baron Burghley, Now at Hatfield House* (Oxford: Roxburghe Club, 1971).

Skelton, R. A. and P. D. A. Harvey (eds.), *Local Maps and Plans from Medieval England* (Oxford: Clarendon Press, 1986).

Skelton, R. A., *County Atlases of the British Isles, 1579–1850* (London: Carta Press, 1970).

Smith, Catherine Delano and E. Morley Ingram, *Maps in Bibles, 1500–1600: An Illustrated Catalogue* (Geneva: Librairie Droz, 1991).

Soja, Edward W., *Postmodern Geographies. The Reassertion of Space in Critical Social Theory* (London: Verso, 1989).

  Thirdspace: Journeys to Los Angeles and Other Real-and-Imagined Places (Oxford and Cambridge, Mass.: Blackwell, 1996).

Somogyi, Nick de, 'Marlowe's Maps of War', Darryll Grantley and Peter Roberts (eds.), *Christopher Marlowe and English Renaissance Culture* (Aldershot: Scolar Press, 1996), pp. 96–109.

Stallybrass, Peter, 'Patriarchal Territories: The Body Enclosed', Margaret M. Ferguson *et al.* (eds.), *Rewriting the Renaissance* (University of Chicago Press 1985), pp. 123–45.

Sullivan, Garrett A., Jr., *The Drama of Landscape: Land, Property, and Social Relations on the Early Modern Stage* (Stanford University Press, 1998).

Taylor, E. G. R., *Tudor Geography, 1485–1583* (New York: Octagon Books, 1968 [first edn. 1930]).

  Late Tudor and Early Stuart Geography, 1583–1625 (London: Methuen, 1934).

  The Mathematical Practitioners of Tudor & Stuart England (Cambridge University Press, 1954).

Thompson, F. M. L., *Chartered Surveyors. The Growth of a Profession* (London: Routledge and Kegan Paul, 1968).

Thrower, N. J. W. (ed.), *The Compleat Plattmaker: Essays on Chart, Map and Globe Making in England in the Seventeenth and Eighteenth Centuries* (Berkeley: University of California Press, 1978).

Tooley, R. V., *Maps and Mapmakers* (London: B. T. Batsford, 1952).

Tooley, R. V., *et al.* (eds.), *A History of Cartography. 2500 Years of Maps and Mapmakers* (London: Thames and Hudson, 1969).

Traub, Valerie, 'Mapping the Global Body', Peter Erickson and Clark Hulse (eds.), *Early Modern Visual Culture* (Philadelphia: University of Pennsylvania Press, forthcoming).

Tuan, Yi Fu, 'Space and Place in Humanistic Perspective', S. Gale and G. Olsson (eds.), *Philosophy in Geography* (Dordrecht: G. Reidel Publishing Co., 1979), pp. 387–427.

Turnbull, David, *Maps Are Territories / Science Is an Atlas* (University of Chicago Press, 1989).

Tyacke, Sarah (ed.), *English Map-Making 1500–1650: Historical Essays* (London: British Library, 1983).

Tyacke, Sarah and John Huddy, *Christopher Saxton and Tudor Map-Making* (London: British Library, 1980).

Vos, Alvin (ed.), *Place and Displacement in the Renaissance* (Binghamton, New York: Centre for Medieval and Early Renaissance Studies, 1995).

Wallis, Helen (ed.), *Historian's Guide to Early British Maps*, Royal Historical Society Guides and Handbooks no. 18 (London: Royal Historical Society, 1994).

Watelet, Marcel (ed.), *Gérard Mercator cosmographe. Le temps et l'espace* (Antwerp: Fonds Mercator Paribas, 1994).

Wayne, Don E., *Penshurst: The Semiotics of Place and the Poetics of History* (Madison: University of Wisconsin Press, 1984).

Wood, Denis, *The Power of Maps* (London: Routledge, 1993).

Woodward, David (ed.), *Art and Cartography. Six Historical Essays* (Chicago University Press, 1987).

Five Centuries of Map Printing (University of Chicago Press, 1975).

Woodward, David and J. B. Harley (eds.), *History of Cartography, Vol 1: Cartography in Prehistoric, Ancient, and Medieval Europe and the Mediterranean* (Chicago University Press, 1987 [first volume of a projected series of six]).

Index